INDIAN COUNCIL OF HISTORICAL RESEARCH
MONOGRAPH SERIES 8

INDIAN HISTORY
A Russian Viewpoint

INDIAN HISTORY

A Russian Viewpoint

edited by

EUGENIA VANINA

Printed in India

PRAGATI PUBLICATIONS

in association with

INDIAN COUNCIL OF HISTORICAL RESEARCH

and

INSTITUTE OF ORIENTAL STUDIES

RUSSIAN ACADEMY OF SCIENCES

First Published 2003

Published by

PRAGATI PUBLICATIONS
4263/3 Ansari Road, Darya Ganj, Delhi 110002
E-mail: pragati1@ndf.vsnl.net.in

in association with

INDIAN COUNCIL OF HISTORICAL RESEARCH
35 Ferozeshah Road, New Delhi 110001

and

INSTITUTE OF ORIENTAL STUDIES
RUSSIAN ACADEMY OF SCIENCES

ISBN 81–7307–080–6

Printed in India

Typeset, printed and published by Vikas Kapoor for Pragati Publications,
4263/3 Ansari Road, Darya Ganj, Delhi 110002

In memoriam of *Dr G.G. Kotovsky*,
distinguished Russian scholar,
whose contribution to this
volume was destined to
become his last one.

Contents

❖ Acknowledgement

The contributors acknowledge their heartfelt gratitude to the Embassy of Russia in India, Russian Centre of Science and Culture (New Delhi), Indian Council of Historical Research, Embassy of India in Russia and Jawaharlal Nehru Cultural Centre (Moscow) for generous assistance in bringing up this volume.

❖ A Note on Transliteration

Given all efforts of editorial control it has been hardly possible to impose a uniform system of transliteration on the essays dealing with different subjects and referring to historical sources in a number of languages. Therefore each contribution uses the system preferred by its author.

Introduction
Russian Studies in Indian History: Past and Present

EUGENIA VANINA

Russian Studies in Indian History: Past and Present

The Russian school of Indian studies has a history of nearly two centuries. The main reason for its emergence was, firstly, Russia's centuries old desire to establish commercial and political contacts with India and, secondly, the interest of the Russian public in the material and spiritual culture of that faraway country. The celebrated *Voyage Beyond the Three Seas* by the Russian merchant Afanasi Nikitin (1468–1472),[1] the active presence of the Indian traders' colony in the Russian city of Astrakhan,[2] persistent efforts of the Russian czars to defy all obstacles and establish direct diplomatic relations with India, the Indian voyages of a number of Russian businessmen and adventurers in the seventeenth and eighteenth centuries[3] – all these were important milestones in not only bringing the two countries closer to each other but in laying down the foundation for the Russian school of Indology at the end of the eighteenth – beginning of the nineteenth century.

The founding father of this new school was G.S. Lebedev (1749–1817), a talented musician who came first to Madras in 1789 and two years later to Calcutta where he earned his livelihood by cello recitals and music lessons, studied Sanskrit, Bengali and Hindi, made friends with many leading Indian intellectuals and established the first European-style drama theatre in Calcutta. Expelled from India by the British authorities, Lebedev returned to Russia where he found employment in the Ministry of Foreign Affairs, established a printing house to publish texts in Bengali and Devanagari scripts and also published his *magnum opus, An Impartial Observation of the East Indian Brahmins' System of Sacred Rites and Customs* – a prelude to all Russian studies of the Indian society, history and culture.

If we distinguish, following Thomas R. Trautmann, the "Indomania" and the "Indophobia" as the two main trends in the nineteenth century European Indology,[4] then the Russian school of Indian studies should, no doubt, be placed in the former category (one may suggest "Indophilia" as a more appropriate name for it). From Lebedev onwards the Russian researches into Indian culture, languages, literatures and society have been marked by the overwhelmingly sympathetic attitude to the country and its people. In this attitude Lebedev and the generations of Russian Indologists who succeeded him were rather close to their Western counterparts like Holwell, Dow or Robertson, but with two extremely important differences. It was not only the classical India that the Russian scholars viewed with sympathy and admiration, but their contemporary India too. While many Western Orientalists praised the wisdom and genius of the sages and poets of the ancient India, for the "jantoos", i.e. contemporary Indians they encountered in their colonial possessions, they spared no derogatory terms to condemn their "moral depravity", "despotism" and "bad religion".[5] For the Russian scholars it was different: in their opinion India had been and still remained a great civilisation which had every right to be proud of numerous spiritual and material achievements, masterpieces of literature and fine arts, great schools of philosophical and religious thought, and high morality. Consequently, the establishment of the British colonial rule was viewed by the Russian scholars and general public not as a blessing for this "barbarous country" but the greatest misfortune that had befallen a highly civilised nation. Such an attitude was well summarised in a report by a Russian military interpreter sent to India in 1901 to practise his Hindustani language: "Endowed in many regions with the richest soil and other treasures of nature, densely populated, in possession of a glorious historical past and of a few most ancient cultures, the cradle of education and intelligence, this country has a full right for a better future, and the cherished desire of its best sons is to see their motherland free from foreign invaders".[6]

Such an attitude that prevailed in the ruling elite, academic circles and general public of Russia throughout the whole of the colonial period in Indian history had in its background a number of important factors, the one pertaining to the Russo-British rivalry in Asia being the least important.[7] More important were Russia's own tragic record of devastating intrusions from the West, the centuries-old tradition of contacts with the Asian peoples, the Eurasian character of the Russian civilisation as a whole that facilitated the sympathetic attitude of the Russian public towards India and the negative perception of the Western impact upon it. Both our countries, India and Russia, were for centuries misunderstood, maligned and slandered by the West which sought to establish the unchallenged superiority of the Euro-American way of life in contrast with the "barbaric" India or Russia: what Ronald Inden has written in this matter about the Western perception of India, fully applies to Russia as well.[8] Both India and Russia had therefore to struggle for preservation of their traditional values, culture and world outlook against the outside forces which strove to suppress and subvert their civilisational identity. Hence they felt each other's pains quite clearly.

Russia's first centre of Indology was St. Petersburg University which became an alumni of many celebrated scholars. The Institute of Oriental Studies in St. Petersburg was founded on the basis of the Asiatic Museum, which has been since 1730s the repository of manuscripts in Indian languages. Towards the end of the XIXth century Indian chairs were established in the universities of Moscow, Kazan, Kharkov, Derpt and others. While the first Russian translations of the Indian classics (some fables from *Pañcatantra* and *Hitopadeśa* in 1762, followed by the *Bhagavad Gītā* in 1788 and *Śakuntalā* in 1792) were not made directly from the Sanskrit original but from the already existing English, French and German versions, the first Russian translators directly from Sanskrit published their works later, in the early 1840s. Since that time and upto the present day translating Indian literary works (ancient, medieval and modern), religious and philosophical texts into Russian has been and remains one of the most important fields of the Russian Indianists' activity.

The major field of Indian studies in Russia throughout the whole of nineteenth and the beginning of the twentieth century was classical Indology with its main emphasis upon Sanskrit linguistics and literature, Pali, Vedic religion, Buddhism and Brahmanism. Uninfluenced, though, in their perception of India by any racial prejudices or feeling of superiority, the Russian scholars still shared some misconceptions of their Western counterparts with whom they maintained close academic contacts. The most significant and ruinous among these misconceptions was the over-emphasis on the ancient period of Indian history (with especial attention to the Vedic epoch, the Maurian empire and the "golden age" of the Guptas) correlated with the under-estimation of the subsequent epochs. The latter were described as periods of "decay" in every possible sphere: the languages prevalent in the post-Gupta (or post-Harsa) times being a corruption of the noble Sanskrit and the undeserved supremacy of the "semi-barbaric vernaculars", the literatures being a collection of vulgarised renderings of the Sanskrit classics, the religions being the crude, chaotic and superstitious cults that replaced the healthy primitivism of the Aryan religion along with the philosophically elevated and logically structured Brahmanism and Buddhism. As for history, it was presented as an encyclopaedia of bloodshed, "Oriental despotism" and caste tyranny. Therefore any research into medieval and modern Indian culture and society was out of the sphere of interests of the Russian Indologists.

Similarly, the history of India which is the theme of the collection of essays hereby presented to the readers was for quite a long time peripheral to the Russian school of Indian studies. It was taught in the universities, especially in the Oriental faculties and chairs, but briefly, the courses were based mainly upon the history textbooks and research works translated from English, German or French. Some scholars did touch upon certain aspects of Indian history (economic and political) while researching into different aspects of world history: the most vivid example was M. M. Kovalevsky (1851–1916), a distinguished jurist, historian and sociologist, a close associate of Marx; in his celebrated book *Communal Landholding: The Reasons, Development and Results of Its Decomposition* (1879) he dwelt upon the development of agrarian relations and village community in India extensively. But Indian history as such was never a subject of his study. The emphasis upon Sanskrit and Buddhist studies did imply some interest of the Russian scholars in the history of ancient and early medieval India, but throughout the whole of the nineteenth and early twentieth century it never emerged into an autonomous field of research. The Indian civilisation was viewed as spiritually and philosophically elevated, but indifferent to the problems of mundane life, and political turmoils were believed to have had no impact upon the secluded worlds of the village communities and the sages' *āśramas.* Some scholars, however, were bold enough to challenge these attitudes that were wide spread in the Western Indology of the epoch. For example, K. A. Kossovich (1815–1883), the reputed Sanskritologist and translator into Russian of several episodes from *Mahābhārata,* Sudraka's *Mṛcchakaṭika* and Somadeva's *Kathāsaritsāgara,* wrote: "They say that India has no history. If history is a depiction of the destinies of a nation which developed independently under the influence of the ideas brought about by its own life, if "the history-minded nations" are mainly those that succeeded in organising their statehood against the spacious background of all possible manifestations of free thought and creativity, if there are impregnable monumental and literary testimonies of their life, then the Indians are nothing inferior to the most historical-minded peoples of the world".[9]

By the end of the nineteenth-beginning of the twentieth century some Russian scholars realised the importance of Indian history studies. S. F. Oldenburg (1863–1934), the celebrated scholar and founder of the renowned *Bibliotheca Buddhica*, stated in a 1919 lecture: "Not so long ago it could be heard both among the general public and among the scholars that India has no history as the Indians are fully devoid of historical feelings. Now we know that it is wrong. India does have its history of which we have failed to have a clear understanding due to the lack of our knowledge and imperfect methods of our research. But we have an idea of some general features as well as numerous details and quite soon the day will come for us to discuss Indian history on equal terms with the history of other countries, with special attention towards its most important and interesting cultural history".[10]

The real emergence of Indian history studies took place in the USSR in the late 20s-early 30s of the twentieth century and implied a certain departure from the traditions of old St. Petersburg-based school of classical Indology. Some important premises for this were laid with the establishment of the army school of Oriental languages in Tashkent (1905) in which Indian studies occupied the most significant place. Unlike other centres of Oriental research, the Tashkent school was oriented towards modern India; the main emphasis of the teachers and students was upon Hindustani language, history and modern state of India, its economy and ethnology. One of the leading professors of this school, A. Ye. Snesarev (1865–1937) pioneered the Russian studies in the national liberation movement in India.

The new wave of the Soviet scholars, who were the founders of the national school of Indian history studies, belonged not to the circles of the traditional Indologists, but to the ranks of diplomats, political activists and educationists who worked in this or that field of practical contacts with India or were personally connected with the emigrant Indian freedom fighters in the USSR. Some of them were brought to the realm of the Indian history research by sheer chance. Thus I. M. Reisner (1899–1958) began his career as a member of the first Soviet diplomatic mission in Afghanistan. A. M. Osipov (1897–1969), the beginner of the studies in early medieval India was for many years associated with the International Agrarian Institute, a subordinate to Peasants' International. The most interesting and even romantic circumstances were behind the entrance of A. M. Dyakov (1896–1974) into the field of modern Indian history. A professional physician, he volunteered in 1921 to serve in Central Asia where he was attached to a Red Army detachment sent on mission to the Afghan border in the Western part of the Pamir mountain range. During the 40-day journey the detachment met a border guard force which was returning from the Pamir. One of the members of that force was Raja Mahendra Pratap Singh, the well-known Indian freedom fighter who had spared no efforts to secure the assistance, first from the czarist and then from the Soviet governments of Russia, for the liberation movement in India. Mahendra Pratap Singh had a long conversation with the Russian doctor about the situation in his home country and this furthered Dyakov's interest in India. Consequently he became the founder of modern Indian history studies in the USSR.[11]

All the founders of the Soviet school of Indian history studies entered the academic realm through contemporary India gates. Unlike the members of the traditional Indologist St. Petersburg school, they were in no way biased in favour of classical heritage and Sanskrit and had a sufficient knowledge of modern Indian languages like Hindi, Urdu or Bengali as well as Persian. Their professional interest in the awakened India of the 20s–30s quite logically required a retrospective view at the preceding epochs too. Thus Reisner, who began his academic career with the works on anti-colonial movement and especially on the agrarian relations in modern India, naturally turned to medieval period and published in 1927 and 1928 two articles *The Indian Peasantry of the Mughal Epoch* and *The Agrarian Movement of the Sikhs.* Noteworthy was the fact that those articles, the beginning of medieval India studies in the USSR, were published in the journals *New Orient* and *Revolutionary Orient* respectively: this itself testifies to the fact that even while researching into the events of the faraway Mughal history the Soviet scholar had their contemporary India in mind. Such an approach had both the positive and negative impact upon the subsequent development of Indian history studies in the USSR/Russia.[12]

The systematic work in the field of Indian history research in the USSR began after World War II and got a great impetus from India's independence and establishment of close friendly relations between India and the USSR. It was between the late 40s and 60s that the founders of the school published their major works that became both the classics of research and textbooks for the following generations of scholars. In the sphere of ancient history it was Osipov's *A Short Outline of the Indian History Upto the Tenth Century* (1948), in medieval history *Essays on Social Relations and Political System of the Mughal India in Akbar's Epoch (1556–1605)* by K. A. Antonova (1952), a student of I. M. Reisner. Reisner's own book *Popular Movements in India in the Seventeenth and Eighteenth century* his *magnum opus* and even now a classic on medieval

India, was published in 1961, after the author's death. The Soviet scholars' considerable interest in the Indian history of the nineteenth and early twentieth century culminated at that time in the publication of the two bulky collections of essays *The People's War in India in 1857–1859* (1957)[13] and *National Liberation Movement in India and the Activities of Bal Gangadhar Tilak* (1958).[14] In the history of the late colonial and early independent India most important were Dyakov's books *The National Question and British Imperialism in India* (1948) and *The National Question in the Present-Day India* (1963).

The founders of the Soviet school of Indian history studies distinguished themselves not only as scholars but as very efficient teachers who brought up a number of talented students – the second and the most successful generation of Soviet researchers into Indian history. Among I. M. Reisner's pupils we have already mentioned K. A. Antonova, whose book on the India of Akbar's epoch was quite well documented and even bold enough to question some postulates of the Stalinist approach to history. The works of another pupil of Reisner's, C. Z. Ashrafyan (1924–1999), were based upon a huge number of chronicles and original documents in Persian; they discussed the most important problems of socio-economic and political history of the thirteenth-eighteenth century India.[15] Another of Reisner's pupils, V. I. Pavlov (1924–1992), distinguished himself in the field of economic history of late medieval and early modern India.[16] The field of economic history of pre-colonial India attracted A. I. Chicherov (1932–1999) too: his book on crafts and trade in the sixteenth and eighteenth century India was published in 1965.[17] While Pavlov and Chicherov worked mainly in the field of industrial and commercial history of medieval and early modern India, L. B. Alayev (the pupil of Osipov) centred his studies around the socio-economic history of village communities in India, as well as upon the history of the South.[18] Among other pupils of Osipov, G. F. Ilyin (1914–1985) and E. M. Medvedev (1932–1985) distinguished themselves in the study of ancient and medieval history.[19] The most renowned scholar in this field is G. M. Bongard-Levin, whose work have won him high international repute.[20] A number of important works and collections of essays on the history of colonial and independent India were also published.[21] One of the most important projects of the Soviet Indologists was the publication of the "History of India" by G. M. Bongard-Levin, K. A. Antonova and G. G. Kotovsky in 1973: it covered political, economic, social and cultural history of India from the Harappan civilisation upto the early 70s of the twentieth century. This book was ran into several editions in Russian, as well as in English (1979), French, Hindi, Malayalam, Bengali and other languages. Another significant field of research has been attached to the study of the documents that are available in the Soviet/Russian archives and throw light upon various aspects of Indian history, and the relations between the two countries. The result of this more than three decades long work was the publication of the four volumes of archival documents pertaining to the Russo-Indian relations from seventeenth to nineteenth century and early twentieth century.[22]

The events that followed the disintegration of the Soviet Union had an unsetting effect upon Russia's whole academic sphere and Indian history studies as its integral part. More ideological openness allowed the scholars to discard some obsolete dogmas, in a number of cases, however, that was done only to acquire new ones. Some scholars hastened to condemn the Marxist methodology which had been for decades the sole instrument of history research in the USSR and turned to other methods: structuralist, Foucaultian, subalternist, etc. Others, disgusted by such opportunism, became even more strict and conservative in their Marxist positions. Still others tried to find more reasonable and flexible combination of different methods. Economic crisis, lack of financial support for the research works and publications made a number of scholars, mostly belonging to the younger generations, look for more profitable fields of activity and that had an extremely adverse impact upon all research fields, including Indian history, especially after the demise of many renowned scholars. Nevertheless, the School continues to exist and, defying all hardships, does its best to carry on the traditions and at the same time to expand the horizons of history research.

This collection of essays was compiled to offer the readers an insight into the present state of Indian history studies in Russia. The importance of this volume can be judged from the fact that with the exception of the already mentioned "History of India", Chicherov's book, and a few other works,[23] other Russian studies in Indian history are not known to the Indian scholars and reading public. The contributors belong to different generations and follow various research methodologies, they express dissimilar views that are their own and in no way represent any kind of an "official" position. Nevertheless, all these authors represent the national school of Indian studies which, as the readers might have seen even from these preparatory remarks, has worked out certain traditions, views and methods that may be close or similar to the approaches of the Indian or European scholars and yet be different in many ways.

The contributors to this book follow a wider perception of the field of their study: this allows them to include into the category of "history" not just political events and socio-economic developments, but ideas, beliefs, values and perceptions, too. The first part, titled *Russia, India and the Neighbours* discusses various aspects of the centuries-long contact between Russia, India and their common neighbours like Central Asia, China and Tibet. The relations are realised and presented by the scholars in different aspects and dimensions: economic, political and human; the latter aspect implies the influence of political links and alliances, rivalries and conflicts upon the individual lives and destinies. Most of the contributions included in this part are based upon materials and documents preserved in various archives of Russia and the former USSR. Thus Kalandarova's presentation depicts India's commercial relations with one of the mightiest Central Asian Khanates, Bukhara, in the nineteenth century. It also throws light upon the life and activities of the Indian merchants in Bukhara, their impact upon economic and cultural life there as well as their place in the growing Russo-British commercial and political rivalry in Central Asia. Zagorodnikova's article describes the life and activities of Ramachandra Balaji, an Indian adventurer, who came to Russia in the 70s of the nineteenth century and passed as the nephew of Nana Sahib, one of the leaders of the Great People's War of 1857–1859. The archival material analysed in the article reveals not just an adventure story but Russia's significant interest in the Indian affairs in the period of Russo-British rivalry in Asia and the propaganda campaign about the so-called "Russian threat" to India launched by the British colonial administration. At the same time it shows that, on the one hand, some political forces in India itself wanted to use this rivalry for their own purposes and even to secure the Russian military assistance for the liberation movement in India and, on the other hand, the Russian government was reasonable and cautious enough to avoid being provoked and involved in an open conflict with Great Britain. This topic is carried further to the end of the nineteenth-early twentieth century by Shaumian whose paper deals with one more dimension of the Russo-British rivalry in which colonial India was involved viz. the Tibet problem. This dimension was in no way less important than the more exhaustively researched and discussed Central Asian one; moreover, it remained significant for the Asian politics and inter-state relations in the subsequent decades too. Mitrokhin analyses the archival materials as well as the witnesses' testimonies (that is oral history) to reconstruct the lives and tragic destinies of the three Indian freedom fighters who emigrated to the Soviet Union after the October revolution, played an important role in national liberation and Communist movement in India and fell victim to the Stalinist repression thus sharing the tragic fate of many Soviet people. Another interesting document is brought to life in Kashin's article. It is the report of K. V. Novikov, the first Soviet Ambassador to India, presented on 5 July, 1949, to the Foreign Policy

Commission of the Central Committee of the Party. These remarks of a broad-minded, friendly and unbiased observer offer an interesting view of the economic, social and political situation in the newly independent India and show how difficult the first steps of the Soviet-Indian relations were, how many bureaucratic obstacles, ideological dogmas and prejudices both sides had to discard in order to build, since the mid-50s, the vast and stable network of multi-dimensional, equal and mutually beneficial relations.

Part II, *Socio-Economic History Studies* comprises three contributions into the field which has been the most developed in the Soviet school of Indian history studies (and in India itself too), with the main emphasis upon the agrarian sphere of socio-economic life. Unfortunately, some distinguished contributors to this field like Pavlov, Chicherov and Ashrafyan are no more. While Alayev's article is of historiographical character and offers the reader an insight into the Russian scholars' understanding of one of India's most important socio-economic institutions as well as the author's own vision of the problem, Kotovsky in his work discusses the intricate system of land ownership and proprietary rights in the Mughal empire. Komarov's contribution evaluates the rural social structure and economic life on the basis of the data pertaining to the late eighteenth-early nineteenth century Bengal.

Part III, *Texts and Ideas* comprises the textual studies and the contributions to the history of ideas within a wide temporal range. Vigasin's juxtaposition of the geographical data from Pliny's "Natural History" with those from various Greek, Latin and Sanskrit sources allows us to reconstruct the ethno-political map of the ancient India and adjacent regions. Samozvantsev's analysis of the composition of the *Āpastambadharmasūtra* discusses the development of this celebrated legal text within the framework of a broader *dharmasūtra* tradition. Tyulina's study of the *Garuḍa purāṇa* is both textual and cultural, it throws light upon the ancient and early medieval perceptions of Man and the Universe as reflected in and expounded by this celebrated text.

The mystical movements of medieval India like *Bhakti* and Sufism have been and are widely studied and discussed by the Indian, Russian and Western scholars, but more by the specialists in literature, culture and religion than by historians. Vanina, however, attempts not only the historical evaluation of those movements but their comparison with their medieval European counterparts. Suvorova's article discusses one of the most important phenomena of medieval and early modern Indian history and culture, the Indo-Muslim cultural synthesis and touches upon some literary and aesthetic implications of this process that do not very often attract the historians' attention. Yurlova's contribution analyses the socio-political and ethical views of Dr B. R. Ambedkar, one of the celebrated thinkers and political figures of modern epoch whose legacy is still, decades after his death, studied and debated in India and outside it.

The book may be reproached for a haphazard and random selection of contributions thus producing a *khicḍī* or hotchpotch of topics. Indeed, it would have been much better if just one important problem had been chosen and the contributors dealt with different aspects of it. But, as the readers have already learned from this very preface, due to the adverse impact of the economic and political changes in Russia, the demise of many renowned scholars and the lack of new blood hardly two researchers remained engaged in the same problem: the number of scholars has declined so much that those who keep working sometimes feel themselves as the "last of the Mohicans". Nevertheless, the Russian school of Indian history studies (along with the schools of Indian literature and language studies which deserve a special study) continues to exist and carry on the traditions bequeathed by its founders. It draws inspiration from the Russian public's never ending interest in Indian history and culture, from the objective necessity for both the Russian and the Indian peoples to know each other better and thus to strengthen the links of our friendship and cooperation.

Notes and References

1. The English translation of Afanasi Nikitin's travelogue is available in: Major *B. H. India in the Fifteenth Century. Being a Collection of Narratives and Voyages to India in the Century Preceding the Portuguese Discovery of the Cape of Good Hope, from Latin, Persian, Russian and Italian Sources, Now First Translated into English,* London, 1857.
2. The documents of the Indian trading colony in Astrakhan were translated from Russian: Surendra Gopal. *Indians in Russia in the Sixteenth and Eighteenth Centuries,* Calcutta, 1988.
3. For more details see: Eugenia Vanina, 'Of Russian Spies and Itinerants: Different Perspectives on the Eighteenth Century India', *Indian International Centre Quarterly,* Spring, 1997, p. 33.
4. Thomas R. Trautmann, *Aryans and British India.* Berkeley-Los Angeles-London, 1997, pp. 62–98, 99–130.
5. Ibid., pp. 103–5; see also: P. Spear. *The Nabobs. A Study of the Social Life of the English in the XVIIIth Century India,* London, 1963, p. 197.
6. *Rossiisko-Indiiskiye otnosheniya v 1900–1917. Sbornik documentov i arkhivnikh materialov* (Russo-Indian Relations in 1900–1917. A Collection of Documents and Archival Materials), Moscow, 1999, p. 67.
7. Discussed in more detail in: Eugenia Vanina, 'Russian Studies in Medieval Indian History and Society: an Insider's View', *Medieval History Journal,* Vol. 2, pt. 2 (1999), pp. 364–65.

8. R. Inden, *Imagining India*, Cambridge, 1992, pp. 2–3, 39.
9. Quoted in I. D. Serebryakov, *Literaturi Narodov Indii* (The Literatures of the Peoples of India), Moscow, 1985, p. 13.
10. S. F. Oldenburg, *Kultura Indii* (The Culture of India), Moscow, 1991, p. 126.
11. L. R. Polonskaya, 'Alexei Mikhailovich Dyakov (1896–1974) – revolutsioner i uchyony (Alexei Mikhailovich Diakov (1896–1974) – A Revolutionary and Scholar', O. K. Dreyer, G. D. Tyagai, P. M. Shastitko (eds.), *Slovo ob uchitelyakh* (The Word About the Teachers), Moscow, 1988, pp. 184–85.
12. This was discussed in more detail in: Eugenia Vanina, *Russian Studies in Medieval Indian History and Society*, pp. 367, 380–81.
13. This was an international project, to which the Indian scholars like K. M. Ashraf, R. C. Mazumdar and S. N. Sen contributed, along with some British and Chinese colleagues.
14. Among all well-documented contributions to this book noteworthy was the one by A. I. Chicherov, *Process B. G. Tilaka v iyule 1908 goda i bombeiskaya zabastovka* (The Process of B. G. Tilak in July, 1908 and the Bombay Strike) which was mainly based upon the dispatches of A. A. Geiking, the Russian Consul in Bombay in 1908. These dispatches are available in the Russian archives and have been published recently in the collection titled *Russko-indiiskiye otnosheniya v 1900–1917 gg* (Russo-Indian Relations in 1900–1917), Moscow, 1999.
15. C.Z. Ashrafyan, *Deliiski Sultanat* (The Delhi Sultanate), Moscow, 1960; *Agrarni Stroi Severnoi Indii* (XIII-seredina XVIII v.) (The Agragian System of Northern India (XIII-mid XVIIIth Century), Moscow, 1965; *Feodalism v Indii* (Feudalism in India) Moscow, 1977; *Srednevekoviy gorod Indii XIII-seredine XVIII veka* (Medieval City in India, XIIIth to mid XVIIIth Century), Moscow, 1983; *Deli. Istoriya i kultura,* (Delhi. History and Culture), Moscow, 1987.
16. V.I. Pavlov, *Formirovaniye Indiiskoi burjuazii* (The Formation of the Indian Bourgeoisie). Mosocw,1958; *Sotsialno-ekonomicheskaya struktura promyshlennosti Indii* (The Socio-Economic Structure of the Indian Industry), Moscow, 1973;. V.I. Pavlov, 'K stadialno-formatsionnoi kharakteristike vostochnykh obschestv v novoye vremya (Towards the Stage-Fromation Characteristics of the Oriental Societies in Pre-Modern Times)' in E.M. Zhukov, M.A. Barg, E.B. Chernyak, V.I. Pavlov (eds.), *Teoreticheskiye problemy vsemirno-istoricheskogo processa* (Theoretical Problems of the World Historical Process), Moscow, 1979, pp. 173–327.
17. In 1971 its English translation *Indian Economic Development in the 16th-18th Centuries: Outline History of Crafts and Trade* was published from Moscow, in 1998 Manohar brought a new edition of this book from Delhi.
18. L.B. Alayev, *Yuzhnaya Indiya. Sotsialno-ekonomicheskaya istoriya XIV-XVIII vv.* (South India. Socio-Economic History in the XIVth-XVIIIth Centuries), Moscow, 1964; *Sotsialnaya struktura indiiskoi derevni (territoriya Uttar-pradesha, XIX vek)* (The Social Structure of the Indian Village [the Uttar Pradesh Territory, the XIXth century]), Moscow, 1976; *Selskaya obschina v Severnoi Indii. Osnovniye etapi evolutsii* (The Village Community in Northern India. Main Stages of Evolution), Moscow, 1981.
19. G. F. Ilyin, *Drevii indiiski gorod Taksila* (The Ancient Indian City of Taxila), Moscow, 1958; *Drevnyaya Indiaya. Istoricheski ocherk* (The Ancient India: A Historical Outline) Moscow, 1969 (co-authored by G. M. Bongard-Levin); *Indiya*

v drevnosti (The Ancient India) Moscow, 1985 (co-authored by G. M. Bongard-Levin); E. M. Medvedev, *Ocherki po istorii Indii do XIII veka* (Essays on the History of India up to the XIIIth century), Moscow, 1990.

20. Among his most significant books are: G. M. Bongard-Levin, *Indiya epokhi Mauryev* (The Maurian India) Moscow, 1973; *Drevneindiiskaya civilizatsia: filosofiya, nauka, religiya* (The Ancient Indian Civilisation: Philosophy, Science, Religion), Moscow, 1980, *Indiya v drevnosti* (The Ancient India), co-authored by G. F. Ilyin) Moscow, 1985.

21. To name just a few: A. V. Raikov, *Natsionalno-revolutsionniye organizatsii Indii v borbe za svobodu, 1905–1930* (The Indian Nationalist Revolutionary Organisations in the Struggle for Freedom, 1905–1930) Moscow, 1979; *Amritsarskaya tragediya 1919 i osvoboditelnoye dvizheniye v Indii* (The Amritsar Tragedy of 1919 and the Liberation Movement in India), Moscow, 1985; E. N. Komarov and A. D. Litman (eds.), *Ideologicheskiye porblemy sovremennoi Indii* (The Ideological problems of Modern India), Moscow, 1970; A. I. Reginin, *Indiiski natsionalny kongress; ocherki ideologii i politiki* (The Indian National Congress: Essays on Ideology and Politics), Moscow, 1978; A. I. Chicherov, *Jawaharlal Nehru i nezavisimaya Indiya* (Jawaharlal Nehru and Independent India), Moscow, 1990. It has to be noted that some new fields of research like economy, sociology, political science emerged from the history of independent India.

22. *Russko-Indiiskiye otnosheniya v XVII v* (Russo-Indian relations in the XVIIth century) Moscow, 1958; *Russko-Indiiskiye otnosheniya v XVIII v* (Russo-Indian relations in the XVIIIth century), Moscow, 1965; *Russko-Indiiskiye otnosheniya v XIX v* (Russo-Indian relations in the XIXth century), Moscow,1997 (published in English by the Asiatic Society of Calcutta in 1999); *Russko-Indiiskiye otnosheniya v 1900–1917 gg* (Russo-Indian relations in 1900–1917), Moscow, 1999.

23. V. I. Pavlov, *The Indian Capitalist Class: A Historical Study*, Delhi, 1964; *Historical Premises for India's Transition to Capitalism (Late 18th to Mid 19th century)*, Moscow, 1978; G. M. Bongard-Levin, *Ancient Indian Civilization*, Delhi, 1985; *A Complex Study of Ancient India: A Multi-Disciplinary Approach*, Delhi, 1986; L. B. Alayev, 'The Systems of Agricultural Production: South India', 'Non-Agricultural Production: South India', Tapan Raychaudhuri and Irfan Habib (eds.), *Cambridge Economic History of India*, Vol. I, Cambridge, 1982.

PART I

India, Russia and Neighbours

ONE

The Indians in Bukhara: With Special Reference to the Nineteenth Century

M. S. KALANDAROVA

THE ECONOMIC AND CULTURAL communications between India and Central Asia may be traced back to remote antiquity. Thus Strabo mentioned, on the basis of the evidence from different Greek travellers and authors, that down the river Oxus (Amu-Darya) "large quantities of Indian wares are brought . . . to the Hyrcanian (Caspian – M. K.) Sea, and thence on that sea transported to Albania and brought down on the Cyrus river and through the region that comes next after it to the Euxine (Black Sea-M. K.)".[1]

Due to the favourable geographical situation Central Asia was an important intermediary between the East and the West. Merchant caravans from India travelled to Central Asia, and from there the Indian goods found their way into the European countries. However archaeological excavations of the Kusana epoch[2] (first to third centuries AD) and later period testify, that Central Asia was not just an intermediary, but an active trading partner of India.

Valuable information on the trade relations between Central Asia and India in medieval times was supplied by the well-known Arab traveller Ibn Battuta. He threw light on the export of war-horses from the Golden Horde steppes, perhaps the most important item of commercial links between India and Central Asia. Despite many losses during the tiresome way to India, robbers' rides and heavy taxation to which the horse merchants were subjected over and again during the journey, the business was extremely profitable as in their native land a horse was bought for a *dīnār* while "they sell the cheapest of them in the land of India for a hundred silver dinars . . . and often sell them for twice or thrice times as much. The good horses are worth five hundred [silver] dinars or more".[3]

The second half of the sixteenth century was a turning point in the political history of both India and Central Asia. It was the period when in India, as well as in Central Asia, strong centralised states were under formation. Akbar, one of the greatest rulers of the Mughal empire, ascended the throne in 1556; almost simultaneously (1557) the power in Bukhara came to the hands of Abdullah, the last Khan from the Shaybanid dynasty.[4] And while Akbar as a result of his numerous war campaigns expanded the territories of the state considerably from the borders of Tibet in the North to the river Godavari in the South and from Gujarat in the West up to the Bay of Bengal in the East, the Bukhara Khanate during the reign of Abdullah Khan, also emerged as a mighty state that succeeded in uniting, politically and militarily, a rather extensive territory comprising Mawarannahr (Samarqand), Dashti Qipchaq (the Qipchaq or the Golden Horde Steppe) and Khurasan (the Northern and the North-Western part of modern Afghanistan, the South of modern Turkmenia, the North-Eastern part of modern Iran).

Hormuz played a significant role in the trade of India with Central Asia. In the fourteenth-fifteenth century it was the centre for the Middle East and Central Asian states' commercial transactions with India. Innumerable caravans from Egypt, Iran, Mawarannahr (Samarqand), Dashti Qipchaq used to head for Hormuz. But after 1510 when Hormuz was captured by the Portuguese followed by their invasion of the most important coastal areas of Western India (Goa, Diu, Daman, Chaul), the maritime trade of India passed into their hands. The caravan road through Kabul and Qandagar came to be even more actively used by merchants as a substitute for the opportunities lost with the Portuguese invasions.

Kabul, located on the crossroads of trade routes linking India and Central Asia, became the centre of transit trade. There, Indian and Central Asian merchants exchanged their goods. The assortment of those goods was rather extensive: textiles, sugar powder, spices, medicines. From Central Asia even fruits were exported. This was the shortest caravan route and led to an increase in the number of commercial camel loads from 3 to 14 thousands annually.[5]

According to Jenkinson, an English traveller who visited Bukhara in 1558, the Indian merchants imported fine white textiles (for making turbans), and other sorts of white cloth, cottons, and exported silk fabrics, raw leather, slaves, horses.[6]

The high-status Indian and Bukhara dignitaries actively participated in commerce through their special representatives, whose authority was attested by special documents signed by the Mughal emperor or the Amir of Bukhara and recognised reciprocally. According to one such document, available in the manuscript depository of the Academy of Sciences, Tajikistan (unfortunately, undated), a merchant by name Akhund Khwaja Awaz and his associates were allowed to freely transport the goods "... from the metropolitan city of Shah Jahan up to the distant boundary province with the centre in Kabul". Both import and export of the goods by these specially authorised merchants were reciprocally exempted from all taxes. The decree obliged the *mubashirs*[7] to seal the document thus attesting the free passage of the caravans through the Bukhara territory as well, and also to carry out strictly all the provisions of the document.[8]

Commercial relations between India and Central Asia grow further in the second half of the sixteenth century. It must, however, be noted that the information about commodity circulation is in most cases of a fragmentary character, since the Indian merchants and travellers had no habit of writing travelogues. But even the hitherto available data allows us to have an idea of the general scope and character of the Indian trade with Central Asia. The eighteenth century sources provide more information. The peak was reached by the beginning of the nineteenth century.

But by this time Great Britain had acquired key positions in India, and in order to expand and protect her imperial interests. She continued subjugating the neighbouring states. The attention of the military and diplomatic circles of Great Britain gradually centred around Central Asia. The English missions penetrated into Central Asia from India, in order to make a detailed survey of political, military-strategic and economic conditions in Bukhara and the adjacent Khanates, thus strengthening the British positions in the region. And while the Anglo-Indian expeditions penetrated into Central Asia from the South, the numerous Russian expeditions with similar mission were sent to the Central Asian Khanates from the North. Thus Bukhara was visited by the Indian travellers and the agents of the East-India company: like Mir Izzatullah, W. Moorcroft and G. Trebeck, Mohan Lal Kashmiri, Alexander Burnes, etc. From the Russian side there were G. Meyendorff, N. Khanykov, the Russian officers P.I. Demezon and I.V. Vitkevich, etc. The participants of English and Russian expeditions left numerous accounts and reports of their voyages, providing the future researchers with valuable materials on India-Central Asia trade.

It has to be noted here that in using terms like Indian, Bukhara, Russian commerce we usually bear in mind the nationality of merchants who carried trade operations. It is known, however, that the Indian merchants along with the products of their own country had a successful business in Central Asian, Persian or Russian goods. Similarly the Bukhara merchants imported into Russia not only Central Asian but also Indian, Persian, Chinese merchandise. The Indian cotton fabrics were highly appreciated in Russia as they were more durable than the English ones that had been imported into Bukhara since the 30s of the nineteenth century by the Afghan and Indian Muslim merchants. The trade in these fabrics was carried on by not only the Bukhara and Indian businessmen, but also by the Armenians and the Khiva merchants. The traders usually dealt in those kinds of goods that were most profitable, notwithstanding the country of manufacturing. Therefore while studying the commodity circulation it is necessary to take into consideration not so much the nationality of a merchant but the affiliation of the imported and exported goods.

Through Kabul, which was border town, the Bukhara merchants traded with Kashmir, Punjab and Peshawar. They used several routes leading to India, but the two most frequented of them were the northern Bukhara – Amul-Jahun (Charjou) – Merv – Serakhs – Meshhed – Herat – Qandahar – Kabul – Peshawar, and the southern Qandahar to Dadui Shikarpur. Multan was halfway between the ends of both routes – Lahore and Shikarpur.[9] Indian and Central Asian merchants preferred the southern way running between the basins of the Amu-Darya and the Indus.

The Bukhara merchants imported into India golden thread, cotton fabrics, garments, cloth, velvet, horses, Dutch thaler coins. The Bukhara merchants could freely move within the whole territory of India, the Indian merchants enjoyed similar privilege in the whole of Turkestan. However the Bukhara merchants had to pay duties in every city of India they passed though and therefore their expenditures were high indeed.[10] As recorded by the Russian travellers, the transportation of one *pud* [11] of merchandise from the coast of Sind through Kabul to Bukhara would cost from six to seven roubles.[12] The duties comprised approximately 6 per cent of the cost of the goods.[13]

The Afghan merchants too were active in bringing the Indian and British merchandise to Bukhara. According to Burnes, the assortment of Indian goods exported by them to Bukhara was similar to the one brought to Afghanistan itself: indigo, sugar, white fabrics of all grades, calico, muslin, velvet, chintz of European manufacture, shawls, brocade, Dacca muslin, Punjabi turbans, etc. Up to two thousands camel loads arrived in Kabul from India annually, half of which was intended for trade in the Central Asian Khanates.[14] From the Punjab into Bukhara the nomad Afghan tribes known as Logani imported indigo which was widely used for dyeing cotton and wool in dark blue – the official Bukhara colour. Sometimes this dye was imported in so huge quantities that all the Afghan *caravanserais* were filled up with it and this resulted in a crash in prices. The merchants had to sell it on credit for 3–4 years and wait for the return of their capital. From the vicinity of Lahore raw sugar was imported.

Indian merchants were extremely active in Bukhara. They brought world famous Kashmiri shawls and woollens of different kinds: *riza* – one-colour; *rahdar* – striped; *buteda* – patterned with palms, flowers, bouquets; *quss* – plain (for turbans), *shamli* - for waistbands, *alvan* – for waistbands and dresses, one colour *dastgush* – for making Kashmiri wool gloves, *jurab* – for making long woollen socks.[15] Kashmiri shawls were extremely popular with the most fashion-minded ladies in Europe and Russia. In Bukhara their cost was from 100 up to 300 *tilla* (golden coin) equalling 250–300 Russian roubles per piece. In Russia their price was from 400 up to 1000 roubles per piece. This price was affordable for the very rich only. In February, 1809, following the imperial order the Orenburg General-governor G. S. Volkonsky purchased Kashmiri shawls of different colours for a sum of 6 thousand roubles.[16]

G. Meyendorff, during his Bukhara voyage, met a Kashmiri merchant who informed the Russian traveller that in his native town 30 thousand looms were engaged in manufacturing shawls.[17] Annually they produced 100 thousand shawls, 20 thousand remained in Kashmir, 60 thousand were sent to other cities of India, 20 thousand to Kabul. Of them 5 thousand went to the inhabitants of Afghanistan and 12 thousand would go on sale in Persia, Turkey, Arabia and Africa. 3 thousand shawls were dispatched to Bukhara, from there 2 thousand were imported into Russia. Naturally these figures changed from year to year, but they throw light upon the scope of manufacture of and market demand for the shawls. Apart from them, the merchants carried brisk trade in silk fabrics, gold-patterned cotton cloth, white fabrics for turbans and printed ones for linings, pearls and precious stones,[18] *qalamdans* (ink-pots), elegant spoons made of gold-plated wood and manuscripts in beautiful handwriting. From Peshawar they imported to Bukhara white and light-blue turban cloth (*lungi*), rice (of much better quality than the local one). The Bukhara people preferred the Peshawar tobacco to the Russian one and had much liking for the tobacco cases made of the Indian coconut. Among the Bukhara traders the Indian-made scales made from the camel leather were very popular. Apart from the above-mentioned products, more than 20 types of other merchandise were exported from India to Bukhara.[19]

According to A. Burnes the demand for the Indian goods was

constant in Bukhara. In his account he made a special reference to the Indian textiles and their prices in Bukhara. Annually about 500 pieces of the celebrated Benares brocade (*kinkab*) were brought there. The white turban cloth from Peshawar was used by both women and men. A piece of such cloth, 30 yards long and 1 foot wide would sell for one *tilla* in the Bukhara market. No less in demand was the Dacca muslin priced 20 *tilla* per piece. The narrower muslins were cheaper. Between 1790 and 1800 the Bukhara merchants re-exported to Russia the Indian textiles worth more than 50 thousand roubles. These were muslins, blankets and coverlets, curtains, chintzes, coarse calico, *alacha* (silk fabric), as well as medicines, jewels, spices, which were not only profitable articles of trade, but easily transportable too.[20]

The densely populated commercial city of Bukhara occupied an important place in the commercial world playing the role of an intermediary between Europe and Asia. In the noisy roofed bazaars of Bukhara, which according to different sources, numbered from two[21] to five,[22] there was a brisk trade and exchange of goods. Apart from the roofed markets, there also existed about 50 open air shopping centres (*attars*). Here medicines, perfumery, foodstuffs, sweetmeats, etc. were on sale.

The favourite place of the city-dwellers and visitors was Registan – a spacious square in front of the Amir's palace. Here one could come across the merchants from India, Afghanistan, Turkey, Persia, Russia, China, as well as Turkmen, Kalmyks, the representatives of the Caucasian and Central Asian peoples. In Registan on sale were Indian textiles and Kashmiri shawls, haberdashery and hardware goods of European manufacture, Chinese tea and spices from Manila. In book stores one could buy books in Turkish and Persian languages, apart from theological literature poetry and history books were available. For example, Alexander Burnes, the agent of British East India Company, who visited Bukhara in 1832 under the guise of a merchant purchased *Kitab-i-Akhbar-i-Bukhara* by Narshahi[23] and presented it to the Royal Asiatic society of Great Britain and Ireland.[24]

The merchants who arrived in the Bukhara Khanate with their goods were housed in special *caravanserais*. From the travellers' account we know that numerous *caravanserais* were constructed according to a uniform plan. It was usually a large square-shaped two-storey building; its outside walls had no windows. The ground floor was occupied by narrow and deep store-rooms, with the doors opening towards the yard; on the first floor lived the merchants. The rooms were equipped with small fireplaces. For a room, merchants would pay, according to some sources, 2–4 *tanga* (1 *tanga* equalled 20 Russian *kopecks*[25]) per month, for a storehouse rent – 7–14 *tanga*; stables were used free of charge.[26]

Within three days the goods of a merchant who came to stay in a *caravanserai* were surveyed and estimated by the officials in the presence of leading tradesmen and brokers. The duties were to be paid in cash only on the spot. The deferment of payment for several days and even up to two weeks was possible only if a reliable guarantee was provided by some influential Bukhara merchants. One fortieth part or 2.5 per cent was charged as tax on the value of all goods belonging to the Sunni Muslims, the traders who belonged to other creeds (Hindus, Russians, Armenians, Jews) had to pay 5 per cent.

During Mir Izzatullah's Bukhara trip in 1812–1813 there were five or six solidly constructed *caravanserais,*[27] in 1820 their number was recorded as 14,[28] in 1835 as 25.[29] Some of them were private, others belonged to the state and were leased out. The travellers said that sometimes the *caravanserais* belonged to the Amir's relatives, however the real owner was the ruler himself. Each *caravanserai* had a name; in a majority of cases it was named after the owner. One of them was referred to as Serai Hindi; it can be safely presumed that it was owned by or leased to the Indian merchants.

In the 20s–30s of the nineteenth century there were about two thousand Indians from Shikarpur and Sind along with 50 Sikhs from Multan and Punjab permanently residing in the Bukhara Khanate. "One of the *caravanserais* and roofed markets is always occupied by the men from one of these two peoples or the other", the travellers informed.[30] Like all other visiting merchants they stayed in the *caravanserais.* According to the travellers, the Indian merchants usually resided in the *serai* Mirzachul, *serai* Qarshi, *serai* Khwaja Jubair, the above-mentioned *serai* Hindi and *serai* Kush-begi.[31] Other sources inform that the Indian merchants, mainly from Shikarpur, rented *serai* Alim Khan and Abdulla Jan that were the property of the Amir of Bukhara.[32]

By the 40s–50s of the nineteenth century the number of Indians in Bukhara increased to five thousand. Most of them hailed from Peshawar and were engaged in trade and usury. Indian merchants stayed not only in Bukhara, but also in other Central Asian cities. In Kokand, for example, they occupied six *caravanserais.* "Here they make wholesale exchange of the goods brought from India, Tibet, Kashgar, Bukhara, Afghanistan and Russia", a traveller reported.[33] Another example was Samarqand, where the Indians occupied three *caravanserais.* The Indian merchants and usurers also resided in other cities of the Bukhara Khanate like Gijduvan, Vobkent, Qarshi.[34]

There was no market, even in the remotest area of the Khanate, without an Indian usurer. "By some unknown means they have taken possession of the whole of the money transactions in the country, – wrote

A. Vambery, the Hungarian Jewish traveller. – Showing deepest obedience like the Armenians in Turkey, they cheat the Uzbeks terribly, and as a pious qazi is always in concert with a worshipper of Vishnu, it is impossible for an unfortunate victim to escape from their hands".[35]

The Indian usurers managed to deeply penetrate into the Bukhara economy: their clients were feudal lords and rich merchants who took huge loans from them as well as petty craftsmen who asked for trifling sums. The Indian usurers had fixed days for visiting their debtors and collecting interest money. The accounts were recorded on special labels, which the usurers pinned upon long sticks and carried with them on their rounds. By the time of P.I. Demezon's Bukhara expedition in 1833–1834 the Indian usurers were the only rich class of the Khanate. The local merchants, always in need of working capital, applied to the Indian usurers, who supplied the required sum for a certain security or high interest rate. Being always in possession of free capital, they purchased the goods by wholesale and then, taking advantage of a favourable market situation, sold the merchandise with a large profit for themselves.[36]

Alexander Burnes, during his Bukhara mission also had a number of encoun-ters with the Indian merchants. In the Indian *caravanserai* about 300 of them stayed. The Indians from Shikarpur whom Burnes met were satisfied with their life, notwithstanding the fact that, according to Burnes, if one listed all the oppressions to which they were exposed there, it would create an impression of heavy persecutions.

The "persecutions" referred to by Burnes were the strict and humiliating regulations that all the non-Muslims or *ẕimmīs* permanently residing in Bukhara Khanate were forced to observe. The laws allowed the *ẕimmīs* to follow their religion, to own property, to make deals among themselves. However in all criminal cases and in their transactions with the Muslims they were subjected to the Islamic laws. They were prohibited to marry Muslims and to keep Muslims as slaves. The Indians were to wear coarse clothes and belt them with a rope; they were prohibited to ride horses and could use only donkeys. If a Muslim passed by the Indians (like the Jews, Armenians and others) had to respectfully let him pass first. They were not allowed to build houses higher than those of the Muslims.[37] Whenever possible, all *ẕimmīs* were settled in special quarters or *caravanserais,* as already mentioned.

During the Russian diplomatic and military missions of G. Meyendorff and I.V. Vitkevich the Amir prohibited the Indians to observe the funeral ceremonies according to their traditions (later on the prohibition was lifted). However it is necessary to note, that unlike the Bukhara Muslims the Indians and other *ẕimmīs* had certain privileges, too. The Indian,

Armenian and other foreign merchants were free within the *caravanserai* premises to drink wine, to smoke, to have fun without the risk of being beaten up by the guards; these enjoyments even within the same premises a Bukhara Muslim could not allow himself.[38]

Between the Amir's officials and Indian usurers there existed close and complicated interactions. The Amir claimed full authority over the property and the incomes of the Indian merchants in the Bukhara state. The Amir nominated the *yasaul* or headman of the Indian usurers. His duty was to keep an account of all the profits earned by the usurers and also render assistance in having the debts paid back. If an Indian usurer died heirless, the whole property after his death was confiscated by the state. The *yasaul* constantly kept the property of the usurers under control so that before their death they could not transfer anything to their compatriots.[39]

These measures were prompted by the fact that the Indian merchants and usurers exported from Bukhara huge quantities of coined gold and silver. That led to such a scarcity that, according to the Russian travellers, it was sometimes difficult to get two to three golden coins at once. Worried by the situation, the ruling circles of Bukhara banned the export of precious metals and coins. I.V. Vitkevich who visited Bukhara in 1836 recorded that "the Indians are hard pressed nowadays and they are going to fully abandon Bukhara. They are not allowed to export more gold and silver into India, indeed, they have really got hold of almost all available gold here".[40] Instead of the gold and silver coins exported by the Indians the Bukhara mint even began to produce and circulate adulterated coins.[41]

The Indian merchants concentrated in their hands nearly the entire trade activity in the Central Asian cities of their residence. They had their own *caravanserais*, highly developed credit system, especially the one based upon usury. The Indian businessmen enjoyed considerable respect in the ruling circles of the Central Asian Khanates. But, at the same time, penetrating into the remotest cities and villages, they brought with them not only goods, but also the great culture of their country. The activities of the Indian merchants therefore extended to not only commercial, but cultural spheres as well.

This can be corroborated by the recollections of Sadr ud-din Aini (1878–1954) the founder of the Soviet Tajik literature. As a youth he used to meet in a *caravanserai* called after its owner Alimjan an Indian jeweller whose name Aini would spell as Boyarchi (Pavarji?). This intelligent Indian "could write and read well in Tajik in the Arabian alphabet". In his cell he kept Indian books such as *Gulistān-i Massarrat*, the *dīwān* of the celebrated eighteenth century Sufi saint and poet Mirza Mazhar

Jan-i Janan and the biographical collection *Khazānā-i Umarā*. Many books were in Hindi. The Indian jeweller allowed the young Aini to use his collection of the Indian and Tajik books.[42]

The problem of the India-Central Asia trade relations cannot be researched adequately without the analysis of the Russo-British political and economic rivalry in the Central Asian Khanates. For many decades it had been Britain's aspiration to penetrate and establish itself in the markets of the Bukhara Khanate. The first fragmentary information on the British products in Central Asian markets appears in 1825. And though the British import was insignificant, the Russian government sounded the alarm.

The anxiety of Russian government increased especially during A. Burnes' expedition to Bukhara with the purpose of establishing a new trade route from India to the Central Asian Khanates by the Indus. Previously the European goods were exported into Central Asia by two routes, through Kabul and through Meshhed. From Kabul and Meshhed the caravans moved to Northern India and to Bukhara. From Bukhara the European goods reached all Central Asian markets. The transportation of the British merchandise to Central Asia was the business of a class of Indian Muslim traders known in these regions as *parasha.* (Similarly the Russians employed the Tartar traders for bringing their goods to Central Asia). The British entrusted their merchandise to the *parasha* on most favourable conditions. From Peshawar the *parasha* brought the goods to the Khanates through Bukhara, where they sold their loads to local merchants on beneficial terms. The *parasha* stayed in all Central Asian cities, but mostly in Kokand.

The Indian caravans brought the British merchandise to Bukhara by the shortest way. The Russian travellers were informed by the merchants that annually the caravans comprising 10 to 15 thousand camels and carrying 160 to 240 thousand *puds* load passed through Kabul.[43] During P.I. Demezon's stay in Bukhara one caravan brought three large bales of English fabrics, painted cottons, chintzes, muslins. These fabrics were of better quality than those brought to Bukhara from Russia, and were sold out easily. The Russian officer reported "... about the constant efforts of the British merchants to completely catch hold of the trade in this part of Asia, which after a very short time may be flooded with the British goods".[44]

In 1833 the Orenburgh General-Governor V.A. Perovsky informed in a report to the finance minister E.F. Kankrin, that a significant quantity of British goods brought by Afghans from the Indian city of Benares appeared in Bukhara and was sold there at much lower prices than the Russian products.[45] The Indian merchants, who previously imported goods from their native country only, now began to import the British merchandise. According to the information communicated to Burnes, 2/3 of goods brought to Bukhara from Russia and India were manufactured in Great Britain.

However, Russia's more convenient geographical situation vis-a-vis the Central Asian Khanates made it possible for the Russian merchants to deliver the goods to the inland areas of Asia by water. It was emphasised by Vambery, that "suffice is to have a look at the markets of Bukhara, Khiva and Qarshi to be convinced that the Russian trade develops significantly and it may be said without exaggeration that there is no house nor tent in the whole of Central Asia where one would not come across a Russian product".[46]

During that period Great Britain faced many obstacles in the development of her trade in Central Asia. Firstly, to transport the goods from the banks of the Indus through the still independent principalities where all kinds of duties were arbitrarily collected by the local potentates meant great losses and the transfer through the territories of the warlike nomads implied a constant risk of robbery too. Secondly, the trade in the Khanates was carried out by the British either through Indian, or through Afghan merchants and that made the business unprofitable. And thirdly, the remoteness of the Central Asia separated from Europe by the ocean and mountain ranges made it difficult to import heavy and large-sized goods. Despite all these hardships the British spared no efforts to overcome the obstacles hampering the development of their trade in Central Asia. They spent many years trying to secure the Amirs' sanction for establishing their factories on the coasts of the Amu-Darya. In return, the British promised to purchase the Bukhara raw materials for the same prices as were offered by Russia and to import into Bukhara British textiles and metal wares at cheaper rates than those offered by the Russians. However all attempts of the British to occupy a dominant position in the Central Asian commerce failed.

By the 70s of the nineteenth century Great Britain had completed the annexation and colonisation of India. Almost at the same time, in 1868, the Bukhara Khanate was likewise annexed by Russia, and the direct trade relations between India and the Central Asian states ceased to exist.

Notes and References

1. *The Geography of Strabo With an English Translation by Horage Leonard Jhones*, Ph.D., LL.D, in Eight Volumes, London, 1932, Vol. 5, p. 253.

2. During the period of its prosperity the Kusana state included the main part of modern Central Asia, Afghanistan, Pakistan, Northern India and probably parts of Sinkiang. The most important excavations of Kusana settlements were made in Bagram and Baghlan (Surkhotale, Afghanistan), in Taxila (Pakistan) and in the towns of Northern Bactria (Tajikistan and Turkmenia). It was in the Kusana epoch that Buddhism spread from India into Central Asia. For more information see: B. A. Litvinsky, *Outline History of Buddhism in Central Asia*, Moscow, 1968; G.M. Bongard-Levin and M.I. Vorobyova-Desyatovskaya, *Indian Texts from Central Asia*, Moscow, 1983.
3. Ibn Battuta, *Travels in Asia and in Africa.* Tr. by H. A. R. Gibb. Cambridge, 1958–62, Vol. 2, p. 478.
4. The Shaybanids were a Turko-Mongol clan whose founder Shayban (Shiban) was the son of the famous Mongol ruler Juchi, the elder son of Chenghiz Khan. The founder of the dynasty was Muhammad Shaybani (1451–1510) who conquered the Timurid capital Mawarannahr (Samarqand) in 1499 and founded the Shaybanid state.
5. N.M. Goldberg 'Russko-indiiskie otnoshenia v XVIII v. (The Russo Indian Relations in the XVIIIth Century)', *Uchonie Zapiski Tihookeanskogo instituta.* (The Occasional Papers of the Pacific Institute), Moscow-Leningrad, 1940, Vol. 2, p. 135.
6. Jenkinson. 'Puteshestvie v Srednyiyu Aziyu v 1558, 1560 gg. (The Travel into Central Asia in 1558 and 1560)' *Angliiskie puteshestvenniki v Moskovskom gosudarstve v XVI v.* (The British Travellers in Russia in the XVIth Century) Leningrad, 1937, pp. 184–85.
7. *Mubashir* was a class of officialdom in Central Asia and Middle East.
8. This valuable document is kept in the Manuscript Depository of the Academy of Sciences of the Republic of Tajikistan, N 102.
9. N.B. Baikov, *Rol Srednei Azii v russko-indiiskih torgovih svyazyakh (pervaya polovina XVI-vtoraya polovina XVIII v.)* (The Role of the Central Asia In the Russo-Indian Trade Relations (first half of the XVIth-second half of the XVIIIth century). Tashkent, 1964, pp. 21–22.
10. G.F. Gens, 'Nekotorie svedenia o Bukharii (Some Information on Bukhara)', *Otechestvennie zapiski* (The Country Records), Vol. 14, St. Petersburg, 1821, p. 303.
11. This old Russian measure of weight was equal to 16 kg.
12. At that period the Russian rouble and the Indian rupee had an approximately equal rate against the British pound –10:1.
13. E.K. Meyendorff. *Puteshestvie iz Orenburga v Bukharu* (The Voyage from Orenburg to Bukhara), Moscow, 1975, p. 129.
14. Alexander Burnes, *Travels To Bokhara.* London, 1836, Vol. 2, pp. 416, 428.
15. *Zapiski o Bukharskom khanstve* (The Notes On the Bukhara Khanate) Moscow, 1983, p. 79.
16. A. Gra, 'Materiali po istorii Orenburga (Sources for the History of Orenburg)', *Trudi Orenburgskogo ucenogo arkhivnogo komiteta* (Research Works of the Orenburg Archival research Committee), Vol. XI. Orenburg, 1903, pp. 141–42.
17. It is not mentioned to which particular town that merchant belonged. But it may be safely presumed that it was Srinagar the capital of Kashmir. In the beginning of the XIXth century Raphail Danibegashvili, a Georgian businessman and

diplomat, visited Srinagar (which he like many other foreign travellers called Kashmir) and recorded that in that city and its vicinities there were 24 thousand looms engaged in making shawls. For more details see: *Russko-Indiiskiye otnosheniya v XIX v*/(The Russo-Indian Relations in the XIXth Century) Moscow, 1997, p. 50.

18. E. K. Meyendorff, *Puteshestvie,* p. 129.
19. *Zapiski o Bukharskom khanstve,* pp. 79, 77.
20. A. Alektorov, 'Torgovie puti v Srednyuyu Aziyu (The Trade Routes to the Central Asia)', *Orenburgski listok,* (The Orenburg Paper), 17 February, 1891.
21. N. Hanykov, *Opisanie Bukharskogo khanstva* (The Description of the Bukhara Khanate). St. Petersburg, 1843, p. 92.
22. *Zapiski o Bukharskom khanstve,* p. 58.
23. This is a celebrated chronicle of Bukhara written in the 40s of the Xth century in Arabic by Abu Bakr Muhammad ibn Jafar an-Narshahi (899–959). In 1128 it was translated into Persian by Abu Nasr Ahmad ibn Muhammad al-Qubavi who abridged it and extended the narration up to his own epoch. In the XIIIth century an anonymous author extended the account of the history of Bukhara up to 1220. It was in the latter edition that this valuable source on the history of Central Asia became available to modern scholars.
24. Alexander Burnes, *Travels to Bokhara,* Vol. 1, p. 278.
25. 100 kopecks make 1 rouble.
26. *Zapiski o Bukharskom khanstve,* pp. 58, 99; E.K. Meyendorff. *Puteshestvie,* p. 100.
27. U.A. Sokolov, 'Bukhara, Samarkand, Kelif', *Trudi Sredneaziatskogo gosudarstvennogo universiteta* (Research Works of the Central Asian State University), New series, Vol. XC, book 4, 1957, p. 202.
28. E.K. Meyendorff, *Puteshestvie,* p. 100.
29. *Zapiski o Bukharskom khanstve,* p. 99.
30. 'Noveishee opisanie Velikoi Buharii (The Most recent Description of the Grand Bukhara)', *Aziatskii vestnik, izdavaemii Grigoriem Spasskim* (The Asian Newsletter Published by Grigory Spassky), St. Petersburg, 1825, p. 306.
31. *Zapiski o Bukharskom khanstve,* p. 99.
32. U.A. Sokolov, *Bukhara,* p. 202.
33. 'Obozrenie Kokandskogo khanstva v nineshnem ego sostoyanii (The Review of the Kokand Khanate in Its Present State)', *Zapiski Russkogo Geograficheskogo Obschestva* (Occasional Papers of the Russian Geographical Society), Vol. III, St. Petersburg, 1849, p. 213.
34. A.P. Horoshhin, *Sbornik statei, kasayuschihsya do Turkestanskogo kraya* (A Collection of Essays Related to Turkestan). St. Petersburg, 1876, p. 508; Sadr ad-din. Aini, *Vospominania* (Reminiscences). Moscow-Leningrad, 1960, pp. 428–28.
35. Vamberi A. *Puteshestvie po Srednei Azii* (Travels in Central Asia). Moscow, 1874, p. 324.
36. *Zapiski o Bukharskom khanstve,* p. 83.
37. A. A. Semenov, 'K proshlomu Bukhari (Towards the Bukhara's Past)', Sadr ad-din Aini, *Vospominania,* pp. 981–82.
38. *Zapiski o Bukharskom khanstve,* p. 60.
39. Sadr ad-din Aini, *Vospominania,* pp. 428–29.
40. *Zapiski o Bukharskom khanstve,* p. 104.
41. Ibid., p. 105.

42. Sadr ad-din Aini, *Vospominania*, p. 427.
43. *Zapiski o Bukharskom khanstve*, p. 25.
44. Ibid., p. 25.
45. Arkhiv Vneshney Politiky Rossiiyskoy Imperii (Foreign Policy Archives of Russian Empire), Fond Sankt-Peterburga (St. Petersburg Depository), Glavnii arhiv (Main Archive), 11–13, 1833, op. 34, d. 6.
46. Vamberi A. *Puteshestvie*, p. 369.

TWO ❖ Nana Sahib's Nephew in Russia

T. N. ZAGORODNIKOVA

In 1878–1880 INHABITANTS of St. Petersburg, the Russian capital, used to meet a strange dark-skinned person with a scar on his cheek walking along the streets. His shabby clothes and deep dark eyes full of pain, with sometimes even hungry looks, were somehow in disharmony with his proud way of behaviour. He was earning his living by small loans here and there and by tutoring in rich families – this was a typical way of earning one's living by poor students, but he was not a student. He had powerful friends and sponsors among different strata of Russian society: Professor V.V.Grigoriev, a famous Orientalist and specialist in Central Asian problems, baron Jomini and Von der Osten-Saken, top officials of Ministry of Foreign Affairs, Grant Duke Nicolai Konstantinovich Romanov, famous traveller Semenov-Tyan-Shansky, M.N. Katkov, the editor of *Moscow Vedomosty* newspaper and others. He had friends among diplomats of Japanese and Persian embassies. All of them tried to get work for him or to help him in any other possible way. Who was that strange fellow?

He came from India. His name was Ramchandra Balaji from Bithoor. "I am the nephew of Nana Sahib, the leader of the Mutiny", he used to add.

There are many documents left about that person and his activities in Archives of former USSR, most of them either in Moscow or in Tashkent. The majority of these documents are in Russian or in French.[1]

He claimed to have been born in 1850 and brought up in the harem of Nana Sahib. In 1857 when the Mutiny was almost suppressed by the British army during the siege of the Peshwa's palace in Bithoor by English soldiers he fell out of the window and broke his cheekbone. An English officer, Captain Brandon or Pradan, captured him and afterwards took the boy first to Calcutta and then to London. The childless wife of the English officer felt affection for the little orphan. Unfortunately, the climate of Great Britain did not suit him and he had to live mainly in Italy, visiting his stepmother from time to time. In 1859 he was send to Lausanne in Switzerland where his studies began. Ramchandra lived there in a boarding house till 1868. Every summer he used to come to Great Britain to visit the family of Captain Brandon and his compatriots, who lived in England. There he learnt the language and faith of his motherland from a Brahman, who came to Great Britain with Dulip Singh, another captive, the last Maharaja of Punjab. All expenses were paid from India Office funds. Ramchandra was given 10 francs as pocket money. During his last years in Lauṣanne he earned some money by teaching English and music. So when he heard that a relative of his, the Raja of Kolhapur, had come to Italy Ramchandra was able to pay the fares and visited him. The Raja of Kolhapur died in Florence and left everything he had to Ramchandra. That was enough to buy a ticket to India and in 1869 he found himself once again in his native land. After several months' of his stay in India the British located him and he was escorted back to Switzerland under the false pretext of completing his education.

In 1870 Ramchandra joined Berlin University. There he made the acquaintance of professor Weber, specialist on Sanskrit, who later recommended him to K.A. Kossovich, one of the first Russian Sanskritologists. One of the Japanese princes was among his friends. All of these people played a role in his later life. He continued spending his vacations in Britain where he made friends with Iskandar Khan of Afghanistan.[2] The latter, annoyed by the attitude of British authorities towards him, made up his mind to go to Persia and invited Ramchandra to join him. Ramchandra was not yet ready to quit and returned to Berlin.

Suddenly he received an official invitation, or rather an order, to go to London. But one of his friends warned him that in Britain he would be seized upon and sent by force to West Indies, to Jamaica. The only possible explanation was that the English were aware of Iskandar Khan's proposal and were afraid that from Persia he would again attempt to penetrate into India. Ramchandra therefore abandoned his studies and left for Tehran. He did try to reach India via Herat. There he found that he was under strict surveillance of the British agents. On his way to Kashmir he was robbed by Afghan rebel tribes and forced to return. In Tehran he launched agitation in favour of Persian-Japanese commercial treaty to import green tea to Persia from Japan instead of Bombay and thus to damage British commercial interests in that part of the world.

In 1878 the Russo-Turkish war was over and peace treaty had to be signed in San-Stephano. Ramchandra, who had reached Turkey by that time, came across a Japanese officer, whom he used to meet in Berlin. It was this officer, who introduced him to the Russians. His new friends invited him to visit Russia. That year he appeared in St. Petersburg.[3]

That was the story, which he narrated to Russian authorities when he was asked about the circumstances of his birth. The information about the life of Ramchandra before 1878 differs in some details if we compare the report of Colonel Korolkov, the article of S.B. Petrov-Baturich (see below) and other documents. We tried to compile it from different sources so that it was quite coherent and contained minimum inconsistencies. His activities in Russia can be easily reconstructed from the documents of military archives.

Before analysing Ramchandra's life in Russia it is necessary to describe the situation in world politics between peace treaty of San-Stephano and Berlin Congress, that is between March 3 and July 13, 1878. Russo-Turkish war of 1877–1878 though it ended in victory for the Russian army, strained the country's economy and human resources heavily. That is why the peace treaty of San-Stephano was welcomed not only in Istanbul, but in St. Petersburg as well. The attitude of Great Britain, which had been an ally of Turkey in this war, towards this treaty was negative. The British did not recognise the treaty, which was signed by the two belligerent powers, Russia and Turkey, both exhausted by war. Therefore Russia was facing another war in Europe. One of the possible ways to prevent this war was to begin a military expedition to India, the most precious British colony.[4] Ramchandra, who understood the situation, decided to make use of the moment and to initiate an expedition in order to liberate his native country. Unfortunately for him, he came too late. We don't know the exact date of his arrival in St. Petersburg, sometime in summer, but even if the Berlin treaty had not been signed by that time, he still would not have enough time to make the acquaintance of proper influential persons for initiating such a plan.

The first year of Ramchandra's life in Russia was full of hard work. He could hardly make two ends meet. Professor V.V. Grigoriev showed great kindness to him and recommended him to Grant Duke Nicolai Konstantinovich Romanov and to Governor-General of Russian Turkestan, P.K. von Kaufman as an expert in the Orient. Military authorities' response gave Ramachandra some hope but nothing more. In June-November, 1879, upon the recommendation of Professor V.V. Grigoriev, Ramchandra took part in the third expedition of Grant Duke Nicolai Konstantinovich Romanov to Central Asia. According to Grant Duke he turned out to be very industrious, helpful and competent member of the team. "To my mind, this person may be very useful for Russians in the East. That is why I invited him to take part in my travels along Turkestan next year also. Next spring he is going to explore a coulee of Amu river hitherto unknown to the world".[5] Ramchandra also wanted to continue his cooperation with Grant Duke Nicolai Konstantinovich, to take part in his expedition next year. His main aim was to explore the route to India from the Russian Central Asia,[6] but by that time his friends in the capital had succeeded in making the Russian nobility and authorities, especially in military and diplomatic circles, interested in him.

The Russian nobility was always interested in every stranger, especially in those who had suffered. In the eyes of the ladies the dark-haired Indian with his romantic looks and glamour of a martyr turned out to be a hero. He received a lot of invitations to parties. Once he was told that an opera was being written about his life.[7] An article about his adventures appeared in one of the periodicals.[8] Thus he became a celebrity.

The attitude of official circles was a bit different. For one thing, they had known about him from the very beginning of his stay in Russia in 1878 and had tried to collect all information about him and his previous activities. Colonel L.N. Sobolev, Head of the Asiatic Department of General Headquarters, had submitted a report about Ramchandra to the Head of General Headquarters as far back as in autumn of 1878.[9]

The second half of the nineteenth century was the time when two great empires, Russia and Great Britain, were bitter enemies. In the Russo-Turkish war of 1877–1878 Great Britain was on the side of Turkey. Confrontation in Central Asia was about to turn into the second Anglo-Afghan war. That was why every Indian in Russia was regarded at that time as a potential British spy. Besides, Ramchandra had several letters of introduction from Iskandar Khan,[10] who after his departure for Great Britain was considered to be a highly suspicious person.

Russian ambassador to Persia I.A. Zinoviev wrote that while in Tehran Ramchandra and his friend were selling medicines and he had not claimed to be the relative of Nana Sahib at that time. The Russian diplomat suggested that this Indian should not be trusted.[11] The rest of the references collected by the military were perfect. There was no doubt that this Indian was of a noble origin, well educated (he knew several European languages, spoke a little Russian and understood everything in that language, knew history well), his judgements and comments were very interesting and unusual. By no means was he a British spy, in fact he was an arch enemy of Britain. His aim was to return to India and liberate it. Colonel Korolkov, Assistant to the Head of Zaravshan district, who knew Ramchandra personally, wrote about him: "The supposition that Ramchandra is a British spy to my mind is not proved by any fact. The English themselves must have invented it. The attitude of the Hindus in Samargand and his desire to go to India by an extremely dangerous route from Samarqand to Kashmir contradict that supposition. All Indians of Samarqand, including the famous envoy of tribe of Sikhs Guru Charan Singh and Brahman from Central India (Gwalior) treated Ramchandra with deep respect. If Ramchandra had been a British spy, than by all means the British would have given him an opportunity to travel to India by a more comfortable way than is the route from Samarqand to Kashmir. And finally, by my personal acquaintance with Ramchandra I am convinced that he is the last person to be suspected to like for the British and in intention to support their rule in India. To my mind Ramchandra is able to accept any risky affair in order to do harm to the British."[12]

In the 1880s no modern Indian language was taught in Russia, and as a result there were no interpreters of Indian languages in Russian Empire. If the need arose they had to translate from Hindustani or any other Indian language into Persian and then from Persian into Russian. So Ramchandra might have been of great help to the Russian authorities, both diplomatic and military, but mainly in Turkestan. On the 13th of March 1880 the Czar's decree (*ukaz*) was issued to the effect that Ramachandra be accredited to the Asiatic Department of General Headquarters and put at command of Adjutant General M.D. Skobelev.[13] Mikhail Dmitrievitch Skobelev, the famous hero of Russo-Turkish war of 1877–1878, military governor of Ferghana district, was then preparing for his second campaign to Trans-Caspian region.

The financial problems of Ramchandra were at last also settled: he was given a generous allowance both from the General Headquarters budget and Ferghana district budget.[14]

The military authorities in Petersburg and Tashkent were planning that Ramchandra would help in some unknown problems of Indian and Central Asian geography and ethnology. Adjutant General M.D. Skobelev thought that this Indian might be useful in his relations with Iskandar Khan of Afghanistan and some nobles of Trans-Caspian region. The collective opinion was that he would be very useful in talks with the envoys of Indian native rulers, who from time to time came to seek support from the Czar. In order to be ready in case of war with Great Britain in Asia it was necessary to arrange intercommunication with our possible allies in India, especially with the Maharaja of Kashmir.[15] They were even planning for Ramchandra's trip to India or to Herat. The Russian authorities hoped that with his help they would be able to facilitate Indian youngsters' coming to Russian Turkestan to make them interpreters or agents or to join Russian army. If there were enough of them to form a special unit it had to be used during any confrontation, either military or diplomatic, in Russian Turkestan, Afghanistan or even in India.

Pieces of useful information had already been dipped out from conversations with Ramchandra by the time of the royal decree. Some of them were true to life, for example, in 1876 the Chitral ruler Aman-ul-Mulk really declared himself a vassal of the Maharaja of Kashmir, others were mere rumours: Badakhshan never seceded from Afghanistan and became part of the Bukhara state.[16] According to Ramchandra the events of the second Anglo-Afghan war had inspired the Burma ruler to expel the British from his state and to declare himself independent from Britain,[17] which was not true. Ramchandra's data about the routes in Turkestan and Afghanistan were especially valuable because he had himself travelled there and assessed them from the military point of view.[18]

Ramchandra had peculiar thoughts about the situation in India and perspectives of British Raj there. According to him Indian people lived in extreme poverty, because of scarcity of tillable land as compared to the size of population. The best cultivated fields were in the hands of the British who had vast plantations of indigo, opium and other herbs for export. So, according to Ramchandra, the Hindus would be somehow satisfied if Great Britain conquered Afghanistan because their two enemies, the Muslims and the British, were thus destroying each other and as a result some of the Indians would be able to move to Afghanistan and settle there.[19] Another way out was to move to waste lands of Russian Turkestan and, as Ramachandra stated, there were many Indians eager to do so. Such emigration might lessen the stress of poverty and oppression that were at the root of British Raj in India.[20] The British did their best to propagate the negative image of the Russians. Nevertheless, many Indians looked upon the Russians as their liberators from British Raj. The Maharajas of Kashmir, Patiala and Gwalior were eager to cooperate. They were, according to Ramchandra, "representatives of 150-million population, truly devoted to Russia".[21]

Before beginning his work in Turkestan Ramchandra asked for permission to go to Persia as he had some urgent matters to sort out there. He was given necessary orders, money and papers.

On the 6th of June he wrote his first letter from Baghdad, addressed to Colonel L.N. Sobolev. There he renounced his service in Turkestan because of some misfortunes which he had faced while in Russia. He wanted to go to Abdurrahman Khan, the Amir of Afghanistan.[22] The second letter, dated 12th of August, came from Shiraz. There he was not so resolute about his resignation. He wrote that the Japanese mission, in favour of which he had launched agitation, was welcomed in Persia and now he wanted to establish relations between Afghanistan and Japan.[23] Simultaneously Ramchandra wrote to Adjutant General M.D. Skobelev that he was ready to start working under his command. On receiving this letter Adjutant General M.D. Skobelev sent a telegram to Major-General[24] L.N. Sobolev: "Are you in want of Ramchandra's service? . . . I don't know what he was doing during 4 months. I don't foresee any use for this work. He is mentally ill".[25] Major-General L.N. Sobolev proposed not to answer him officially but privately.

In autumn of 1880 Ramchandra once again appeared in Adjutant General M.D. Skobelev's camp in Trans-Caspian region. The instructions, which were endorsed by the Czar himself, were very clear: ". . . Let Ramchandra be attached to Trans-Caspian troops, but under strict surveillance. Do not let him intrigue or interfere in our policy".[26]

In the February of 1881 another telegram from Trans-Caspian region was sent to the capital to Major-General L.N. Sobolev: ". . . His stay here is quite useless, the best way out is to call him back".[27] Ramchandra didn't want to wait for the answer from the General Headquarters and escaped. He was caught in Ashkhabad en route to Herat. This time Adjutant General M.D. Skobelev used more violent language in his telegram: he called the Indian "an evil person".[28] The order was to send Ramchandra to General Headquarters at St. Petersburg under police escort.[29]

In March 1881 Ramchandra found himself in Moscow. His escort was removed and he was allowed to go anywhere he wanted. He was free again but without work and without money. He was down on his luck. So he went to the Capital and tried once again to seek his fortune in the General Headquarters. The military authorities didn't want to deal with him any more. Then he decided to go abroad, but where was he to get the money?[30]

A petition was forwarded to the Czar requesting an allowance of 1000 roubles to Ramchandra. "I think this is too much. Send him to our border at the expense of the Government, he does not deserve any allowance." – That was the decision of the Czar, written in his own hand on the margins of the petition.[31]

This is the end of Ramchandra's story, his almost three years' stay in Russian empire.

The documents from the Russian archives did not provide us with the answers to three main questions: Who was Ramchandra? Did he want to gain any benefit for himself? What happned to him after this?

To our mind, he could hardly be a relative of Nana Sahib. Nana Sahib was the eldest adopted son of the last Peshwa. His only nephew from the Peshwa's side was Panduranga Rao, son of the Peshwa's second adopted child. His own kinsmen were rather poor, they belonged to the same *gotra* as the last Peshwa. As far as we know there also were no nephews from that side.

Moreover, on July 17, 1857 during his retreat from Bithoor Nana Sahib had taken his harem, women and children of the palace, and escorted them to Nepal. On the July 19, when the British troops walked into practically deserted palace, there was hardly any big siege or battle.[32]

To our mind, Ramchandra was a nationalist who wanted to strike the right chord in the hearts of the Russian people for India's liberation and was therefore, trying to explore the attitude that the Russian people had towards Nana Sahib, leader of the Mutiny and Indian national hero. His desire was to take advantage of the Anglo-Russian confrontation in Europe and Central Asia just after the Russo-Turkish war of 1877–1978, to liberate his country with the help of Russian troops. That was maybe the only right moment for initiating such an expedition but he had only several months from March till July 1878 to do it and he missed that opportunity and failed. I doubt if even a more influential person than Ramchandra could have managed such an achievement.

His failure as a civil official of Turkestan military administration was inevitable because of his own character. He was an ill-tempered person, always quarrelling with those who turned out to be near by. During the expedition to Central Asia he quarrelled with count N.Y. Rostovtzev,[33] who was the Czar's special agent attached to Grant Duke. In one of his letters, mentioned above, he accused Adjutant General M.D. Skobelev of being unfair to him. Another letter in which he described his way back from Central Asia discloses its author as an absent-minded person leaving behind pieces of luggage, his pet-animal etc. It was not himself he blamed for these misfortunes but a person accompanying him.[34] Besides, in spite of his life in Europe and European education, Ramchandra had a strong sense of high caste superiority and contempt for the common people.[35] One can imagine the attitude of Russian battle-tried general M.D. Skobelev towards such a person, who simply failed in the duties he was entrusted to fulfil.

The attitude of the Russians, who dealt with him, changed from blind admiration first to incomprehension and even to compassion and then to negativism, distrust and suspicion. But in any case nobody supposed that he wanted to gain anything for himself by planning for military campaign and liberation of his country.

The documents from Russian Archives narrate the story of Ramchandra, offer us some information to answer the first and the second question posed above, but, unfortunately, provide no answer for the third.

Notes and References

1. French was the language of official correspondence and the language of Russian nobility for almost the whole of the XIX century.
2. Iskandar Khan was a grandchild of Amir Dost Muhammad Khan of Afghanistan and a nephew of Amir Sher Ali Khan, one of the pretenders to Afghanistan throne. He was loser in the dynastic strife and fled to Russia. Here he joined the army and tried to receive support in his dynastic struggle, but failed. In 1871 he moved to Great Britain with the same aim and also failed. In 1877 he left England for Turkey, and after that settled in Persia.
3. The information about Ramchandra was specially collected by military authorities from different sources, including Ramchandra himself, and the whole story was related by Colonel Korolkov in his report submitted to the Head of Military Scientific Committee of the General Headquarters in January of 1880. Rossiyskiy Gosudarstvenniy Voenno-istorocheskiy Arhiv (RGVIA) (Russian State Military-Historic Archives) f. 400, op. 1, f. 657, pp. 14–27.
4. In fact the Russian military authorities in Turkestan started mobilization of local forces, regiments moved towards the border.
5. RGVIA, f. 400, op. 1, file 657, p. 88.
6. RGVIA, f. 400, op. 1, file 657, pp. 88–89.
7. Gosudarstvenniy Arhiv Rossiyskoy Federatzii (GARF) (Russian State Archives) f. 1155, op. 1, f. 2830, pp. 1–2 and op.
8. S.V. Petrov-Baturich, 'Vstrecha s plemyannikom Nana Sahib v Peterburge (Meeting with a nephew of Nana Sahib in Petersburg)', *Russky Vestnic,* 1879, N 6.
9. RGVIA, f. 400, op. 1, f. 657, p. 3.
10. Ibid., p. 25.
11. Arhiv Vneshney Politiki Rossiyskoy Imperii (AVPRI) (Russian Empire Foreign Affairs Archives), f. SPb. Glavny arhiv, II-8, op. 45, 1878, file 2, p. 2.
12. RGVIA, f. 400, op. 1, f. 657, p. 16 and op.
13. Ibid., pp. 5–6.
14. Ibid.
15. Ibid., p. 32 op.
16. Ibid., pp. 3–4 and op.
17. Ibid., pp. 45–48 and op.
18. Ibid.
19. Ibid., p. 4 op.
20. Ibid., p. 45.
21. Ibid., p. 48 and op.
22. Ibid., p. 52.
23. Ibid., pp. 52–53.
24. L.N. Sobolev was promoted to the rank of Major General on the 30th of August 1880.
25. Ibid., p. 51.
26. Ibid., p. 65.

27. Ibid., p. 69.
28. Ibid., p. 73.
29. Ibid., p. 86.
30. Ibid., pp. 113–14 and op.
31. Ibid., p. 108.
32. A.S. Misra, *Nana Saheb Peshwa and The Fight for Freedom,* Lucknow, 1961, p. 297.
33. Ibid., p. 36 op.
34. GARF, f. 1155, op. 1, f. 2830, pp. 1–2 and op.
35. Rossiyskiy Gosudarstvenniy Arhiv Literaturi i Iskusstva (RGALI) (Russian State Archives of Literature and Arts), f. 472, op. 1, f. 84.

THREE

❖ Russia's 'Threat' to British India: The Tibetan Dimension

T. L. SHAUMIAN

SITUATED IN THE heart of Asia and bordered by the mighty Himalayas, distinguished as the geographical, historical, economic and religious centre of the Himalayan region, Tibet is a junction which cradled the largest Asiatic civilisations. It remained inaccessible, "forbidden" for the Europeans and through the centuries was shrouded in a veil of mystery and enigma. Preserved there is a unique socio-political and economic structure with political and economic supremacy of the Lamaist church. The religious leader – the Dalai Lama is the living divine and also the temporal ruler of Tibet.

Tibet had a long history of trade relationship with China and India. Tibet exported the famous Tibetan wool, gold dust, silver, stone salt, borax, medical herbs and animal products and imported tea, silk, porcelain, enamel, footwear and garments from China and cotton, woollen cloth, tobacco, sugar, glass and metal utensils, firearms, etc. from India.

Being a highly important residence of the Lamaist religious head, the Dalai Lama, Tibet was visited by many pilgrims not only from neighbouring India, Nepal, Sikkim and Bhutan, but also from Mongolia, Russia, Trans-Baikal area and Kalmyk Steppe. A large number of Buddhists lived in India and they compelled the British colonial authorities to establish firm connections with Lhasa, which would also promote and consolidate the British power and influence in India. These factors were made use of by the governments of Great Britain and Russia to conceal the true motives of their interest in Tibet, with its favourable strategic position in the heart of Central Asia, under the guise of their concern about their Buddhist subjects.

Since the end of the eighteenth century Great Britain attempted to actively and regularly penetrate into China from the Indian territory across the Himalayas, gradually seizing parts of the Himalayan principalities like Bhutan, Sikkim and Nepal to get nearer the Tibetan borders.

In 1898 Lord Curzon became the Viceroy of India. It is well known that the British Government in London determined only the general guidelines for the policy of Great Britain in Central Asia. Concrete implementation of it was in the hands of the Viceroy of India. It is not surprising that at the end of the nineteenth and beginning of the twentieth century the Asiatic policies of Great Britain reflected the political views of nationalist circles of the British establishment whose worthy spokesman was Lord Curzon.

The main task of Lord Curzon in India was to further expand and strengthen the British possessions. Russia's active penetration into Central Asia was used by Curzon to forward the theory that the conquest of India was Russia's main purpose and Central Asia was a spring-board for attacking that British colony.

As is known there were no common borders between the Russian possessions in Asia and India. They were divided by Sinkiang and Tibet which belonged to the sphere of the influence of Ch'ing China. Therefore Curzon was extremely watchful of the success of Russian policy in Sinkiang and of the signs of the growing Russian influence in Tibet.

Lord Curzon accelerated his efforts to establish relations with the government of Tibet. But the unfriendly attitude of the Tibetan ruling circles dismayed the Anglo-Indian administration, particularly as the British agents and later the Russian press reported that the Dalai Lama had sent letters to the Russian Czar through special Tibetan missions. Lord Curzon was at the end of his tether when the Russian governmental newspaper "Journal de Saint Petersburg" in October 1900 reported, that on 30th September, 1900, Russian Emperor Nicholas II had received in Livadia, his summer palace, Ngawang Lozang Dorjieff, the first *Tsenyi Khenpo* (a high-ranked scholar of the Tibetan religious and philosophical tradition and the tutor to the young Dalai Lama). A Russian Buryat by origin, Dorjieff was in the service of the High Priest in Tibet. Consequently he became not only the ideologist, but also direct performer, of the basic measures pertaining to the implementation of the policy of rapprochement between Russia and Tibet.

Thus the British, justified their expansion in the Central Asia, to the North-East and North-West of the borders of India, as a measure to protect the Indian borders but they came into conflict with, were Russian interests who also sought to strengthen their position in Central Asia. Therefore the relations of the Anglo-Indian colonial authorities with the borderland territories went beyond the limits of local border conflicts and were determined by the terms of the so called "great game", the Anglo-Russian rivalry in Central Asia. They also directly affected the European interests of both the powers.

According to the British version, Great Britain was only defending her Indian possessions, while the Russians, seizing one Central Asian region after another, were seeking to add India, "the Jewel in the British Crown" to their possessions. This viewpoint is at least disputable. It appears that both Russia and Great Britain pursued offensive policies from the strategic point of view, in the interests of developing trade, acquiring new sources of raw materials and market for the growing bourgeoisie of these countries. And it was in Central Asia that these two streams of expansion clashed.

In the majority of the research works discussing the Russo-British collision of interests and the alleged "Russian threat to British India" the problem has been analyzed mainly in terms of the Central Asian and Afghan dimension. But the Tibetan dimension of the Russo-British rivalry was of no less importance. moreover, it remained extremely significant for the subsequent development of the Asian politics as well. One of the episodes of that "great game" is dealt with in the present work. It makes use of many original sources from the Foreign Policy Archives of the Russian Empire (Arkhiv Vneshney politiki Rossiyskoy Imperii, AVPRI) and the National Archives of India, including correspondence between the Russian Czar and Dalai Lama XIII, reports and letters from Russian and British diplomatic representatives and agents from London, Petersburg, Calcutta, Peking and Urga.

The reportedly warn reception to the Tibetan representative Dorjieff, by the Russian Czar in September 1900, caused great anxiety in London and Calcutta. The British diplomats in Petersburg were instructed to ascertain its implications on the spot.[1] The charge d'affairs of Great Britain in Petersburg, C. Hardinge, got in touch with the Tibetan doctor P.A. Badmaev, who had played a role in the Tibetan orientation of Russian policies. In a report to Marquis Salisbury of the Foreign Office on 31st October, 1900 he said that after talking with him, he had come to the conclusion that the mission, in contrast to the previous one, was of an official nature, although Badmaev had asserted that it was a courtesy visit by Dorjieff. Hardinge himself considered it possible that Dorjieff had visited Petersburg to clear up purely religious issues between Lhasa and the Russian Buddhists. However, Hardinge wrote, whatever might have been the aim of the mission, the Russian government would benefit from it and seize the opportunity to propagate the opinion that it would be natural for Asiatic peoples to be under the Russian patronage.[2]

Curzon, at first, dismissed the report saying that Dorjieff was a swindler and his mission to the Czar was a "fraud" and entirely fabricated. Of course, Curzon knew that Russia had for a long time been attempting to penetrate into Lhasa, but the presumption that the Tibetan Lamas might have shed their usual suspicious attitude towards the Europeans and openly sent a direct mission to Europe, was from his point of view unlikely. Curzon was also convinced that Tibet would sooner ask for support from Great Britain than from Russia.[3] Besides, assuming that it would take not less than ten years for Russia to make Tibet her protectorate, he believed that the British still had sufficient time to drive Russia away from Tibet. To achieve that aim, it was first necessary to establish direct relations with the Dalai Lama. "A Russian protectorate over Tibet is to be stopped, and the only way to stop is by being in advance ourselves". In case it could not be done by friendly correspondence, which Curzon's persistent effort had tried to establish, albeit without any results. On 11th June 1901, he wrote to Hamilton, the Secretary of State for India: "It is really the most grotesque and indefensible thing that at a distance off little more than 200 miles from our frontier this community of unarmed monks should set us perpetually at defiance. Future use of force might become necessary."[4] It must be said that even these attempts of Curzon to establish correspondence with the Dalai Lama were regarded by the Foreign Office as needless; the latter was afraid, and with reason, that harder pressure on Tibet might make the latter come closer to Russia.

As regards the sending of a smallest expedition to Tibet, because of serious differences with both Germany and Russia, any measure of a military nature, especially at the time of the Anglo-Boer war, was supposed to create for the British Empire a complicated military and political situation. Curzon was sure to realise that. In the letter to Hamilton he wrote that for the British it would be a madness to cross the Himalayas and occupy Tibet. But if it was important that nobody else captured it so was it necessary to convert it into a buffer between the Indian and the Russian empires.[5]

From the correspondence between Curzon and Hamilton on the question of relations with Tibet, it is evident that there was serious disagreement between the Anglo-Indian government and the London Cabinet that manifested itself whenever any matter of external policies concerning India cropped up. Thus it what happened in the case of Tibet. What Curzon could not secure by negotiations, he was prepared to secure by force, while the London government was more cautious and dealt with the matters of foreign policy in the context of the interests of the British Empire as a whole.[6] As regards relations with Russia, the foreign minister Salisbury wrote that Curzon wanted him to negotiate with Russia, pretending as if they (the British) had "500,000 soldiers" to back them up.[7]

Meanwhile rumours about Russia's penetration into Lhasa were becoming more and more persistent. The British press was receiving numerous inquiries from the readers about the situation on the North-Eastern frontiers of India.[8] The ruling circles in India loudly voiced the necessity to include this province into the sphere of English influence.[9]

Reports in the Russian press about another visit to Russia by Dorjieff in June 1901, this time with a whole group of Tibetans, greatly increased concern about the Tibet situation.

Having learnt that on June 23, 1901, Czar Nicholas II had received the extraordinary ambassadors of the Dalai Lama in his summer residence Peterhof, the British Ambassador in Petersburg tried to find out the details of the reception. He informed his Government that, according to Dr. Badmaev, the Tibetans had requested Russia to help them in case of British aggression. The Chinese Charge d' affairs in Petersburg supposed that Dorjieff came to Petersburg to request the Czar not to prevent his Russian subjects to penetrate into Tibet (evidently, the Russian diplomacy still tried to convince the Chinese diplomacy of their desire to preserve the integrity of China). The international press also differently interpreted the reported Tibetan mission. Some of the Indian newspapers reported that the mission like that of 1900 was only of a religious nature.[10] The press in Colombo, on the contrary, asserted that in Ceylon "the explanation, that the aim of the envoy was purely religious . . . was never believed, rather the conviction of its political nature had become stronger owing to the printed descriptions . . . of the difficulties suffered by the envoys when going through India, secretly from the English".[11]

The British Ambassador in Petersburg, A.M. Scott, received instructions from London to meet the Foreign Minister of Russia, Lamsdorff. During their talks on July 3, 1901, Lamsdorff characterised "the Russian press conclusion that the Tibetan guests had come on some diplomatic mission, as absurd and absolutely baseless".[12] According to him, Dorjieff came to Petersburg "probably to collect money for his order" from the numerous Buddhists of the Russian origin. Lamsdorff stated that during Dorjieff's first visit the Emperor had received him in Yalta with the aim of learning about the life in Tibet, which was of interest to him. The Russian Imperial Geographic Society also displayed great interest in this visit which, however, was not of an official nature.[13]

After the Russian press reported that Dorjieff had paid visits to Lamsdorff and Witte, the Russian Finance Minister, Scott again had a talk with Lamsdorff and was reassured by the latter that the mission was not official and could not be regarded as political or diplomatic. It was similar to the missions sent by the Pope of Rome to other countries, said Lamsdorff. In the letter by the Dalai Lama, sent to him through Dorjieff, he only wished him good health and wrote that he himself was in a good state.[14]

However, the reports of British Ambassador in Petersburg, did not satisfy the Foreign Office. Hamilton, the Secretary of State for India, emphasised his surprise that Russia publicly welcomed the Tibetan mission, while the Dalai Lama ignored the Viceroy of India and returned his letters without even opening them. On September 2, 1901, Scott again visited Lamsdorff and conveyed to him that the British government could not be indifferent towards any actions which might violate or change the existing status of Tibet. At that, the Russian Minister once again reiterated his earlier statement that the mission dealt "with purely religious matters and had no political aims or diplomatic nature".[15]

While the British government was still unclear about the nature of Dorjieff's mission, the Viceroy of India, Lord Curzon, openly expressed doubts that "the Tibetan mission to Russia represented only monasteries"[16] and demanded the Foreign Office conclude a treaty in Lhasa guaranteeing permanent relations between England and Tibet. For this Curzon was willing to take any measures, including even an armed invasion of the Tibetan territory. Hamilton wrote that the way proposed by Curzon "may boomerang. It may place Tibet in the Russian hands". Besides, according to the London Cabinet, Britain had no material prerequisites to organise any expedition beyond the Indian borders.[17] However, Curzon ignored these arguments and continued to assert that Dorjieff was a Russian agent. (It is interesting that Curzon overestimated Dorjieff's abilities and said that if the British Intelligence Service had such agents he could have established personal relations with the Dalai Lama without difficulty. Meanwhile, on February 13, 1902, Curzon reported to Hamilton that his letter was again returned by the Dalai Lama[18]).[19]

Thus Curzon and the British government both realized the importance of the events in Tibet, but did not assess identically the seriousness of the events and the strategy to be used in Tibet. The differences on the Tibetan issue between Calcutta and London further aggravated.

As far back as August 1901, Hamilton had written to Curzon that "the Tibetans are but the smallest of pawn on the political chessboard, but castles, knights and bishops may be all involved in trying to take that pawn".[20] This was testified by the scope of the campaign started in the British press about the Russo-Tibetan rapprochement. It showed that the ruling circles in Britain had vested interests in it. (Let alone the English press, even the Russian newspaper *New Times (Novoye Vremya)* had published openly provocative materials on Dorjieff's visit!). The reports of the British press coincided with the signing of the anti-Russian Anglo-Japanese treaty and the Russo-Chinese Agreement on the withdrawal of the Russian troops from Manchuria, that meant the weakening of the Russian positions in the Far East.

The spread of rumours in the press and in some diplomatic circles about the Russo-Chinese Agreements on Tibet, about Russian agents in Lhasa etc. gave the Curzon government a new pretext to intensify the anti-Russian propaganda and the justification of the "offensive policy" by the Russian threat to India.

In May 1902, V. Klemm, the Russian Consul-General in Bombay reported to the Russian Foreign Ministry that the Anglo-Indian newspapers were almost daily printing "cock and bull stories of war and outrageous slanders about Russia." All Indian libraries contained collection of books "which wrote with a suppressed fear and undistinguished spite of Russia's intentions vis-à-vis India and the possible outcome of this allegedly inevitable struggle of the whale and the bear for appropriating that treasure".[21]

During a talk with Klemm, a British officer acknowledged that false information spread about Russia, especially about the Russian civil and military authorities and about their treatment of people, was a part of a programme to train the Indian native troops. According to Klemm, the editor of a native newspaper told him that "malicious attacks directed at the Russians are welcome to the government, and to please the British public as a means to strengthen the British charm and the sympathies of the native Indians for the British regime". Klemm concluded that "by this way the Indian people or at least the educated classes receive absolutely false ideas of Russia, in the first place, and secondly, are imbibed with the fear and awareness, that this ignorant, barbarous country, the embodiment of tyranny, lack of rights and bribe taking, etc. may one fine morning lay its heavy paw on India".[22]

The British authorities attempted to ascertain Tibet's attitude. Ravenshaw, the Resident in Nepal, spoke to a merchant who recently had come from Tibet and said that Tibet at present seeks Russian help since China has lost her power there".[23] A. Lamb writes that, according to a Tibetan monk it is said in Lhasa that now Tibetans can be tranquil and need not fear either British or the Nepalese".[24] It was also said that in 1901, the Dalai Lama had sought Russia's help and now Tibet had become her protectorate. China came to an understanding with Russia about the Chinese withdrawal from Tibet, so that the Russians might probably enter Lhasa by the end of the next year, 1903.[25]

However, despite the stepped up anti-Russian propaganda, the Indian public opinion believed that Russian threat to India was being greatly exaggerated. For example, the newspaper *Times of India* wrote on September 4, 1902, that Russia for many years would be busy with the assimilation and development of its acquired territory, therefore British Indians should not think that Russia would dream of invading India during the life of the present generation. A distinguished member of the Anglo-Indian government, a well-known expert on Asian problems, Henry Cotton, in an interview on December 3, 1902, stated that he did not believe that Russia had any plan regarding Tibet." Tibet is located at a distance of 1500 miles from the nearest point in the Russian territory and has nothing in common with the Russian sphere of activities in the Chinese territory. . . . In the present case, again the old slogan "Russia is interested in India" is repeated. "I do not believe that this is really the case; but even if it were, I am sure that Russia could never do this". Cotton thought that Russia could never cross the Himalayas at the present level of technological development.[26] But as far back a in 1898, an British military agent reported to the Intelligence Department that any relatively big contingent of the Russian troops would starve to death and the non-numerous detached force could be easily routed and pushed away by a superior strength from India.[27]

Although the British Defence Ministry was anxious over the development around Tibet, the British army strategists at times showed sobriety and realism appraising the real situation in connection with the rumours about the "Agreement" of Russia with China and Tibet. Lieutenant-Colonel V. R. Robertson prepared a "Memorandum on the alleged agreement between Russia and China concerning Tibet",[28] in which the position at the North-East border was compared with the position at the North-West border. He wrote that from the purely strategic point of view, it is difficult to believe that some day, the Russian protectorate over Tibet may convert the Himalayan principality of Nepal "sandwiched" between the British India and Tibet, into a "second Afghanistan". Despite of strengthening of Russia's position in Sinkiang and Mongolia, "the distance from Tibet is too far, the country is poor and to penetrate there from the North in Nepal is too complicated and the roads from Tibet to Nepal are difficult to access". Hence, continued V. R. Robertson, Russia will never move as many soldiers across the Tibetan border as she may move across the border of Afghanistan. So it might be considered that the threat to Tibet from the Russian side lies not in the intention to capture their firm strategic position, but in the desire to divert the attention of the British from the regions where they were really trying to concentrate their efforts, i.e. from Afghanistan and Persia.

Besides, Robertson wrote, after achieving a nominal protectorate over Tibet Russia would do everything possible to complicate the political situation, create disturbances amongst the local tribes and prevent the development of trade. So it was necessary, according to V.R. Robertson, to take steps to prevent Russia from making Tibet its protectorate. Above all, it was necessary to receive exhaustive information about the developments in Tibet, and the best way to do that – to have a resident in Lhasa, irrespective of what China would say or do in response.

Thus it was clear that the British Cabinet, the representatives of the Defence Ministry and the Indian press soberly evaluated the situation realising that the Anglo-Indian government need not fear the Russian threat to Tibet. At the same time, the idea of Russian penetration into Tibet justified the plans of the most bellicose representatives of the British colonial circles, who used it as a pretext for the armed invasion into the Tibetan territory.

So, in 1902–1903, the Anglo-Indian authorities under the pretext of the intensification of activities against "the aggressive plans of Russia" and the necessity to take timely measures against them, employed more active means to consolidate their position in Tibet. This was further manifested, in the first place, in the attempt to ensure the implementation by Tibet of the conditions laid down by the Convention of 1890 and Trade Rules of 1893.

Lord Curzon and the Anglo-Indian authorities did not have any comprehensive proof of the existence of treaty between Russia and Tibet. However Curzon, Lansdowne and Hamilton conjectured that there must have been some sort of negotiations, or, if not a secret treaty, then surely a secret agreement between China and Russia, concerning Tibet.[29] Curzon considered it his duty "to foil this petty game, while there is still time". On May 28, 1902, he wrote to Hamilton: "As you probably know my open answer to any such action of Russia will be very simple. Without the slightest difficulty, I would put a British army into Lhasa".[30] Thus Curzon only looked for a pretext to fulfil his plan to invade Tibet.

On January 8, 1903 the Viceroy of India sent to Hamilton, Secretary of State for India, a letter in which he formulated the main principles of the Indian government policies vis-vis Tibet. He enumerated the main developments in Anglo-Tibetan and Russo-Tibetan relations. He reminded that "the Russian border nowhere even touches that of Tibet, and the nearest point of the Russian territory is more than a 1000 miles short of the Tibetan capital, which is situated in the extreme south and in close proximity to the northern frontier of the Indian Empire". No other states or powers had any connection with Tibet, and only "China who possesses a nominal suzerainty over the country; secondly Nepal, a state in close connection with India; and, thirdly the British Government itself". Russia had absolutely nothing to do with it. Thus Curzon insisted upon resolute action to the extent of using military force in Tibet.[31] (Finally, since the beginning of February 1903, British troops had been gradually beginning to invade the Tibetan territory. One of the members of the expedition, A.Woddel, attempting to justify the invasion, wrote that England was "compelled" to prevent very important geographical point situated so near India from finally getting into the Russian orbit).[32]

On February 2, 1903, the Russian Embassy in London sent a memorandum to the Foreign Office stating that the Russian government had learnt from a reliable source that the British military expedition had reached Komba-Ovaleko on the way to the northern part of the Chumbi Valley. The Russian government drew the attention of the British government to that information because such actions might force the Russian government to take suitable measures to safeguard its interests in that region.[33] Thus the Russian government, on their part, attempted to use the threat of the British invasion in Tibet to put pressure on the ruling circles of Great Britain to gain concessions on other controversial matters.

On February 4, the contents of the Russian memorandum were forwarded to the Indian government with a request to clarify. On February 6, Curzon replied that the information of the Russian Ambassador had no basis that there had only been the discussion of border issues (between India and Tibet) in an atmosphere of mutual understanding and friendship.[34]

On February 11, 1903 talk tooks place between Lansdowne and Benkendorff, the Russian Ambassador to Great Britain on the Russian memorandum of February 2, 1903. Lansdowne said that in his opinion the memorandum was written in a somewhat unusual threatening tone, that it dealt with the country in the direct vicinity of the Indian borders and it was strange enough that Russia had so resolutely spoken of the immediate defence of her interests in that region. Lansdowne suggested that the Russian government should, in case it wanted information on that matter, directly approach him. He repeated that the information was baseless and pointed out that the Chumbi valley was situated close to the Indian border, and had always served as a trade route between the two countries. Benkendorff, on his part, remarked very cautiously that all the rumours of such kind were possibly being spread to aggravate relations between Russia and Great Britain. He did not see any reason why the two countries should quarrel because of Tibet. Neither Russia and, as he thought, nor Britain had political interests in that country. Lansdowne answered that Britain had no intention to conquer Tibet or annex the Tibetan territory, but regarding other issues he did not give any definite assurances. It was natural that the Indian government wanted to develop trade relations with Tibet and would take necessary measures in that direction.[35]

On February 18, Lansdowne and Benkendorff met again. The British minister stated that the Indian government was extremely perturbed by the Russian memorandum. Indian interests in Tibet were of a special character, he reiterated. Lhasa was in close proximity to the northern borders of India, while the Asiatic possessions of Russia were more than a thousand kilometres away from Lhasa. So, any manifestation of Russia's interests or activities in that region might perturb the population or create an impression that the British influence was being pushed into the background and that Russia was quickly moving into the regions which never had been within the sphere of her interests.

Lansdowne also told Benkendorff that rumours had reached the British government that Russia had concluded an agreement about establishing Russian protectorate over Tibet and was despatching a resident or a Consul to Lhasa. Benkendorff promised to clarify this matter with the Russian Minister of Foreign Affairs. Lansdowne, finally, asserted that since Britain had greater interest in Tibet than Russia, so, in response to any action taken by Russia, Great Britain would be "compelled" to take more active action. If Russia sent its mission to Tibet, then Great Britain would also reciprocate with a mission but a more serious one and significantly exceeding the Russian mission in numbers. As far as Tibet was concerned, Lansdowne continued, the British would demand only the implementation of the conditions laid down in the 1890 Convention concerning the demarcation of Sikkim's border and trading privileges for their country. The Anglo-Indian government had discovered the insignificance of the Chinese influence on Tibet. It considered the Chinese suzerainty over Tibet as a mere "constitutional fiction and political affectation" and, therefore endeavoured to establish personal contacts with the Dalai Lama.[36]

On the February 19, 1903, the British Cabinet reviewed the Tibetan question and concluded that it could not sanction sending an armed mission into Tibet. The British Prime Minister Lord Balfour expressed the view that since Tibet was a part of the Chinese Empire, a British Mission to Lhasa might be regarded as an attack upon the integrity of China, and other powers might press the Chinese Government to offer them some compensation elsewhere.[37] Lansdowne informed the Viceroy of India on February 20,[38] and Curzon expressed, "deep regret", regarding the decision of the British government, which according to him exposes "interest of India on Tibetan borders to undesirable risks".[39]

Lord Curzon believed that Great Britain did not have such serious doubts about taking extreme action in any other part of Asia. If Great Britain delayed, declared Curzon, then in future "some gross and irrelevant insult is offered to our honour or our flag". He maintained that the resolution to take action would have served the interests not only of India, but of the British Empire as a whole, that Britain's prestige should be unconditionally recognised in any point of the "glasis" which surrounded it.[40] The leader of the military mission in Tibet, F. Younghusband, wrote in his memoirs that only "irresponsible persons, at a comfortable distance in England" could ignore the rumours about Russian intrigues in Lhasa, but the Indian government, vitally interested in those matters could not "with a clear heart" repudiate those rumours. Younghusband considered Russia's interest in Tibet to be quite natural and expressed the opinion that Russia would not restrict herself to expansion in Manchuria, Sinkiang and Mongolia, and that at this particular moment it was necessary to stop her, otherwise she would take Tibet under her control, which would make her the topmost power in Asia. Younghusband wrote that "a full-dress Russian invasion of India through Tibet no responsible person ever dreamed possible". But he was seriously afraid of Russia's strengthening her influence in Lhasa. "In practical detail it would mean the increase of our army in the North-Eastern frontier by several thousand men".[41]

The British government, which took the rumours of Russian penetration into Lhasa seriously, examined the situation from a wider point of view than Lord Curzon, taking into account the interests of England in Europe and Asia, as a whole.

Great Britain was preparing for an open encounter with its main rival-Germany. In 1903 started the Anglo-French negotiations regarding all colonial problems. During that period, England showed the tendency to come closer to Russia, which was actively supported by France. In 1903, the discussions between the Russian Ambassador in London, Benkendorff and Lansdowne became regular.

Considering all these circumstances, on February 27, 1903 Hamilton wrote to Curzon that a careful study of his January 8, proposals was made not only from the point of view of difficulties on the Indian border with Tibet, but "from the wider point of view of the relations of Great Britain to other powers, both European and Asiatic". Hamilton wrote that the British government was of the opinion that employment of force to establish British influence in Lhasa would be undesirable, particularly at a time when negotiations between the British Foreign Secretary and the Russian Ambassador in London were under way. Both the British and the Indian governments, no doubt, considered it necessary to guarantee the interests of British India in Tibet, to neutralise the influence of any other foreign state in that region situated in direct proximity to the British possessions. Although the British government had "no desire either to declare a Protectorate or permanently occupy any portion of the country", yet steps, such as an armed mission undoubtedly would entail the establishment of a firmer footing in Lhasa. But "measures of this kind might, however, become inevitable if we were once to find ourselves committed to armed intervention in Tibet". Therefore, the British Government "think it necessary before sanctioning a course which might be regarded as an attack on the integrity of the Chinese Empire, to be sure that such action can be justified by the previous action of Tibet and Russia". Of course, despatching an armed mission to Tibet could be assessed as a legitimate reply to such actions of the Tibetan government, as the returning of three of Curzon's letters unopened, and disregarding the Convention with China of 1890, "the validity of which was repudiated by the Tibetan officials". However, in the emerging situation such measures would be premature. In connection with it, Hamilton wrote that they must exploit the Russian memorandum of February 2, and force them to make a clear-cut announcement of their policies. They must be warned that Great Britain would counter any action on Tibet taken by them. The explanations from the Russian government would make it easier for the British government to decide on the question of further negotiations with China and about other steps necessary to defend the interests of India against the danger of the establishment of foreign influence in Tibet.[42]

However, Curzon was not convinced by these arguments, and while expecting a reply from the Russian Ambassador, the Viceroy of India again wrote to Hamilton that time was ripe and further delay could result in the appearance of a Russian agent in Lhasa. He reiterated his proposals put forward on January 8.[43]

On 20th March, 1903, Russian Minister of External Affairs, in a letter to his Ambassador in London, Benkendorff, formulated the principles of Russian policies in relation to Tibet. He wrote, *inter alia*, that ". . . the Imperial government considers that it is necessary to maintain status quo in Tibet and, if the British would somehow violate that, Russia will not fail to protect her interests, of course, not by taking any direct measures in Tibet herself (as she is removed from us by Anglo-Indian possession), but most probably in other proper parts of the Asian continent".[44]

On March 24, and April 8, 1903, Lansdowne met the Russian Ambassador Benkendorff in London, who assured the British Minister that the rumours about the secret treaties between Russia and Tibet and between Russia and China regarding Tibet were unfounded. Benkendorff states that Russia had no agents in Lhasa, nor did she intend to despatch any mission there. He stated, however, that although the Russian government did not have any plans regarding Tibet, it could not remain indifferent to any attempt to violate the status quo in Tibet. Russia would protect her interests in Asia, not only in Tibet, but also in any other place. The Russian government considered Tibet as a part of the Chinese Empire and was interested in its integrity. He expressed the hope, that Russia would not be forced to take such action.[45]

Lansdowne made it clear that Great Britain had no intention of invading the Tibetan territory; however, she would insist upon the implementation by Tibet of the provisions of treaties and trade Agreements. In case Tibet violated its commitments, Britain would be forced to exercise its rights. Anyway, Great Britain did not desire to encroach upon the independence in Tibet.[46]

The British government did not find it possible to accept the Russian government's assertions and concluded that in order to counter the Russian aspirations, "it is not necessary to send an armed mission to Lhasa". Reporting this to the Viceroy of India, Hamilton requested Curzon to suggest how negotiations with China and Tibet should be conducted under the existing circumstances.[47] Curzon, in a letter to Hamilton on April 16, 1903 that they must immediately start negotiations with China and Tibet on the implementation by the Tibetan side of the obligations stipulated in the treaties.

Thus it seemed that Great Britain and Russia exchanged definite commitments regarding Tibet. Nevertheless, the British continued their military preparations at the Tibetan border, moving in men and material. Younghusband explained that the English were still apprehensive of the Russian influence in Tibet, believing that even if the Russians did not intend to help the Tibetans, the latter "might and did think they could count upon Russian support". He further stated that the Tibetans expanded "ordinary amenities" from the Russian side "into a promise of thick-and-thin support against the English".[48] However, it was clear, that the Anglo-Indian government would not like to miss an opportunity to capture Tibet which ultimately came in 1903.

In stopping up their military preparations, the British authorities found a ready excuse the reluctance of the Chinese and Tibetan authorities to start negotations with them Yu Tai, just appointed the Chinese resident in Tibet, in a conversation with the then Charge d'Affairs of Great Britain in Peking, did express the desire to do everything within his power to reach an agreement with White on the border question.[49] In a letter to Curzon dated April 6, 1903, Yu Tai wrote that as early as 1902 he had sent his representatives to Yatung. They were there for over three months and repeatedly tried to negotiate with White. Yu Tai suggested starting negotiations without further delay, at any place of the Viceroy's choice.[50] Curzon on his part expressed the opinion that Khamba-Dzong situated close to the disputed part of the border in Giagong would be the best place to hold such negotiations.

Concern over the British mission in Tibet was also expressed by the Chinese Ministry of External Affairs. Amban (the Chinese resident) in Lhasa, had said that the British representative should be told of the necessity of peace negotiations and to desist from sending English forces into the Tibetan territory.[51]

In a letter to Hamilton dated March 7, 1903, the Viceroy of India suggested Gyangtse, an important trading centre en route to Lhasa and Shigatse, as the place for the trade market and the residence of the British agent. While working out the trade rules, Curzon said, that the British should make it clear to the Chinese and the Tibetan authorities that the British representative should be given all possible facilities to establish direct links with the Tibetan government. In case there was any resistance, the idea of shifting him to Lhasa should be put forward as a threat. Curzon suggested appointing F. Younghusband as the chief representative at the negotiations, because he had recently been promoted to the rank of Colonel and had great experience in the Asian affairs; G.White, the resident in Sikkim, would assist him.[52]

As a matter of principle, Hamilton was not against the transfer of the market to Gyantse.[53] However, before taking the final decision he wanted to know, whether, if Tibet rejected Gyantse, would there be any other alternative to armed invasion into Tibet. Thus the British government continued to be very cautious and did everything possible to avoid an offensive on Tibet.

After consulting Younghusband and White, Curzon wrote to Hamilton on May 21, that the Tibetans and the Chinese were so much perturbed by the long silence (of the British) and by the construction of the road in Sikkim, and were so afraid of the armed invasion in Lhasa, that to avoid this danger they would be prepared to agree to any deal. As an alternative to the invasion into Tibet, Curzon suggested: (1) deportation of all Tibetans from British India and blockading all trade routes (although that might be futile or expensive), or (2) occupation of the Chumbi valley, which obviously would be a form of an armed invasion. According to him, the main thing was that the Tibetans should know the seriousness of the British intentions, because as soon as they realized it and saw "our military detachments behind", invasion might not be necessary.[54]

The British government in London made a close scrutiny of the messages of the Viceroy of India of May 7 and 21, 1903, and agreed upon the need to conduct negotiations in Khamba-Dzong regarding the border. Lansdowne and Hamilton did not consider it advisable to put on the agenda the question of the residence of the British Agent (either in Lhasa or in Gyantse). Hamilton wrote to Curzon that complications which might arise due to such a step might in the existing conditions overweigh the probable advantage of the proposed measure.[55] According to Lansdowne it might lead to a serious breach of status quo in Tibet to which the Russian Ambassador, Russian government would not remain indifferent.[56] The British government did not wish the proposals made to Tibet to be accompanied by a threat, especially, as Hamilton stated, Russia's assurances had changed the previous views about the extent of their political influence in Tibet.[57] Thus the British government continued trying to restrain the activities of the Anglo-Indian authorities in the context of its own interests which it believed lay in a rapprochement with Russia.

On June 3, 1903, the Viceroy of India informed the Chinese *Amban* in Lhasa that Younghusband would lead the British mission and that Khamba-Dzong would be the place for negotiations. Curzon wanted to secure the attendance of the Chinese and the Tibetan emissaries by July 7, 1903.[58] The Chinese authorities in Peking, on their part, informed the Charge d'Affairs of Britain that the Dalai Lama had appointed a representative to conduct the negotiations,[59] however, only in Gyagong or Yatung.[60]

Meanwhile, the British colonial authorities continued military preparations along the Tibetan border, chalked out extensive plans for the expedition, its composition, and the possibilities of its supply with provision and ammunition and drew-up the estimate of necessary expenditure, etc. Younghusband received detailed instructions on what issue he should conduct negotiations with the Tibetan and the Chinese emissaries.[61]

The situation in the border region was gradually aggravating. The British, using the reports of the military preparations of the Tibetan side, of the decision of the Tibetan Assembly to launch armed struggle against the British,[62] of the supply of arms to the Tibetan forces quartered in Lhasa, Pari and Shigatse,[63] etc. pressed for fulfilment of their terms or else they would increase their military escort's strength.[64] Younghusband himself continued to emphasise the Russian intrigues in Tibet and sent a memorandum to the Indian government regarding Russian penetration in Lhasa. He stressed that even if Russia did not intend to help Tibet the latter, like the Chinese, believed that they could use Russia to put pressure on Great Britain in the solution of the border question.[65] He further said that the display of courteousness and friendliness by the Russian, might have been interpreted by the Tibetans as the promise of help during the anti-British struggle.[66] Younghusband referred to the reports of the British agents in Tibet about a substantial Russian detachment being located in the area to the North of Lhasa.[67] The British press also continued to spread rumours about Russian penetration into Tibet and of 143 Russian engineers who had arrived in army uniforms in the Eastern border of Tibet and of a Cossack detachment coming to Tibet from the north and so on.[68] No doubt, the British authorities used these reports to prepare for invasion into Tibetan territory.

Younghusband continued to supply information about the Tibetan military preparations and their refusal to hold negotiations in Khamba-Dzong stating to the Chinese representatives at the negotiations that if he wanted to save the country from future trouble, he should convince the *Amban* in Lhasa to task necessary measures while it was still not too late.[69] Reporting to London, the Viceroy of India added that Younghusband did not hope for the peaceful solution of the question and foresaw the possibility of occupying the Chumbi valley and simultaneously sending a mission to Gyantse. Curzon stated that the Tibetans were not aware of British strength and unconditionally counted on Russia's help. He said that the situation was getting desperate owing to the coming November, after which it would become extremely difficult to take any action, and the mission would have to wait till the spring in Khamba-Dzong. In that case some other power might interfere.[70] Besides, the Tibetans had imprisoned two British nationals in Shigatse. The British demanded their release and a compensation of 2 million rupees, and in retaliation they captured herds of Tibetan sheep in the area of Gyagong.[71]

Hamilton informed Curzon that the British representative in Peking had been requested to report all these facts to the Chinese authorities (although, he wrote, it was doubtful, whether, taking into consideration the existing relations between China and Tibet, it would yield any result) in case it might be necessary to use forcible measures in Tibet in future. He thought also that the occupation of Chumbi Valley would be sufficient to make the Tibetans realise the seriousness of the intentions of Great Britain.[72]

The Peking authorities acting on the request of the *Amban*, approached the British diplomatic representative in Peking with the request to wait for the arrival of the newly appointed *Amban* Yu Tai in Lhasa and not to increase the strength of the British forces in Khamba-Dzong area by another 300 men (as it was planned) as in that case serious difficulties might crop up as regards supplying them with provisions.[73] However, the British Colonial administration continued to point out to the Chinese government that the Tibetans were against holding peace negotiations and insisted that it send appropriate instructions to Lhasa and explain the seriousness of the situation to the Dalai Lama. Prince Ch'ing replied that the Chinese Government was interested in the peace settlement of all questions with the Tibetan side (in a talk with the British diplomats, Prince Ch'ing repeatedly showed disrespect for Tibetans, called them foolish, ignorant, etc.).[74]

The British government informed China that their sole aim – to establish friendly relations with Tibet – did not mean that the latter should continue to keep in prison the British nationals. Great Britain expected that the Chinese government would put immediate pressure on the Dalai Lama so that he sent a plenipotentiary emissary to negotiate without delay, and release of two British nationals, otherwise Britain would be compelled to take necessary measures to ensure the safety of the mission.[75]

At the end of September 1903, in order to consolidate the positions in the border regions, Colonel MacDonald was placed in command of all the forces stationed there. He was also in charge of the construction of a road from Siliguri up to the border.[76]

On October 3, 1903, Colonel F. Younghusband sent to the Anglo-Indian government in Simla a plan of invasion of Tibet and the capture of Shigastse by the joined forces from Khamba-Dzong and Chumbi Valley under MacDonald's command. He also wrote that he had established friendly relations with the associates of the Panchen Lama in Shigatse, so that the latter's support to Lhasa would be nominal. The Nepalese detachment would also take part in the invasion into the territory of Tibet.[77] As a matter of principle this plan was approved by the Anglo-Indian authorities.[78] The entrance into the Chumbi valley was expected after October 26.[79]

Thus Tibet's fate was sealed. The British colonial authorities took advantage of the weakness and unpreparedness of the country to resist such a powerful and highly experienced neighbour as the British masters of India. The inability of China, due to the complexity of her internal situation, to defend her vassal, and the aggravation of the situation in the Far East which diverted Russia's attention from Tibet, allowed the British armed forces to march into Tibet.

Notes and References

1. National Archives of India (further abbreviated as NAI), January 1901, Ns 80–95. Doc. 90.
2. NAI, Doc. 95.
3. A. Lamb, *Britain and Chinese Central Asia*, London, 1906, p. 225.
4. Lord Ronaldshay, *The Life of Lord Curzon*, London, 1928, Vol. II, p. 205.

5. A. Lamb, *Britain and Chinese*, p. 260.
6. Lord Ronaldshay, *The Life*, Vol. II, p. 205.
7. Lord Ronaldshay, *The Life*, p. 206.
8. A. Lamb, *Britain and Chinese*, p. 225.
9. Arkhiv Vneshney Politiky Rossiiyskoy Imperii (Foreign Policy Archives of Russian Empire, further abbreviated as AVPRI). Fund Central Asian desk, file No. 915, list 58.
10. A. Lamb, *Britain and Chinese*, p. 256.
11. AVPRI, Fund Chinese desk, file No. 1448, list 112.
12. Great Britain, Foreign Office. Papers relating to Tibet. Cd 1920, p. 116.
13. Papers, p. 116.
14. Papers, p. 117.
15. Papers, p. 123.
16. A. Lamb, *Britain and Chinese*, p. 256.
17. Lord Ronaldshay, *The Life*, Vol. II, p. 207.
18. A. Lamb, *Britain and Chinese*, Vol. II, p. 207.
19. Curzon considered that the diplomatic failure of England was one of the most significant outcomes of the transfer of political functions to the local administrations (in this case of Bengal), who were incompetent and inexperienced and had no people to do such work. The British intelligence service suffered a serious setback and it was necessary to prevent in future such things as Dorjieff's mission. Therefore Curzon thought it urgent to take the entire control of the Anglo-Tibetan relations in his own hands demanding that all information from the border reaches him without delay. National Archives of India, July 1901, Ns 81–86, Docs 82–84.
20. A. Lamb, *Britain and Chinese*, p. 262.
21. AVPRI, Fund Central Asia desk, file No. 920, list 81.
22. AVPRI, Fund Central Asian desk, list 81
23. A. Lamb, *Britain and Chinese*, p. 276.
24. A. Lamb, *Britain and Chinese*, p. 276.
25. A. Lamb, *Britain and Chinese*, p. 276.
26. *Amrita Bazaar Patrika*, 3 December, 1902.
27. P. Fleming, *Bayonets to Lhasa*, New York, 1961, p. 55.
28. National Archives of India, February 1903, Ns 1–88, Doc. 61.
29. A. Lamb, *Britain and Chinese*, p. 275.
30. A. Lamb, *Britain and Chinese*, p. 276.
31. NAI, February 1903, Ns 1–88, Doc. 82. Papers relating to Tibet. Cd 1920, pp. 150–53.
32. A. Woddell, *Lhasa and Its Mysteries*, London, 1906, pp. 37–38.
33. NAI, April 1903, Ns 130–72, Doc. 145, Enclo 1.
34. Papers relating to Tibet. Cd 1920, p. 179.
35. NAI, April 1903, Ns 130–72, Doc. 142, Enclo 2.
36. NAI, April 1903, Ns 130–72, Doc. 145, Enclo 3.
37. Lord Ronaldshay, *The Life of Lord Curzon*, Vol. II, p. 275.
38. NAI, April 1903, Ns 130–72, Doc. 131.
38. NAI, April 1903, Ns 130–72, Doc. 131.
39. NAI, Doc. 132.
40. Lord Ronaldshay, *The Life*, Vol. II, p. 275.

41. F. Younghusband, *India and Tibet*, London, 1904, p. 75.
42. NAI, April 1903, Ns 130–72, Doc. 142.
43. NAI, April 1903, Ns 130–72, Doc. 149.
44. AVPRI, Fund Chinese desk, file No. 1455, lists 37–38.
45. NAI, July 1903, Ns 38–95, Doc. 42.
46. NAI, Ns 130–72, Doc. 164.
47. NAI, Doc. 169, 170.
48. F. Younghusband, *India and Tibet*, p. 82.
49. National Archives of India, April 1903, Ns 130–72, Doc. 130.
50. NAI, July 1903, Ns 38–95, Doc. 41.
51. NAI, July 1903, Ns 38–95, Doc. 44.
52. NAI, July 1903, Ns 38–95, Doc. 46.
53. NAI, July 1903, Ns 38–95, Doc. 48.
54. NAI, July 1903, Ns 38–95, Doc. 49.
55. NAI, Doc. 55.
56. NAI, Doc. 77.
57. NAI, Doc. 55.
58. NAI, Doc. 69.
59. NAI, November 1903, Ns 118–58, Doc. 129, Enclo 1.
60. NAI, November 1903, Ns 118–58, Doc. 139.
61. NAI, July 1903, Ns 38–95, Docs. 56, 58, 67, 79.
62. NAI, November 1903, Ns 118–58, Doc. 152.
63. NAI, November 1903, Ns 118–58, Doc. 155.
64. NAI, Doc. 137
65. NAI, July 1903, Ns 38–95, Doc. 66. Enclo 1.
66. F. Younghusband, *India and Tibet*, p. 82.
67. NAI, November 1903, Ns 118–58, Doc. 152.
68. P. Fleming, *Bayonets to Lhasa*, p. 82
69. NAI, November 1903, Ns 118–58, Doc. 155.
70. NAI, November 1903, Ns 159–234, Doc. 66
71. NAI, November 1903, Ns 118–58, Doc. 127.
72. NAI, November 1903, Ns 159–234, Doc. 174.
73. NAI, Doc. 186, Enclo.
74. NAI, Doc. 194.
75. NAI, November 1903, Ns 159–234, Doc. 201.
76. NAI, Doc. 207.
77. NAI, Doc. 223.
78. NAI, Doc. 224.
79. NAI, Doc. 226.

FOUR

Triple Trap: A Story of Three Indian Comintern Activists

L. V. MITROKHIN

THE FATE OF A political immigrant has never been enviable. The intelligence and police services of the country which has given him asylum keep a watchful eye on him for years and his home country does not leave him alone.

The people whose life story I am narrating here had a special role to play, because in the 1920s and 1930s they were in the files of dozens of police and intelligence services of the "civilised" and "uncivilised" world – France, Britain, Sweden, Germany, Japan, the United States, China, British India, Turkey and Afghanistan. They were also under close surveillance in the Soviet Union, the country of their hope and dreams, which gave them political asylum and made them victims of the Stalinist machine of repression. A time will come when a patient historian will dig out all the facts about their eventful and rebellious lives and compare the documents kept in the European and American archives.

This account is based mainly on the Indian archives, especially the National Archives in New Delhi, which contain a large number of British colonial intelligence documents about Indian revolutionaries, especially those who found themselves in Russia after the Bolshevik revolution. Many facts in their lives are still unknown because the Comintern archives in Russia were opened to researchers just recently. I was nursing the hope that some time I would be allowed to study KGB documents and rather unexpectedly that time has come now.

On January 9, 1990, a Soviet publishing house sent the following letter to the KGB archives: "The Publishing House of Political Literature of the Central Committee of the CPSU is planning to publish a series of materials about foreign activists of the Comintern. One of them is a story by Leonid Mitrokhin, holder of a Ph.D. in history and Jawaharlal Nehru Award Winner, entitled "The Fate of Indian Revolutionaries", which relates to the life and activities of three prominent Indian revolutionary immigrants in the Soviet Union, Virendranath Chattopadhyaya (Chatto), Abani Mukerji (Oboni Mukharji) and Ambia Ghulam Ahmad Khan Lugani (Lohani). They all worked in the Comintern in different years and information about them is available in Indian archives and memoirs. Leonid Mitrokhin met Prof. Mukerji's wife, Rosa Fitingof, and Virendranath Chattopadhyaya's wife, Lydia Korunovskaya, in Leningrad who told him that in the late 30s Mukerji and Chatto were arrested by the Soviet security forces and no one knew what became of them. As for Lugani, foreign documents on the Comintern members say that in the 30s he faced persecution in the USSR.

We request you to help us obtain reference or documentary material about the three above-mentioned Indian revolutionary immigrants to enable the author of the story to create a true picture of their lives".

The answer from the KGB came less than a month later:

> "The following facts have been established as a result of a study.
>
> "Virendranath Chattopadhyaya, born 1880, Hyderabad (India), Indian, member of the German Communist Party since 1927, senior research associate of the USSR Academy of Sciences, Institute of Anthropology and Ethnography; arrested on July 15, 1937, by the Leningrad NKVD[1] on suspicion of espionage and on September 2, 1937, sentenced by the military collegium of the Supreme Court of the USSR to death by firing squad. The sentence was implemented on the same day. On April 28, 1956 rehabilitated by the military collegium of the Supreme Court of the USSR.
>
> Abani Mukerji, born 1891, Jubbalpore (India), Indian, member of the Indian Revolutionary Party, member of the Russian Communist Party (Bolshevik), since 1925, professor at the Moscow State University, was arrested by the NKVD on June 2, 1937, on suspicion of espionage and on October 25, 1937, sentenced by the military collegium, of the Supreme Court of the USSR, to death by firing squad. The sentence was carried out on October 28, 1937; rehabilitated by the military collegium of the Supreme Court of the USSR on May 26, 1957.
>
> Gulam Abdul Khan Lugani, born 1892, Sirajganj (India), Indian, member of the Russian Communist Party (Bolshevik) since 1928, editor-translator of the National Committee for Radio Broadcasting; on February 27, 1938, arrested by the NKVD on suspicion of espionage and on September 17, 1938, sentenced by the military collegium of the Supreme Court of the USSR to death by firing squad; the

sentence was carried out on the same day; rehabilitated by the military collegium of the Supreme Court of the USSR on July 9, 1957. We have no other information about the above-mentioned persons".

Since this terse report gives little information about the men, I shall try to reconstruct their character to do justice to the people who sought to liberate their own people from oppression and tyranny, but were caught in a lethal trap.

The Passionate Chatto

It so happened that we know more about Chatto than the other two men. This is not by chance. He came from a well known family of Indian intellectuals, which made a great contribution to the liberation of the country from colonialism. Someone may write a full story about this family some time.

Chatto's sister, Sarojini Naidu, a close associate of Mahatma Gandhi, was a famous Indian poetess, known as the "Indian Nightingale". His brother, Harindranath, who died recently, was a leading writer and poet. He was the first to translate the "International" into Hindi language. His younger sister, Suhashini Jambekar, was a prominent Communist activist and graduate of the Communist University of the Toiling Peoples of the East in the USSR.

Loyal friends of the Soviet Union, they made great efforts for the promotion of Soviet-Indian mutual understanding. Sarojini Naidu was President of the All-India society of "Friends of the Soviet Union", which was founded during the Second World War; Harindranath was one of the founders of the Indian People's Theatre movement as well as author of some of the best books about the Soviet Union in India; Suhashini Jambekar organised countless fund-raising campaigns in India for helping the Soviet people during the World War II ordeal in 1941–1945.

Virendranath Chattopadhyaya, more known in the history of the Indian revolutionary movement as Chatto (Jawaharlal Nehru called him by that name in his letters), chose his own way of struggle for the liberation of his country. Unfortunately, it was a futile tactic based upon the view (it was particularly widespread at the beginning of the century and during the World War I) that India would not be able to gain independence without the assistance of the European powers hostile to Britain. Hence his decision to emigrate from India and find allies in the struggle against the hated British colonialists. Under different aliases (in the British intelligence service he was known as Vincent Chatterton, A. Alfieri and Mohammed Jafar) he visited many European countries.[2]

The best personal reference source about his Soviet years are the reminiscences of his wife, the late Lydia Korunovskaya, a leading Soviet ethnographer. "I am happy to have met this man", the 80-year-old woman told me in 1970. "I fell in love with him and I have loved him all my life".

Chatto first appeared in the Institute of Ethnography, USSR Academy of Sciences, early in March 1933. An Oxford graduate who later obtained a diploma in anthropology in Germany, he was welcomed in the institute with great interest. Later it became known that he was an Indian revolutionary whose political activism provoked a sharply negative reaction from the British government. Chatto was the leader of a secret society founded in London in 1907–1908, which fought for India's independence from Britain. While in London, Chatto earned his living by teaching Hindi to Oxford and Cambridge graduates. His main occupation, however, was politics and journalism.

After a terrorist act committed by an Indian who was connected with Chatto, the latter had to flee from Britain to France, the centre of Indian political emigration at the time. In 1910 he joined the French Socialist Party.

In Europe he edited several periodicals (the *Oriental Review* and *Indian Industrial Review* in London and the *Anti-imperialist Review* in Berlin) and contributed many articles on political and historical problems and the national-liberation movement.

Early in May 1917 Chatto moved to Stockholm and in September he became the first Indian revolutionary to establish contact with Petrograd. Indian intelligence archives corroborate Lydia Korunovskaya's information about Chatto's stay in Sweden.

There is a document[3] making it clear that in August 1920 Chatto was still in Stockholm. According to a rumour, he lived there on "Bolshevik money", though he actually subsisted on help from his Swedish friends. Chatto regularly received from Indian organisations the anti-British literature published in the United States. According to the document, he was planning a Communist rebellion and was confident of its success. He was reportedly to send this plan to India with some trusted person.

This information was sent from London to Delhi to warn the authorities there that the victorious revolution in Russia had encouraged the Indian revolutionaries abroad to step up their activity and that they had found new allies and were probably harbouring new plans.

Another report (September 1920, No. 71) said that in Stockholm Chatto intended to launch a newspaper, *Indian Communist,* had met Lev Kamenev, a close associate of Lenin, and was in correspondence "through Bolshevik couriers" with Germany and Russia. The document further said that Chatto had complete faith in the Bolsheviks, who were reportedly preparing for a revolution in India next March, and that the Bolshevik Bureau of Propaganda in the East had stepped up its activity in this direction.

According to the report, Chatto planned to convert all Indians to Bolshevism and conspired for this purpose with Rabindranath Tagore, whom he expected to meet in Stockholm in September or October and whose latest statements encouraged Chatto.[4]

Chatto came to Moscow in 1921 as a member of the Indian delegation to participate in the Third Congress of the Comintern. That visit was a failure. M. N. Roy, a prominent Indian emigrant revolutionary, had a great influence in the Comintern (he parted company with it and the Communist movement in the 30s) and was viewed as an ambitious and selfish man by many Indians who knew him personally. He did not want to see such a brilliant and educated man as Chatto in the Comintern.[5]

"In 1918 Vorovsky[6] sent me a telegram from Petrograd (to Stockholm), inviting me to come", Chatto said in one of his statements, "I could come later to Moscow where Roy had been since 1919. I came to the Third Congress of the Comintern in 1921 with some Indian comrades – Dutta, Lugani and Khankoje. We were not yet organized in a party and hoped to do so in Moscow. But Roy teamed up with a group of adventurers and imperialist agents and, unfortunately, wormed himself into the confidence of Comintern comrades (. . .) Unable to convince our comrades about the true character of Roy and his people, we had to leave 11 months later. Arguing against Roy's position, we wrote several theses on the Indian question and sent them to Lenin. Lenin sent us the following message in English: "To Comrades Chattopadhyaya, Lugani and Khankoje. I have read your theses with great interest. Why new theses? I shall soon talk with you about this. With fraternal greetings, Lenin".

(Chatto later lamented that he had failed to take the original of Lenin's letter out of Germany. It was confiscated along with the other documents in a Gestapo raid on the Berlin office of the Anti-Imperialist League.)

"We were looking forward to an interview with Lenin," Chatto continued. "But our opponents foiled that meeting and we had to return without meeting the leader".[7]

All subsequent British sources confirm this statement. According to reports by secret agents, Roy managed to convince the Soviet leaders that Chatto was "a nationalist rather than a Communist". So, Chatto, who insisted that the Comintern establish direct ties with the national liberation movements in the colonies, left Moscow without any results.[8]

Nevertheless, in December 1921 he founded a new organisation in Berlin, the Indian News and Information Bureau, to conduct open propaganda and secret revolutionary activities. His aim was to create a true Communist party to replace the sham party of Roy. A little later he was joined by Maulvi Mohammed Barkatullah, a prominent Muslim leader who had met Lenin twice[9], and Indian communist Abani Mukerji, who had broken away from Roy.[10]

Judging by the British intelligence reports, the new group had far-reaching plans and was very active.[11] Later it developed into an organisation that sought complete independence for India and the creation of a federative democratic republic.

Later Chatto visited Moscow once again, but that was preceded by many events. In 1922–1923 the British colonial authorities in India had to admit that all their efforts to isolate India from revolutionary ideas had failed. Marxist groups appeared in India and began to propagate Marxism-Leninism in the country. Indian Communists agitated for their cause inside the country and abroad. The Laskar Welfare League, set up in Britain by Indian and British Communists, had a major role to play in bringing Marxist and anti-imperialist literature to India. Eventually, the British colonial authorities decided to fall upon Indian Communists and their sympathisers in India and abroad.

In February 1923 an official of the Home Department of the Government of India wrote in a memo to the India Office that the question of the application of Regulation No. 3 of 1818 (imprisonment without trial) had been considered and that the Government of India was prepared to use it when necessary. The only question was when this regulation was to be put into effect, though even at that stage the Secretary of State for India suggested that everyone should be interned as soon as he arrived in India and before he got the opportunity to disseminate his doctrines or establish contacts in India.

On July 1, 1923, the Chief Commissioner of the North-West Frontier Province suggested in a secret letter that the government begin a "case of a communist conspiracy in Calcutta", but it was eventually decided to begin the trial in Kanpur, a major industrial centre in northern India.[12]

Unfortunately, the problem was compounded by the atmosphere of distrust and suspicion in Moscow among European and Asian revolutionary democrats. A memo of the Home Department of the Government of India (No. 287 of June 1921) said that Indian revolutionary Dalip Singh Gill, who had met Lenin in the summer of 1919, was arrested by the Soviet government in Moscow as a spy at the request of the Berlin-based Indian Committee.

Unable to convince the Comintern leaders that M.N. Roy's sectarian policy of fighting for the victory of Marxism-Leninism in the East was futile, in 1924 Chatto decided to return to India. He asked the British colonial authorities to grant him a passport for entry to India or Britain. We know this from his letter to the Foreign Office on September 9, 1924. Chatto wrote in it about his earlier application for a passport to the British Consul in Berlin, who had rejected his request and demanded that Chatto send the Consul monthly reports about his activities.

Chatto categorically rejected that demand, saying that after graduating from the Berlin University and obtaining a Ph.D. in anthropology in Hamburg in 1923 he would like to return to India to conduct anthropological research and study social and economic problems in his home country.

"I have Marxistic world views", he wrote. "In 1913 I was a member of the Bronx Socialist Club in New York and often visited the Rand School of Social Science and was a student of the American sociologist, late Prof. Lester Ward. I was preparing myself for social service work in India. As man grows and learns, he is subject to development and change, and I have a new world view today than what I had some years ago. I always stand for the freedom of mankind and naturally I do stand for the political, social and economic freedom of the Indian masses. My articles in the *Hindustan Review, London Review, Servant*, etc., in India will testify to my new views. And I will not buy my liberty by sacrificing my conscience. Therefore I cannot do anything more to satisfy the bureaucracy".

The colonial authorities in London and in Delhi rejected Chatto's request. In 1927 Chatto actively participated in organising the World Anti-Imperialist Congress in Brussels, where he met Jawaharlal Nehru. The two became friends and their confidential and friendly correspondence testifies to this. In July Chatto became Secretary of the World Anti-Imperialist Congress in Frankfurt-on-Main, at which he was elected a member of the General Council of the Anti-Imperialist League. Korunovskaya recalled that at that time he moved from France to Germany, where he joined the German Communist Party, and worked under Georgi Dimitrov.

When the Nazis came to power in Germany in early 1933, Dimitrov advised Chatto to move to the Soviet Union to escape possible arrest. In the USSR Chatto first worked in a Comintern section in Moscow and then, on the suggestion of Sergei Kirov,[13] he was given a job in the USSR Academy of Sciences. Later he was made one of the heads of the India Department of the Institute of Anthropology and Ethnography.

His excellent command of European and Oriental languages, profound knowledge of primitive societies, personal charm and communicative character soon made him popular with his colleagues. Chatto quickly learned Russian and spoke it almost as a native. He willingly helped his colleagues and tutored an American Indian post-graduate, Archie Finney, who had come to study in the Soviet Union from the United States. Chatto also taught Hindustani in the Leningrad Institute of Oriental Studies, conducted Urdu, Hindi and Telugu language courses in the University and contributed articles on India to the Soviet Encyclopaedia.

In 1932 he edited the six-volume collection of Lenin's works in English and in 1933 the English translation of Karl Marx's "The Poverty of Philosophy", which appeared in 1935. In 1936–1937 he worked on an English edition of Frederick Engels' "The Origin of the Family, Private Property and the State".

While working in Leningrad, Chatto never lost contacts with Moscow, especially the Comintern, which, judging by his letters to his wife in 1935, discussed some intricate questions of his status in the organisation. The matter was investigated by the Control Commission headed by Zigmas Angaretis. A document stamped secret was found in Chatto's personal papers (dated November 10, 1932), stating that the commission investigating his case "found no evidence for accusing him of political dishonesty".

Nevertheless, in 1937 Chatto was arrested and executed.

His wife did not know that he had been shot. The NKVD told her that after his arrest he was taken to Moscow. Many years later a Leningrad district office of marriage, birth and death registration gave her a death certificate written in the name of Chattopadhyaya and dated March 22, 1958. It did not say what was the cause of his death or where he died. It said Chatto died on April 6, 1943.

"Chatto left his home country, India, when he was a very young man to fight for its liberation", Chatto's wife recalled (May 1970). "He considered the Soviet Union, the birthplace of Lenin, his second Motherland. He trusted it and was devoted to it. Bitterness and grief fill my heart when I think about his tragic death".

On April 13, 1965, Lydia Korunovskaya wrote to Dr Horst Krueger, an East German researcher: "A tragic fate befell Chatto. He fell victim to Stalin's personality cult. He was arrested on the night of July 17, 1937. He waved me goodbye from the car and that was the last I saw of him. I never saw him or knew where he was. . . ."

The Tragic Fate of Prof. Mukerji

Abani Mukerji, or Abaninath Mukerji, also lived and worked in Europe under different aliases. The British intelligence knew him as Charlu and R. Sahir.

He was born in Bengal in 1891. In 1910 he went to Japan for studies and in 1911 to Germany, probably to continue his education. In 1912 he returned to India and left for Japan again in 1915. In 1923 he secretly returned to India as an emissary of the revolutionary Communist organisation in Berlin.

In February 1924 he was in Europe again. Mukerji had contacts with active members of the Bengal Revolutionary Party. He wrote several books, including *A Short Biography of Lenin, White Terror in India, Rural India* and *India in Transition,* and was the co-author of several appeals and manifestos addressed to the major Indian revolutionary and nationalist organisations, in which he urged them to unite with the Comintern and overthrow the British colonial rule in India by force.[14]

Indian archives in Delhi provide an insight into the tragic life and career of this person, who, like Chatto, was constantly under the watchful eye of the British intelligence. The head of the intelligence department, Lt.-Col. Cecil Kaye, and his successor, David Petrie, kept his dossier in their personal custody.

In a private letter dated June 1, 1924, to a British trade union activist, Bramley, who was under police surveillance, Abani Mukerji wrote that he considered himself a native of Calcutta (1, Sukeas Street). He was arrested in Singapore in 1915 on charges of organising an anti-British armed rebellion and served his term in the Fort prison, from which he escaped 18 months later to the Dutch East Indies.[15]

An ardent Marxist, he joined the socialist movement in 1912 when he was illegally living in Germany. In a letter to Bramley he wrote that he had thought a long time about the causes of his failures and setbacks and had come to the conclusion that "the masses were not with us and could not be with us" because "we did nothing to represent their interests".

That period of rethinking and growing up took three years, after which in 1919 he travelled to Russia, where he lived for two years, participating in the congresses and conferences of the Third International and being one of the organisers of the Indian Communist Party in Tashkent.

However, major differences arose between him and the leaders of the International, especially M.N. Roy. Mukerji was of the opinion that the International was increasingly serving the interests of a small faction and had backslided from its principles. Eventually, Mukerji found himself in isolation and was forced to leave Russia for India.

Abani Mukerji was sent on a secret mission to India for establishing direct contact with the isolated Communist groups in India. He was to meet the leaders of the Indian National Congress and other organisations and persuade them to recognise the Indian Party of Independence in Berlin.[16]

In India, Mukerji managed, in cooperation with several groups of Indian revolutionaries, to work out a manifesto emphasising non-violent methods of anti-colonialist struggle and urging unity of the democratic forces of India and the creation of worker-peasant parties in different regions of the country. The police got to know about Mukerji's arrival from Moscow and he nearly escaped arrest.[17]

He stayed in India under an alias for one year, organising "the Labour Party that is wanted there".[18] After making a study of the living conditions and public mentality in India, he came to the conclusion that they were not ripe "though subconsciously ripe". "I came to the conclusion that to talk about communism with these people who as yet do not exactly know what their interest is, is nothing more than an attempt to exploit them in a new way for certain vested interest, which is termed as phrase revolutionism", he wrote. "But to organise these ever exploited masses I, though in my hard conditions, organised the Hindustan Labour and Peasant Party with headquarters in Madras. The main principle of this party was that it will be an open organisation of the Indian masses. That it will follow the slogan of non-violence. That it will take parliamentary actions (. . .) to protect the labour interests in India. That it will fight with legitimate means (and) will not accept any foreign help (. . .) Its program was to act within the Congress as the Swarajya Party works".

However, Mukerji was soon to learn that he had been expelled from the Comintern. Provocative letters came from Europe to India and fell into the hands of the police,[19] so Mukerji had to flee from the country. In March 1924 he arrived in Berlin. Declaring that he did not represent any government or organisation, Mukerji concluded: "I work as I think it best for India from socialistic principles. I am a Marxist-Socialist. I believe in the evolution of society and people".

Isolation from the national liberation struggle in India, constant travelling from one country to another and disappointing changes in the Comintern compelled Mukerji (as was the case with Chatto) to think about returning to India. They applied for permission to return to India almost at the same time.

Abani Mukerji's "Application for Amnesty and Permission to Return to India" was dated July 24, 1924. The document was considered by the India Office in London.

It followed from intelligence reports that Mukerji was an active participant in the "Indo-German conspiracy" during the war, that is, he collaborated with the Kaiser's Germany against Britain. However, the main charge against him was that he admitted being involved in "Bolshevist propaganda" and illegally coming to India from Russia without a passport as a sailor.

Yet, the decision of the colonial administration in London was inconclusive: "It is the accepted policy not to grant amnesty to Indian seditionist abroad, but to permit them to return provided they are prepared to face the risk of prosecution for their past misdeeds, if this is considered necessary by the Government. In regard to Bengal we have recommended the refusal of passports to persons whose presence is likely to cause embarrassment to the local Government, particularly at the present juncture. This request may be refused on the same grounds. August 6, 1924". Thus, London passed the buck to Delhi, especially the intelligence service, that is Cecil Kaye and David Petrie.

Incidentally, Cecil Kaye wrote in a memo that Abani Mukerji arrived in India as an emissary of the "anti-Roy" party of Indian revolutionaries and that he carried a mandate (copied by the British intelligence), issued on June 21, 1921, in Russian and German, declaring him a voting delegate to the Third Comintern Congress and a certificate of October 31, 1922, confirming that he was a member and Secretary of the Indian Committee for Russian Relief, signed in Berlin by Barkatullah and another leading Indian revolutionary, Bhupendranath Dutta. Cecil Kaye also noted that Mukerji was connected with the "notorious revolutionary" Chatto.

The report said that the only thing known about Mukerji's wife was that her name was Rosa. (Rosa Fitingof worked in Lenin's secretariat. She met Mukerji in Moscow and married him. She was reportedly a member of the Indian Communist Party founded in Tashkent.)

In conclusion Cecil Kaye wrote the following: Mukerji is "a definite advocate of violence and in touch with the Communist International; (. . .) if he was allowed to come to India, he would do so as a propagandist of revolutionary and Bolshevik ideas. In the interests not only of the Government of Bengal, but of the Government of India also, I think his request should certainly be refused. C. Kaye. August 20, 1924".[20]

Judging by everything, Kaye's characterisation of Mukerji did not correspond to reality: over the years Mukerji's views had changed dramatically. Early in 1920 his signature stood next to those of M.N. Roy and Roy's American wife under the *Indian Communist Manifesto* calling for an immediate proletarian rebellion to prevent the creation of a bourgeois government in India ,[21] whereas in later years his programme became far more moderate. Cecil Kaye's reports confirm this too.

Incidentally, this is how the British intelligence service evaluated the possible effect of the *Indian Communist Manifesto* on the worker and peasant movement in the country. This call for a rebellion, a British intelligence report said, with its orthodox Leninism and misunderstanding of Indian politics reminds of a letter sent by Lenin to the British

Labour Party on the eve of its conference in Scarborough. That letter turned the conference against Bolshevism and the Third International. The *Indian Communist Manifesto*, Cecil Kaye wrote, might produce the same effect in India if it ever reached there. At the same time, its author's belief in original Bolshevism in India was of considerable interest.

Thus the extremism of some Indian emigrant revolutionaries did not bother the British colonial administration very much. The latter justly believed that it had no social base in India and even stood in the way of cooperation between the revolutionary and national-liberation forces.

As for Mukerji, he appealed to the top representatives of the British Labour government, which took office after the defeat of the Conservatives, to allow him to go to India. This is the text of his letter to Ramsey McDonald, delivered through the British embassy in Berlin:

> "Sir, with due respect I beg to draw your favourable attention to the following. I am an Indian Socialist from Calcutta. For the last few years a political exile in Europe. I pray for an amnesty for my past deeds. I am willing to sign any official form necessary to get my freedom and passport to return home with my wife and baby.
> I have etc.
>
> (Sd.) Abani Mukerji
>
> June 26, 1924"[22]

In another statement to the British Embassy in Berlin (July 1, 1924) Mukerji promised "not to take part in any secret anarchistic or terroristic activities in India": "I am a Socialist and will devote myself to the economic and social emancipation of the Indian masses by all non-violent means by forming a Labour Party within the Indian National Congress movement", he wrote.

However, as I have already written, the British Labour government decided to pass on all responsibility in that matter to the Indian colonial administration. The latter realised this and sent the "required" answer to London. Here is the text of the reply:

> "No. D. 2695
> Political Branch
> Dated September 4, 1924
> To the Secretary
> Public and Judicial Department, India Office, London
> Sub: Amnesty for Abani Mukerji
>
> Sir, in reply to your letter No. P&J (S) 961, dated July 17, 1924, I am

directed to say that the G.O.I. are unable to agree that an amnesty should be granted to Abani Mukerji in any conditions whatever. The G.O.I. could place no reliance on any promise that Mukerji might give to refrain from further revolutionary activity, and they believe that if he were allowed to come to India, he would do as a propagandist of revolutionary and Bolshevik ideas. The present would obviously be a most inopportune time to allow him to return to Bengal (. . .) The G.O.I. hope that, in view of Mukerji's world views as described above, the Secretary of State (for India) will agree that it is extremely undesirable to grant him an amnesty".

So, Mukerji remained in Moscow where years later he paid with his life for his "vacillation" and "deviation" from Marxist-Leninist and proletarian ideas and "backsliding to nationalism".

Lohani

We have very little information about the third person, who was executed in Leningrad. Ghulam Ahmad Khan Lohani, or Gholam Ambia Khan Lugani, was born in the East Bengali village of Sirajganj of the Pabna district (now in Bangladesh), in 1892.[23] He was known as an active and devoted Communist. In 1914 he went to study law in London. In 1920–1921 he continued his education in Paris. The British intelligence suspected him of being a courier between Moscow and "Bolshevik agents" in London.

In 1921 Lohani visited Berlin where he met Chatto. For some time he headed the Paris office of M.N. Roy's information agency. He maintained close ties with anti-British Indian emigrant organisations in European countries, especially the Worker's Welfare League of India, the Indian Communist Party, the Pro-Hindu Committee and the Indian Bureau in Berlin.

Lohani contributed articles to various communist periodicals, especially the European-based journal *Masses of India.* According to British agents' reports, he went to Moscow in November 1925 and ever since "has worked zealously as a Bolshevik propagandist".

Some time ago in Moscow I met Mathiur Rahman, formerly Secretary of the Central Committee of the Communist Party of Bangladesh, who gave me a photograph of Lohani. He also gave me the Paris address of Lohani's wife.

Mathiur Rahman is planning to write a book about Lohani, which may provide some new insights into the life and activity of this revolutionary from Bengal.

Notes and References

1. NKVD – (Narodny Kommissariat vnytrennich del) – People's Commissariat of Home Affairs
2. See: 'Note on V. Chattopadhyaya (Chatterji), Virendra Nath alias Vincent Chatterton alias A. Alfieri, alias Mahommed Jafar, familiarly known as Chatto, Biren or Binnie', Sir David Petrie, *Communism in India, 1924–1928.* With the Introduction and Explanatory Notes by Mahadevaprasad Saha. Calcutta, 1972, p. 307.
3. National Archives of India, Home Department of Government of India, August 1920, No. 110
4. Sir Cecil Kaye, *Communism in India,* pp. 140, 143.
5. Sir David Petrie, *Communism in India,* 1924–1928, pp. 13–14.
6. Vaclav Vorovsky (1871–1923) – distinguished Soviet publicist and diplomat, since 1917 Soviet ambassador to the Scandinavian countries, in 1921 was appointed ambassador to Italy, in 1932 shot dead in Lausanne by a Russian counter- revolutionary.
7. For more details see: L. V. Mitrokhin, *India on Lenin,* Moscow, 1973.
8. Russian Central Archives for the Documents on Modern History. Comintern files (1918–1928).
9. Sir David Petrie, *Communism in India, 1924–1928,* p. 26.
10. According to the British Intelligence office, "Mukerji Abani Nath alias Charlu alias R. Sahir of Khulna" was "a self-opiniated scoundrel who has been completely overshadowed by Roy in Indo-Bolshevik intrigues" (Sir Cecil Kaye, *Communism in India. With Unpublished Documents from National Archives of India.* Compiled and Edited by Subodh Roy. Calcutta, 1971, p. 328.
11. Sir Cecil Kaye, *Communism in India,* pp. 150–51.
12. Sir David Petrie, *Communism in India, 1924–1928,* pp. 7–9.
13. Sergei Kirov (1886–1934) – prominent Communist party leader, at that time head of Leningrad Regional Party organisation, member of the Politburo.
14. Sir Cecil Kaye, *Communism in India,* pp. 135–39.
15. Sir David Petrie, *Communism in India,* 1924–1928, pp. 312–14.
16. *Communism in India. Sir Cecil Kaye,* p. 39.
17. Ibid., p. 54.
18. Ibid., p. 40.
19. Ibid., p. 39.
20. Ibid., p. 39.
21. Ibid., pp. 174–86.
22. Sir David Petrie, *Communism in India, 1924–1928,* pp. 315–19.
23. ('Note on Lohani, Gulam Ambiya Kibriya (Gulam Ambia Logani)', Sir Cecil Kaye, *Communism in India. With Unpublished Documents from National Archives of India.* Compiled and Edited by Subodh Roy. Calcutta, 1971, p. 323. From another intelligence report we come to know that Lohani during the International Labour Conference in Geneva in 1925 met N.M. Joshi, trade union leader from India (Sir David Petrie, *Communism in India, 1924–1928,* p. 266.)

FIVE

India's Early Years of Independence: A Secret Report by the First Soviet Ambassador

V.P. KASHIN

UNTIL RECENTLY IT HAS been habitual for research and journalistic works to describe the relations between the USSR and India and later Russia and India, as initially friendly and to assert that they have been the same since the establishment of diplomatic relations between the two countries. In fact, such estimates do not wholly reflect the full spectrum of the events and tendencies pertaining to the more than half a century long history of the contacts between the USSR/ Russia and independent India. This is especially true of the formative stages of Soviet-Indian relations, the approximate chronological boundaries for which may be defined as the mid 40s–the beginning of 50s.

Historically, India has had a special place in the international activities and geopolitical plans of the Soviet authorities. This was conditioned by a number of factors, among which of especial significance were political projects of establishing an anti-imperialistic tripartite alliance between Russia, India and China. The author of the idea of this triangle was V.I. Lenin. On March 2, 1923 he stated: "The outcome of the struggle finally depends upon the fact that Russia, India, China, etc., form the giant majority of world population. And this very majority of population is nowadays being unusually quickly envolved into the struggle for its liberation, so in this sense there may be no doubt about the final solution of the world struggle. Therefore the final victory of socialism is quite and undoubtedly ensured."[1]

Later on Lenin's successors referred to the idea of Russo-Indo-Chinese class alliance time and again. They hoped that independent

India would surely join the ranks of socialist camp. The victory of the anti-fascist coalition in the Second World War, the spread of socialism among the peoples of Eastern Europe and the Civil War of 1946–1949 in China generated a great deal of optimism. But the post-war events in India frustrated the tempting perspectives like these.

That is why Stalin and the Soviet authorities of his period showed frank ill-will towards the declaration of independence of the Indian State in 1947 and Jawaharlal Nehru's government policy with its manifest purpose as the building of democratic society, social harmony, political stability and economic progress. Of no small importance in directing the Soviet government policies during the period under review were also ideological aims, far removed from the real scientific understanding of social and political processes going on in the countries of the East.

Firstly, we should refer here to Stalin's pre-war estimate of the national bourgeoisie of colonial and dependent countries like a "collaborationist" and "counter-revolutionary" power, which had allegedly entered into an agreement with imperialism behind its own peoples' back. Included in the "collaborationist" camp were the most influential circles of the Indian bourgeoisie and nationalist movement like Mahatma Gandhi. "Messrs bourgeois expect to flood these countries with blood and rely upon the police bayonets, with the help of people like Gandhi"[2], Stalin argued on June 27, 1930, at the moment when the Second *Satyagraha* was taking place in India.

Under Stalin's immediate guidance, the principle of colonial revolution as the way for the oppressed peoples of the East to achieve independence was introduced into the Comintern programme. The liquidation of the foreign imperialist supremacy was correlated with the violent struggle of the oppressed classes and the simultaneous overthrow of the feudal lords and landowner bureaucracy power, the establishment of a democratic dictatorship of the proletariat and the peasantry on the basis of the Soviets, organisation of the revolutionary workers' and peasants' Army and emergence of a bourgeois-democratic revolution into a proletarian one.

The "transfer of power" process in British India could hardly pretend to be in even distant conformity with such theoretical constructs. It was not by chance that the Soviet periodicals either refused to publish information about the situation in India, or presented the latter's liberation as a "political farce", skilfully arranged and staged by the colonial administration. "There are no reasons to suppose that 50,000 English families stationed in India are likely to leave it during a year"[3], *Pravda* wrote on the eve of the independence and underlined that hoisting the three-colour flag at the Red Fort could hardly improve the position of the Indian proletariat, peasantry and the "untouchables".

Secondly, the Soviet authorities' suspicious attitude to the independent India was conditioned to no small degree by the political status of the dominion as acquired by the Indian Union and Pakistan. They were sure in the Kremlin that in August, 1947 changes in India had touched only the top power echelons and resulted in the replacement of a viceregal administration by the bourgeois government of Jawaharlal Nehru while Viceroy L. Mountbatten had taken a Governor General' s seat in one of the new dominions.

The Soviet military circles supposed that in case of a war with the USA, Britain and their allies, India as a member of the British Commonwealth would inevitably be among the enemies of the USSR, and the Indian air force bases as well as other military-strategic objects would be used for bombing raids against the southern boundaries of the Soviet Union. The alleged Indian orientation towards military-political collaboration with the former metropolis was corroborated, in *Pravda*'s opinion, by the fact that 16 out of 19 British general-majors were supposed to stay in India, and 260 out of 280 brigade commanders were to continue their services too.[4]

And, lastly, what kind of friendship and cooperation with India could be considered when Stalin and his associates considered Nehru as the agent of American imperialism while Foreign Minister Molotov and his subordinates reckoned Nehru among the British secret service agents?

But even in those hard years the impartial assessment of the political processes in South Asia made breaches in the wall of dogmatism.

A bright example of it is the report by K.V. Novikov, the first Soviet Ambassador to India[5] presented on July 5, 1949, to the Foreign Policy Commission of the Central Committee of the AUCP (B).[6] The document has a "top secret" classification. At the present time it is available in The Russian Centre for Maintenance and Research of the Modern History Documents (RCMRMHD), where the main part of the archives of the Central Committee of the CPSU was preserved. The shorthand record of the account is done in 26 typewritten pages. The account itself is in 9 pages and 17 include the Ambassador's answers to the questions from the Commission's members. There were 28 such questions: 9 were asked regarding the situation in the CPI, 8 dealt with the political situation in India, 7–the British-Indian relations and 4 questions concerned the spread of the Soviet publications in India. The page enumeration in the text begins from page 20, because the list includes several documents which are close in contents.

The main task set before the Ambassador by the Commission was to give a detailed analysis of the situation in India and simultaneously to discover the presence of the signs of revolutionary crisis in the country.

Quite understandably a considerable part of the report dealt with the position of the working class and the peasantry as well as the role of the CPI. But to the great disappointment of the Commission's members the Ambassador could not discover a revolutionary situation in India. In his opinion, the struggle of workers and peasantry was exclusively under economic slogans and did not touch the basic of the present political formation.

"There has been no improvement in the economic status of the working class and peasantry in comparison with the British period. Moreover, progressive deterioration is taking place. While under the English rule, till August 15, 1947, a qualified worker earned 50–60 rupees and was also getting, in different branches of industry and in various princely states, roughly speaking, about 20–30 rupees a month as high prices addition; from August 15, 1947, to the present time the subsistence level index grew from 150 to 200 points. For the period the Indian government has been in power it has grown from 200 points to 360 in 1948 and to 560 in this year. The development is not towards the wage increase but towards the abolition of high prices bonuses and, secondly, towards the liquidation of fair price shops where the workers could buy cheap products. It was planned to organise a general strike of railwaymen on March 9. One of the main points of the strike was the question of abolition of a high prices bonuses and liquidation of the fair price shops".[7]

While the workers were dissatisfied with low wages, bonus abolition, etc., the peasantry was angry with the revenue policy of the government as a whole.

"The situation now is that the Indian government has to import 4 million tonnes of grain this year. The Indian government has now to spend all the export profits mainly on the grain import payments. Finding it necessary to cut down expenses and to reduce the import of grain, it introduced a tax in kind instead of the cash one. The Indian officials began to tour the villages and extort grain from the peasantry, which has grain left neither for sowing nor for subsistence; this has inevitably provoked a repulsive reaction against the Indian authorities: separate, uncoordinated, spontaneous peasant revolts against various government grain collectors, landowners, feudal lords and especially against usurers take place here and there. The Minister of the Interior of the Madras province was questioned in the parliament about the number of recent mass shootings in the Madras province. He answered that from the beginning of 1947 till September 1, 1948, the government recorded 52 mass shootings of peasant and workers' campaigns".[8]

Nevertheless severe measures against the strikers hardly caused any serious protest from the democratic-minded circles and the repression victims themselves. "The press features these shootings like order of the day".[9] The reason for this apparent paradox is rightfully described by the reporter as the simultaneous impact of the following three factors: firstly, the organisational weakness and insufficient political orientation of the Indian proletariat and the peasantry; secondly, the spontaneous, local and defensive character of the workers' and peasants' actions, and, thirdly, the absence of a coordinating work among the Indian communist masses. "A great shortcoming and misfortune of the democratic movement is that in the overwhelming majority of cases spontaneous actions take place without any coordinating or guiding activities of the Communist Party".[10] A temporary ban on the CPI and its underground work even more weakened the links between the Party and the people. Emphasising this circumstance, Novikov at the same time declined the supposition of those Commission members, who regarded the anti-Communist repressions as a result of the police provocation, and put forward his own version. "At present both the working class and the peasantry of India are in a somewhat awakened mood. Strikes of the working class and armed revolts of the peasantry take place around the whole country. To tell the truth, these actions of the working class and the peasantry are separate and spontaneous, they are rather of a petty character, but the main thing is that the whole country is engulfed in this movement. Under these conditions many local Communist Party organisations apply persistently to the Central Committee asking for help with arms and munitions. A portion of those documents with the requests for help fell into the Indian government's hands. Apparently it is upon these very documents that the Indian government statements concerning the preparation of an armed revolt by the Communist Party are based".[11]

"Until the Second Congress held in March of the previous year, the Communist Party of India thought that Nehru could turn to the left. Before this Congress of the Communist Party the Central Committee supported the Nehru government, and laid emphasis upon the struggle against the British imperialism. The Communist Party believed that the Indian government could, as a result of criticism and outside pressure, turn not towards a further new-form rapprochement with the British imperialism, but towards the left for the sake of the establishment of a certain kind of democratic government".[12] But during its Congress "the Communist Party rejected the policy of supporting the Indian government and proclaimed the struggle against the British imperialism on par with the struggle against the present regime in India".[13]

Thus, the Ambassador considered the change of CPI's attitude to the government as the main reason for the ruling circles' "displeasure" with the Communists. In its turn a cardinal revision of the party's home policy line implied an inevitable change in its leadership. "The Second Congress of the Communist Party of India condemned the position of the previous Central Committee including the position of the General Secretary Joshi as a reformist one. Joshi was relieved of his General Secretary's post and the staff of the Central Committee was almost wholly renewed. The present CC is not known to us. It was published that Ranadive was elected General Secretary. From the conspirative point of view the Indian Communist Party took the right decision not to publish the names of the new CC members. I am a little bewildered by the fact that they could not inform us even of the head persons of the Central Committee".[14] The report goes on: "At its December meeting Political Bureau carefully analysed the work of provincial Party organisations, in accordance with the decisions of the Second Congress of the Communist Party. In these decisions the Political Bureau strictly underlines that a reformist tilt still exists in the ranks of the Communist Party, that Joshi despite his speech at the Congress, in which he has admitted his mistakes and approved the decisions of the Second Congress of the Indian Communist Party, in reality pursues in essence the old reformist policy. Moreover, these decisions point out that he supported and tried to establish close links with the reformist groups and groupings in provincial Party organisations and princely states. A problem of treason in the Communist Party ranks was discussed at that Political Bureau meeting. The treason came to such a level that the underground organisation network of the Indian Communist Party was discovered by a policeman, so the CC had to reestablish the whole underground organisation network to protect itself from new failures".[15]

Later while considering the political situation in India Novikov made some significant observations that were not only out of step with Stalin's estimates but quite contary to them.

"Before my arrival to India, I was instructed by Comrade Stalin to bear in mind that the Indian government came to power on August 15, 1947, as a result of the deal between the Indian national bourgeois-feudal circles and British imperialism"[16], the Ambassador said in the preamble of his speech. As a result he came to the conclusion that after the achievement of independence absolute power was in the hands of the national bourgeoisie. So the establishment of Nehru' government, the act of transfer of power to the Indian side by the British, the partition of India, and the positive actions of the Indian government, which were directed towards the establishment of diplomatic relations with the Soviet Union and development of the Soviet-Indian cooperation least of all corresponded to the classification of "political farce".

"Has the situation in India changed after August 15, 1947 essentially or formally? I met one Portyannikov in Kabul who had been appointed the Second Secretary of the Embassy, but was going to work as the editor of the TASS bulletin. I discussed this question with him several times and asked how it was viewed in the Sovinformburo[17] circles. 'You see, he answered, the situation in India has not changed substantially. Britain dominates it the same way as before and the domination has changed only its form'. I cannot agree with such a position. Since August 15, 1947, the situation in India has changed not only in form but in essence. In fact the situation is such that the judicial, legislative, political, administrative power in the country belongs to the Indian national bourgeoisie, feudal lords, land-owners' circles and you cannot escape from it. The Indian bourgeois-landowners' circles are free to solve any political, or other problem as they please".[18] In this connection it is noteworthy that the Ambassador comes to this conclusion in a polemic with Portyannikov whose point of view was absolutely in conformity with Stalin's.

At the same time the British had changed the form of their participation in the economic life of the country. "They sell a portion of shares to the Indians, 25 per cent, make the management boards [of the companies – V. K.] Indian, thus the company becomes Indian too. From the other side, they purchase the shares of the companies which are purely Indian"[19], the Ambassador observed.

"The Communist press published only the information that at the present 75 per cent of investment profits are appropriated by the British bourgeoisie and only 25 per cent by the Indian. A part of the leading bourgeois circles is ready to reconcile to such distribution, but a part of the same circles would like to change the situation so that 75 per cent of profits would come into the hands of the national bourgeoisie and 25 per cent – into the hands of the foreigners. Such is the position of the Socialist Party of India".[20]

Novikov's estimation of Jawaharlal Nehru's political role was even more independent and farsighted. Contrary to Stalin's views he described India's first Prime Minister as the leader of liberation movement, a subtle politician, a wise parliamentarian and a faithful Congressist, able to skilfully assess public mood, as a man enjoying great authority and respect in his country. Discussing Nehru's views, he unintentionally foresaw beyond his time and made theoretical statements concerning the variety of methods of transition to socialism in accordance with the concrete conditions of this or that country.

"He [Nehru – V.K.] sometimes opposed Gandhi, styled himself a Socialist and in some cases assessed in a positive way the Soviet system, Communism, and stated that India had the same problems as

Russia had had. At present Indian national bourgeoisie and the Congress intentionally propagate the view that within the Congress and the government Nehru is a progressive figure. This is corroborated by Nehru's repeated statements that he is a supporter of Socialism, but in the conditions of ways and methods of socialist transition must be different from those of the Soviet Union.[21]

Paying homage to Mahatma Gandhi as a recognised leader of the liberation struggle of the people of India, the Ambassador informed that the day after Gandhi's assassination offered his own and the Soviet government's condolences to Nehru, and after a few days condolences on behalf of the Foreign Ministry and the Soviet government were expressed by the special note of the USSR Foreign Ministry. Moreover, the Ambassador behaved as a courageous man of principles and criticized the position of Stalin who did not publicly react to Gandhi's tragic death. "Comrade Molotov asked me if Comrade Stalin was right not to offer his condolences on the occasion of Gandhi's death. I answered that from a practical point of view it was harmful as Truman, Churchill and other government and state leaders of the world sent their condolences while Comrade Stalin did not. From a conjunctural point of view it was harmful for us".[22]

The analysis of the problems of the Soviet film distribution in India was of considerable risk for Novikov, who in his deliberations styled India a "friendly country" and mentioned the Indian government's assessment of Stalin's rule as dictatorship; this was very dangerous not only for the speaker himself but for the whole audience present.

". . . The Indian government looks very carefully after the policy of the Soviet Union and all that the Soviet Union says and publishes. I am not sure whether you know that at present the Indian censorship prohibited showing nearly all Soviet films in India. In fact, they not only refuse permission to show our films but withhold permission, given in 1944–1945 and the subsequent years. As a result of our application only six scientific and geographical documentaries are allowed to be shown: these are "Autumn in Georgia", "Sukhumi", "In the World of Crystals", "A Miraculous Laboratory", "Science and Technology No. 1"; "The May 1, Parade of 1948" was allowed too. Since 1944 the film "She Fights for her Motherland" has been of great success in India. The Indian government has now banned this film and in answer to our application it officially stated that the film was a threat to the interior security of the country, and they informally told me in the Ministry of Foreign Affairs that, you see, "this film teaches our Communists and rebellious elements how to organise a guerrilla war against the present government. Therefore, the Ministry of Interior considered the film to be inappropriate, harmful and even dangerous for the Indian national security".[23] We can hardly have any doubts that later films like this will be banned too. The "Stone Flower" film is in fact banned as well. It is nothing but a fairy-tale, but we were unofficially informed that since in this movie there were such scenes as a stone-carver being beaten up by the landlord's bailiff and it roused the Indian audience's indignation against the landlord and his bailiff, and as a result this film stirs the Indian people up against the landlords.[24]

There is a film "Native Melodies". The Censorship Board wrote that the film could be shown if some sequences could be cut out beginning from the scene of a group of Cossacks in the foreground, a huge figure of Comrade Stalin in the background, and the Cossacks paying homage to "dictator" Stalin. I reported to Moscow. As a result, the Indian government was sharply reprimanded. As you see, it runs even into hooliganism when the officials of a friendly country style Comrade Stalin as dictator'.[25]

This part of the report testifies to the fact that the "cold war" did have an impact upon the initial phase of Indo-Soviet relations. It could hardly be otherwise in the period under review, when sharp ideological confrontation ruled supreme. The Ambassador further said:

> "I must say that there is a document , the instruction of the Indian government which has fallen unofficially into our hands. It instructs the provincial governments to see to it that a minimum of the Soviet propaganda reaches India. It is openly stated there that there is a TASS publishing agency in India, so it is expedient that propaganda authorities do not their allow the TASS information to be published with the exception of those articles and materials that contradict themselves".[26]

K.V. Novikov's objectivity, sagacity, and personal courage as evident from his interpretation of the social and political situation in the newly independent India did not go unnoticed and had a negative impact upon his career. After the end of his Ambassadorial term in India he occupied some secondary post in the Foreign Ministry and retired in 1973.

Nevertheless, in spite of Stalin's unfriendly and prejudiced attitude to India and its leaders at the end of 40s, there were some positive signs in the Soviet-India relations towards a certain rapprochement and establishment of trade and economic contacts. After Nehru's unsuccessful 1949 visit to the USA and the American side's refusal to offer India food help, the government of India made an analogous request to the Soviet Union. In 1951 a contract was signed for the delivery of 100 thousand tonnes of Soviet wheat to India in exchange for the traditional goods of

Indian export.[27] The next year India agreed to participate in the international economic conference organised in Moscow, and the Soviet Union from its side took part in the international industrial exhibition in Bombay. Simultaneously Moscow offered to deliver industrial equipment to India.

The Soviet leadership's growing interest in India was corroborated by the fact that on the March 5, 1952, Stalin received S. Radhakrishnan, the Ambassador of India to the Soviet Union and on February 18, 1953 his successor K.P.S. Menon was also received by the Soviet leader. It has to be noted here that during the last years of his life Stalin personally received only three ambassadors, among them two were of the Republic of India.

As a result, at the initial stage of the Soviet-Indian relations, in spite of the obvious difficulties, the necessary foundation was laid for development and intensification of mutually beneficial cooperation between the two countries. Unfortunately, this positive and constructive process was developing against the background of an unfriendly attitude of the then Soviet leadership to India and this could but negatively affect the development of the contacts between the two countries.

Notes and References

1. V.I. Lenin, 'Better Less But Better', *Collected Works*, Moscow, 1964, Vol. 45, p. 40.
2. I.V. Stalin, 'Political Report to the CC to XVIth Congress of the AUCP.(B)', *Collected Works*, Moscow, 1955, Vol. 12, p. 252.
3. "Pravda", August 14, 1947.
4. "Pravda", August 10, 1947.
5. Novikov Kirill Vasilyevich (1905–1983) was on diplomatic service since 1940. In 1940–1942 he was counsellor in the Embassy of the USSR in Great Britain, 1942–1947 – head of the 2nd European Department of Foreign Ministry, member of the Member of the Foreign Ministry Board. He participated in a number of international conferences like the Yalta (1945), Potsdam (1945), San-Francisco (1945), Paris Peace conference (1946). K.V. Novikov was the Soviet Ambassador to India in 1947–1953.
6. AUCP (B) – All-Union Communist Party (Bolsheviks) was the official name of the Soviet Communist party upto its XIXth Congress in 1952, when it was changed to Communist Party of the Soviet Union (CPSU).
7. RCMRMHD, f. 17, l.128, d. 1187, p. 39.
8. Ibid., p. 29.
9. Ibid.
10. Ibid., p. 30.
11. Ibid., p. 28.
12. Ibid., p. 21.

13. Ibid., p. 28.
14. Ibid., p. 25.
15. Ibid.
16. Ibid., p. 20.
17. Sovinformburo was the abbreviation for the Soviet Information Bureau, the then Soviet news agency.
18. RCMRMHD, f. 17, l.128, d. 1187, p. 32.
19. Ibid., p. 34.
20. Ibid.
21. Ibid., pp. 20–21.
22. Ibid., p. 22.
23. This "dangerous" film was made in 1942 during the war against Hitler. It is the story of a village woman who, after her husband and child were brutally assassinated by the Nazi invaders, joined the anti-fascist guerilla group and soon became its commander.
24. The film "Stone Flower" was a fairy tale based upon the story by the famous Russian writer P.P. Bazhov who adapted the Urals' folklore of the mysterious Stone Flower and its fatal mistress, the Lady of the Copper Mountain.
25. Ibid., pp. 35–36.
26. Ibid., p. 36.
27. P. Shastitko et al (eds.). *SSSR i India* (The USSR and India), Moscow, 1987, p. 167.

PART II
Socio-Economic History

SIX

Indian Village Community in Russian Historical Writings

L. B. ALAYEV

THE PROBLEM OF VILLAGE (rural, territorial) community in India was one of the prime subjects of Russian/Soviet studies in Indian history and society. It was presumed that this is the core of the broader and more crucial problem of specificity of Indian traditional social structure. One of the founders of Russian Indology, I.P. Minayev, basically a Buddologist, in one of his papers presented, for the first time in Russian literature, a description of the Maratha village organisation at the end of the nineteenth century.[1]

M.M. Kovalevsky, who was the leading socio-historian and specialist in "comparative history of law", as he himself called his field of study, made a rather detailed research of traditional Indian (such as *Mānavadharmaśāstra*) and the British colonial sources on village communal structure.[2] But his interest was mainly in general regularities of social history all over the world and in corroborating these regularities with evidence from various concrete societies. He worked in the frame of evolutionist paradigm that was predominant in European social sciences of those days. Therefore he paid no attention to the specifically Indian features of rural life, such as the caste structure and the system of exchange of goods and services inside a locality, which later on became known as the *jajmānī* system. On the contrary, he tried to find in India the forms of land holding familiar to him from the history of other countries and to prove that the process of decay of village communal property was taking place in India as well. For this purpose he put various forms of community in some order according to his ideas of unilinear evolution, irrespective of chronological sequence, often resorting to assumptions when no positive data was available. As a result his scheme of stages which the Indian village community presumably passed through had very little relevance to Indian history.[3]

In the Soviet Indological studies of the 20s–50s of the twentieth century the ideas of M.M. Kovalevsky were very popular. They were supported by the Marxist understanding of property evolution, which were taken as unconditionally the right ones by their very definition. The general scheme of stages of communal property and land-holding, as worked out by K. Marx, differed a little from Kovalevsky's[4], but it was in the same paradigm of evolutionism, of the gradual disintegration of communal property and ripening of private one, with the same presumption that the general regularities are already known.

But K. Marx knew Indian material much better than Kovalevsky did; he had a broader outlook and was interested not only in the history of institutions. His idea of "Asiatic mode of production" (not to discuss the problem of validity of this idea) led him to inquire not only into the common features of all communities, but the peculiar features of "Oriental" rural community as well. It is well known, that he paid proper attention to the *jajmānī* system, although, perhaps he did not understand it quite adequately. For him it was the system of non-commodity, i.e. pre-commodity exchange of goods, a phenomenon of primitive stage of division of labour, when agriculture and crafts were not separated from each other. He did not see the close connection of the *jajmānī* system with the caste system, i.e. with the more advanced stage of development, "class society" in his terminology.[5]

The initial period of Soviet school of Indian studies (up to mid 50s) was not quite productive. It was a period of training of a new generation of scholars both in profession and in the Marxist theory. In this period some discord was already felt between Marx's understanding of Indian traditional social structure as a primitive-communal one, and the obvious high level of contemporary social contradictions (in spite of the possible exaggeration of those contradictions in the Comintern propaganda). But serious researches in the field of traditional Indian institutions, including village community, in this period were not undertaken.

In the 50s a certain breakthrough was made. A shift was made from the generalisation-type approach to the regional researches based upon a broad range of sources. The main part of evidence was obtained from the early British revenue documents, settlement accounts etc. It was presumed that these documents reflected the traces of pre-British Indian social structure too. The influence of foreign research literature on the group of authors listed below was quite weak. It can be explained, firstly, by the general situation of substantial isolation of the Soviet intellectual world from the Western research schools, and, secondly, by the fact that for quite a long time sociology was not acknowledged as a science by the Soviet political as well as academic elite. Therefore field-studies of villages undertaken by that time by Indian and Western sociologists and social anthropologists were completely ignored. As to the classical works of British administrators-*cum*-scholars, like B.H. Baden-Powell and others, they were used as a compendium of facts, but their ideas were rejected, because these authors were stamped as "apologists of private property". If purely ideological arguments for these accusations be ignored, the reason was the non-acceptance by the Soviet scholars of the structural approach to historical material. They were educated within the frame of historical, evolutionary, genesis-oriented paradigm and trained to argue in terms of single-directed development. The ideas, which were not in accord with this direction, had to be either ignored or condemned .

The series of regional studies was opened by I.M. Reisner's papers on Maharashtra[6] and K.A. Antonova's on Southern India.[7] Then the writings by N.I. Semyonova on the Punjab,[8] A.M. Osipov on the North-Western Provinces,[9] E.N. Komarov on Bengal,[10] L.B. Alayev on South India[11] were published.

To understand the general direction of these works, it is necessary to make some preliminary observations. It is interesting indeed that Soviet researchers in Asian history, included those engaged in Indian studies, being quite confident in their ardent Marxism, did not *en masse* accept Marx's idea of "Asiatic mode of production". The "Soviet Marxism" is a fascinating object for research, but this is not the subject of the present article. It is necessary to only point out here, that, as for the study of Non-European societies, the Soviet Indianists as a rule could not agree with idea that major Oriental societies were more primitive than the ancient European ones (the core of "Asiatic mode" concept). Therefore the main efforts of the Soviet researchers, dealing with the problem, were directed towards proving that, although Marx was absolutely right in assessing the primitive character of the Indian rural community, he had in mind some remote periods of Indian history, and that in modern period, on the eve of colonialism, the ("Marx's") community was "in the stage of deep disintegration". With the help of this "disintegration" the scholars explained all the features, non-corresponding to the "model", "classical Indian" type: broadly spread private rights on land, social and economic inequality inside a village, developed commodity production and marketing and so on. As it became obvious that the *jajmānī* system did not embrace all the relations between agriculturists and artisans, it was also understood as being in a process of disintegration.

The findings of these works were such. The forms of territorial community in India by the nineteenth century turned to be very diverse. In the Punjab and Hindustan (Uttar Pradesh and the adjacent territories) the community looked like a coherent group of landholders with some communal land rights, including those pertaining to arable land. Three types of landholding were spread: *zamīndārī* (common holding as a single estate), *paṭṭīdārī* (individual holding by shares), *bhayācārā* (individual holdings without shares). Rural administrative leadership was either absent or comparatively weak. In Maharashtra the full-fledged members of community had also broad landholding rights but more individualised ones. Community as a whole spread its rights only over various waste lands. Nevertheless the communal leaders (the headman, the accountant and some others) were hereditary, strong, dominant over the ordinary members and sometimes struggling against fiscal officers with success. In Bengal the social layer corresponding to the full-fledged community members, possessed land rights to a comparatively smaller extent, and communal "office-bearers" were more dependent on higher "feudal lords". Quite usual were holdings devoid of hereditary rights, and the landless population was numerically strong. Strangely enough, E.N. Komarov did not find in his sources the traces of the *jajmānī* system in Bengal. In South India in some regions (Eastern Tamilnadu) the rural communities were more like the North Indian model (common, shared and individual landholdings, weak leadership), in other regions (Andhra, Mysore) they were more similar to the Maharashtrian type, although with not so strong property rights, as in Maharashtra. In Kerala the system was in general akin to the Bengal one: predominance of large estates, insignificant development (or low level of intactness) of communal institutions, including the *jajmānī* system.

The same works discussed the following general features inherent to a certain extent in the local (territorial) communities in most part of the studied regions:

(1) Socio-economic inequality of rural population groups. Almost always there were around four strictly demarcated groups: (*a*) the community leadership, headmen and some other office-bearers, (*b*) full-fledged members, hereditary holders of land, members of a dominant caste, (*c*) possessors of land on restricted right or at-will, (*d*) servile castes and artisans. Some scholars distinguished also one more group: (*e*) the untouchables who by some parameters might be adjoined to the groups *c* or *d*.

(2) Concentration of land in the hands of a layer belonging to "higher agricultural" or "military-agricultural" castes. Members of other castes either had no land, or received it on a subordinate right, as a sort of a "wage" for serving a collective of full-fledged members, or the landowning individuals. It led to a restricted character of the landholding collective, barring the admission of strangers into their ranks. In this

sense landholding in a village was always "communal", although in other respects private rights might predominate. But stronger degrees of communal regulations of private holdings, such as the allotment of holdings or the redistribution of land between members were in India exceptionally rare, lasted for a very short time and might be explained by this or that exclusive conditions of time and place.

(3) Strength of property right of the community landholders *vis-a-vis* higher and larger landowners. Having fulfilled the main obligation – payment of revenue – the community landholders used the land freely as they liked. They had the rights of possession, usage and disposal of land. Especially amazing was the possibility for a community member to leave the village, preserving his land right for generations.

(4) The system of labour division within the community, when various professionals supplied each other with their products and services, receiving customary fixed payments in kind. Even in Bengal and Kerala, where this system was not traced in the early nineteenth century materials, some features of it were discovered. I. Reisner and his pupils paid proper attention to the fact that the system of "reciprocal services" was in essence a form of exploitation of servants and dependent people by the "full-fledged" members.

Due to the fact that in the Soviet historiography the view of primordial origin of village community prevailed, in the works mentioned above the authors were especially attentive to "vestiges of kin", such as extended family, caste and clan. This contradicted the thesis of "deep stage of disintegration", and led to some archaisation of social and productive relations in the community.

As a result of those works the Soviet Indianists came very close to the proper understanding of the institution conventionally called "The Indian Village Community". In the papers by I.M. Reisner, K.A. Antonova and A.M. Osipov caste stratification of village population was studied and a correlation between high caste status and landed property was pointed out. Only one step was left to the understanding that the caste and the local communities were the two interrelated manifestations of one and indivisible social fabric of pre-colonial India. The particular attention of Soviet historians to the problem of exploitation helped them to discover some exploitative features of intra-community relations. In the 50s it was already clear that the layer of "full-fledged members" included peasants who used their own labour, as well as landlords. In some parts of Northern India fully exploitative communities of landlords were discovered. But all these facts were interpreted as exceptions to the rule, as a result of disintegration and decay of the original model of a community of peasants.

The present author in his works of the 50s and beginning of the 60s was basically on the same positions, being a member of the research school founded and headed by I.M. Reisner. The only substantial difference of my approach from the one depicted above was the resolute demarcation of the Indian village community from the primitive, kin-based forms and stages. Community relations of later medieval period were understood by me as not only an integral part of feudal structure as a whole, but as a result of a process of development of feudal relations.[12] Consequently the emergence of the community land property (i.e. of the right prevailing over the individual rights of the community members) and of the redistribution of land was explained not by process of intra-community development, but by the external factors like influence of ecological conditions or of feudal (fiscal) environment.[13] The land shares in Tamil communities of *pacuṅkarai* type were treated as an example of redistribution which had emerged on the basis of combination of private and communal rights under the pressure of deficit of wet lands.[14] The redistribution of plots in *visapadī* villages of Rayalaseema and *bhej-barrār* villages of Bundelkhand at the end of the eighteenth century were discussed as the examples of transformation of the original model under the burden of unbearable feudal (fiscal) exploitation.[15] In all other aspects I followed the methodology of I.M. Reisner and E.N. Komarov.

However I can definitely fix the time of changing of this position by 1968. It became clear to me, that the majority of Western and Indian writers dealing with the village community problem, do not equate the notion of a "community member" and a "peasant", or understand "a peasant" very vaguely as a rural house-holder irrespective of his participation in physical field labour, and that a close linkage of these two notions ("peasant" and "community member") in the Soviet historiography was determined by the Marxist theory of community and by the fact that in Russia these two characteristics were practically inseparable from each other. The new conception (for the author) of Indian rural community was published in a paper, in which the local community was treated as "a meeting place of castes", as a mode of caste system functioning.[16] But this hypothesis needed to be verified by historical material pertaining to different periods and regions of India.

The new stage of Soviet studies of the problem started with the publication of the book by M.K. Kudryavtzev.[17] He broadly used the results of the studies by the Indian sociologists, made a thorough analysis of the *jajmānī* system as a functioning of the caste system, and finally came to the conclusion that the Indian village community represented a peculiar form of the type of "neighbourhood village community", known in the other countries.

Further researches of the present author were based on the works mentioned above. They were summarised in a monograph,[18] dealing mainly with North-Indian materials from the 1st millennium BC up to the nineteenth century. The main findings of this monograph are as follows.

For a few millennia the structure of Indian village community fluctuated within the limits determined by the two extreme models: (*a*) a peasant organisation of equal (the rights of whom were equally infringed upon) producers and (*b*) a community-estate, acting in the interests of a small part of its members. Originally a collective of respected householders (*gṛhapati*), mainly *vaiṣyas*, using slave, servile and "free" hired labour, this institution evolved for nearly a thousand years in the direction of equalisation of statuses, and by the first century AD became a dependent community of servile peasants. The bulk of agricultural householders became treated as *śūdras*. Later on (eighth-tenth centuries) a new layer of high caste exploiters was imposed upon them and the process of "peasantisation" started anew. This process 700–900 years later was halted by the British and therefore failed to come to the logical end.

The conditions of Oriental despotism were propitious for the consolidation of the upper strata of the rural community. This strata played a crucial role in the functioning of the society. Its members were, firstly, the organisers of households. Secondly, they secured the collection of revenue, which was so important for the maintenance of the bureaucratic structure and of the urban society as a whole. They were first-hand extractors of surplus product from the producers, leaving for the bureaucratic apparatus a comparatively simple job of redistribution. In this capacity the communities of landholders ensured social peace, making class conflicts inside the villages out of question. It is true that the village proprietors (*zamīndārs*, as they were known after the sixteenth century) were in a constant struggle with the ruling strata, and this struggle quite often took the form of revolt. Village proprietors were forced into narrow and rigid limits by high revenue demands and various regulations. But the government usually did not try to do away with this intermediary layer and to equalise the rural population on the level of toiling peasants.

Only Ala ud-din Khalji at the beginning of the fourteenth century made an effort to raise the revenue to the point at which the upper strata of the village would be deprived of the rent due from their holdings, and in the second half of the eighteenth century the Maratha chieftains in some parts of their dominions succeeded in reducing the hereditary proprietors to the level of tenants-at-will. But the attempt of Ala ud-din was evidently a failure, and the Maratha "experiment" ended with ravage and British conquest and we can not definitely know, how long it was possible to rule in India while extracting full rent from the villages. In other periods and other territories strong oriental-bureaucratic state co-existed with the local communities headed by socially high layer, reserving for themselves a part of surplus product.

The lower, toiling layers of the village population, may be summarily defined as producers of mainly slave type (for ancient period), and of mainly feudal type (for medieval period), but during all the periods the social composition of this layer was rather complex. The toilers were split into various economic strata, social statuses, judicial categories. Contrary to the upper stratum, which was marked with definite social activity, the lower layers were passive, as if they were absent at all, their existence may be traced from indirect evidences only.

The *jajmānī* system emerged probably in the central parts of Northern India in the fifth to second centuries BC. In medieval period it spread to other regions of India. Simultaneously the occupational scope of the system broadened from five (blacksmith, carpenter, potter, barber and washerman) to eight and then to twelve specialities (these figures were to a great extent conventional).

But this system even in the middle ages did not tend to the complete self-sufficiency of the communal economy. On the contrary, even in the period of its highest development it presumed that the agriculturists, land holders, as well as artisans had some contacts with the market. On the other side, there were no indications of the decay of the *jajmānī* system up to the nineteenth century.

The territorial scope of locality communal relations turned out to be much more complex than it was presumed earlier when the notion of "Indian village community" was coined. Communal relations were not restricted by the limits of a "village" in any sense of this word. There existed administrative bodies, as well as *jajmānī* network on the levels of a part of a village (ward), a village, several villages and, finally, of a broad territorial unit, comprising up to 100 villages (*caurāsī, khap* in the North of India, *nāḍu* – in the South).

Therefore the problem of Indian "village" community and the "Asiatic society" obtains some new dimension. Socio-economic differentiation turned out to be much more complex and multi-layered than the elementary division of "producer-ruler" type, as in the most widespread models of the "Oriental society". "Rent-tax" appeared to be not the only mode of exploitation, but only one of a few, side by side with the slave, rent, labour-rent, product-rent and money-rent, extracted by private persons. "Rent-tax" was usually a method of redistribution of resources extracted by private means. The "natural" (non-monetary) character of economy appeared to be not a result of self-sufficiency and low level of marketing, but of the objective process of restriction of marketing by limited kinds of goods and services. The reasons for slow and difficult evolution in direction of the predominance of private property and market relations were to be traced not to the total supremacy of natural relations and of state ownership, but the specific combination of private and state, natural and commodity principles.

Notes and References

1. I.P. Minayev, *Staraya Indiya. Zametki na Khozhdeniye za tri morya Afanasiya Nikitina.* (Old India. Notes on the Going over Three Seas by Aphanasius Nikitin). St. Petersburg, 1881.
2. M.M. Kovalevsky, *Obschinnoe zemlevladeniye, prichiny, khod i posledstviya yego razlozheniya* (The Communal Landholding: Causes, Process and Consequences of its Decomposition). Pt.1. Moscow, 1879.
3. M.M. Kovalevsky worked out the following scheme of stages: (1) "Non-divided kin community", (2) "Community with family plots determined by the law of inheritance", (3) community with egalitarian redistribution of land, (4) gradual giving up of redistribution.
4. See drafts of the letter by K.Marx to V. Zasulitch.
5. K. Marx gave the mostly identical descriptions of the Indian type of community twice: in the letter to F. Engels 14 June 1853 (citing from the "Fifth Report" through G. Campbell. Modern India: a Sketch of the system of Civil Government. London, 1852) and in "The Capital", Vol. I, referring to M. Wilks. *Historical Sketches of the South of India,* Vol. I. London, 1810. The best 'story' of the text see in L. Dumont. ' "The Village Community" from Munro to Maine'. *Contributions to Indian Sociology.* No. IX Paris – The Hague, Dec. 1966.
6. I. M. Reisner, 'Nekotoriye danniye o razlozhenii derevenskoy obschiny u marathov v XVII – nachale XIX v. (Some Data on the Decomposition of Village Community Among the Marathas in the XVII – Beginning of the XIXth Centuries)', *Uchyoniye Zapiski Instituta vostokovedeniya.* (Memoirs of Institute of Oriental Studies). Vol. 5. Moscow, 1953.
7. K.A. Antonova, 'K voprosu o vvedenii sistemy rayatvari (klassovaya suschnost mirasdarov) (Towards the Question of Introduction of the Rayatwari System (Class Nature of the Mirasdars)', *Kratkiye soobscheniya Instituta vostokovedeniya* (Short Notes of the Institute of Oriental Studies). Vol. 10. Moscow, 1953.
8. N.I. Semyonova,'Selskaya obschina i feodalnoye zemlevladeniye v gosudarstve Ranjit Singha (Village Community and the Feudal Land Property in the State of Ranjit Singh)', *Uchyoniye zapiski Instituta vostokovedeniya (Memoirs of the Institute of Oriental Studies),* Vol. XII, Moscow, 1955.
9. A.M. Osipov, 'Krestyanstvo severo-zapadnikh provinziy nakanune vosstaniya 1857–1859 gg (The Peasantry of North-Western Provinces on the Eve of the Revolt of 1857–1859)', *Narodnoye vosstaniye v Indii 1857–1859 godov (The Peoples' Revolt of 1857–1859 in India),* Moscow, 1957.
10. E.N. Komarov, 'Bengalskaya derevnya i krestyanskoye khozyastvo vo vtoroy polovine XVIII v. (The Bengal Village and Peasant Household in the Second

Half of the 18th century)', *Uchyoniye zapiski Instituta vostokovedeniya (Memoirs of the Institute of Oriental Studies).* Vol. XVIII. Moscow, 1957.

11. L.B. Alayev, 'Formy obschinnogo zemlevladeniya v Yuzhnoy Indii v XIV–XVIII vv.(The Forms of Communal Landholding in Southern India in the XIV–XVIII Centuries)', *Indiya i Afganistan. Ocherki istorii i economiki* (India and Afghanistan. Sketches of History and Economics), Moscow, 1958. To the same series may be attributed somewhat later papers: L.B. Alayev, 'K voprosu o severoindiyskikh obschinakh tipa zamindari, pattidari i bhayachara (On the Question of North-Indian Communities of the Zamindari, Pattidari and Bhayachara Types)', *Narody Azii i Afriki* (Peoples of Asia and Africa), 1962, No. 5; L.B. Alayev. Ñekotoryye voprosy razvitiya indiyskoy obschiny v kontse XVIII–nachale XIX v.(Some Questions of Development of Indian Village Community in the end of the XVIIIth – beginning of the XIXth Centuries)', *Voprosy istorii* (Questions of History), 1962, No. 8.
12. L.B. Alayev, *Yuzhnaya Indiya. Sozialno-Economicheskaya istoriya XIV–XVIII vekov.* (South India. Socio-Economic History of the XIV–XVIIIth Centuries), Moscow, 1964, p. 85.
13. L.B. Alayev, *Formy obschinnogo zemlevladeniya,* p. 8.
14. Ibid., p. 8, 15; L.B. Alayev, *Yuzhnaya Indiya,* p. 78.
15. L.B. Alayev, *Formy obschinnogo zemlevladeniya,* pp. 30–32; L.B. Alayev, *Nekotoryye voprosy razvitiya.*
16. L.B. Alayev, 'Tipologiya indiyskoy obschiny (The Typology of Indian Community)', *Narody Azii i Afriki* (Peoples of Asia and Africa), 1971, No. 5.
17. M.K. Kudryavtsev, *Obschina i kasta v Khindustane (Iz zhizni indiyskoy derevni)* (Community and Caste in Hindustan. From the Life of Indian Village), Moscow, 1971.
18. L.B. Alayev, *Selskaya obschina v Severnoy Indii. Osnovnyye etapy evolyutsii.* (Rural Community in Northern India. Main Stages of Evolution), Moscow, 1981; a short synopsis of this monograph is available in English: L.B. Alayev, *Rural Community and the Traditional Indian Social Structure.* Paper presented at the 32th International Congress for Asian and North African Studies (Hamburg, 1986). Moscow, 1986.

SEVEN

On the Nature of Land Property in the Late Medieval India: Sixteenth to Eighteenth Centuries

G. G. KOTOVSKY

Economic and social history of the Asian societies has put before historians the basic problem: why did these societies first of all India and China – which by the end of the fifteenth century had attained the level of material production that was higher than that of the Western Europe, in the era of the so-called Merchant Capitalism begin to lag behind the Western world creating thereby the pre-requisites for the emergence of colonialism.

The present author is convinced that the answer might be given by a comparative study of economic and social systems and modes of production of East and West during the late medieval-early modern periods. Within this framework the author makes an attempt to denominate the economic and social character of landed property in India in the sixteenth-eighteenth centuries. A student of medieval Indian history may be disappointed finding here neither new historical facts nor new sources brought to light. The author has only tried to re-interpret the enormous material summarised in the works of Indian historians, by S. Nurul Hasan,[1] Irfan Habib,[2] Satish Chandra,[3] B.R. Grover,[4] Shireen Moosvi,[5] M. Athar Ali,[6] N.A. Siddiqui,[7] I.H. Qureshi,[8] A.R. Khan,[9] A.D. Khan,[10] Muzaffar Alam[11] and others.[12] The author has also utilised the studies of the Russian historians, especially I.M. Reisner,[13] K.A. Antonova[14] and C.Z. Ashrafyan.[15] There are also important contributions by the Western scholars.[16]

Before elaborating upon the main subject it is necessary to introduce some preliminary remarks of a conceptual nature.

Firstly, the initial postulate is the well-known one by Marx who equated the property relations with production-based, economic relations (naturally, here the property refers to means of production, not items of consumption).

Secondly, comparative historical research of various types and forms of property may be possible only as the disclosure of their common qualities. These common qualities are the inner essence, inner structure of property as a historical and economic category. The latter pre-supposes the denomination of two sides of the property relations: (*a*) controlling the very process of production, its organisation, (*b*) controlling the outcome of production, the results of labour in their kind and cash denominations.

These two sides of property are conventionally styled by the present author as the **property attributes or functions**. It is in these two functions that property is realised as an economic category.

As property realisation is, however, nothing but a certain set of relations entered by the people during the social reproduction process, the above-mentioned functions are bound to be in this or that way appropriated, attributed by the sides participating in this process (here the readers may be reminded of Marx's wonderful denomination of property as **appropriation**!).

Throughout the whole history of human civilisation these sides have been only three in number: society as a whole (represented by the state), private owners and primary producers.

The three above-mentioned sides are conventionally styled by the present author as **property agents**.

Thus the inner structure of property consists of its objects and subjects. The functional distribution of property attributes, i.e. control over the process of production and its results, constitutes in given historical epochs both the different types of property and their evolutionary forms.

The author has verified the possible distribution of the two property functions between its three agents, using algebraic formula C_m^n where m = 3 and n = 2 and obtained 9 possible variants: 5 main, basic types of property corresponding to the following modes of production: state slavery, private slavery, state feudalism, private feudalism, state capitalism, private capitalism, state socialism, primary producers' property related to small-scale commodity production of peasants and artisans, collective and cooperative property.

The remaining four variants are various forms of co-participation of the three property agents in the realisation of the two functions of property (for example, different types of lease, mixed state – private enterprises, etc.).

It has to be noted here that different variants of property relations, as obtained from this formula, in various historical epochs have been conditioned by dissimilar socio-economic meaning as facilitated by the changing character of the property agents themselves. The latter has been determined by the change of stages of historical development of mankind or, according to Marx, socio-economic formations.

It is also important to note that in a given space and time different types of property, representing successive stages of socio-economic evolution, i.e. formation, may coexist and interplay. The total sum of economies based on the same type of property form an economic structure (in the Russian terminology – *uklad*, literally 'layout').

Before elaborating upon the main topic of this article we find it necessary to remind that the relations of feudal landed property are denoted by us as a totality of relations entered by the peasants who were the immediate producers, individual feudals and the state or the 'collective feudal' during and due to the process of agricultural production and consequent distribution of its results. The research into the character of these relations which makes it possible to attribute them to one of the two main structures of the feudal society, viz. **state feudal or private feudal**, has to be undertaken by analysing the **ownership rights** of the three above-mentioned subjects of land property. By their very essence these rights are divided into two groups: (1) pertaining to the relations of the property subjects towards land as the object of economic activity; (2) pertaining to the relations of the property subjects towards distribution of surplus product (or realisation of feudal rent) which pre-supposes a certain demarcation between the necessary and surplus product (or the amount of feudal rent) and form of its appropriation, as well as appropriation of surplus product as such with its subsequent distribution within the ruling feudal class.

Therefore, a methodological basis for the reconstruction of the inner structure of the ruling class and denomination of the proprietary rights of its different groups will depend on answers to the following questions: (1) by whom, how and in which forms feudal rent was exacted from the peasant households; (2) between which social groups and how the exacted and appropriated feudal rent was distributed.

By the beginning of the eighteenth century nearly the whole of the Indian territory belonged to the Mughal empire, the mightiest feudal state on the Indian soil. Previously independent feudal states, conquered by the Mughals during endless wars in the sixteenth-eighteenth centuries, were absorbed in the empire either as semi-autonomous vassals or as parts of its major territory, controlled by the military and fiscal-administrative apparatus of the empire.[17]

The destiny of a previously independent principality was by and large determined by geopolitical factors that enabled the Mughals to practice a real military-political control over the conquered territories. Therefore the vassal principalities remained, as a rule, in the border areas of the Mughal empire or in some uneasily accessible territories. The acknowledgement of the Mughal suzerainty was expressed by the vassal princes by paying a fixed form and amount of tribute (*peshkash*) and participating in the imperial military campaigns as well as guarding borders and communications. According to S. Nurul Hasan, the strengthening of the Mughal control over the vassal principalities made their rulers gradually lose control over their own vassals who thus became more dependent upon the central government, and over the principality's fiscal-administrative apparatus that became a part of the imperial one. Consequently the territory of such a vassal principality merged with the imperial domain and its ruler became a part of the feudal class of the Mughal empire as a holder of a conditional land grant (*jāgīr*).[18] In cases when a previously independent principality, conquered by the Mughals or other feudal state, remained, for whatever reason, autonomous in managing its administrative, fiscal and judicial system, it acquired the status of a semi-independent vassal.

As has been ascertained by the numerous works on the Indian history of the sixteenth-eighteenth centuries, in the Mughal empire (and its successor states too) the lands that belonged to the imperial domain were governed by the unified system of taxation.[19] All arable lands (*ārāẓī*) were subjected to land revenue (*kharāj, māl*) fixed as half of the land produce[20] and usually payable in cash. Apart from this land revenue that constituted main, "normal" form of feudal rent T, the tax-paying agriculturists (*ri'āyā*) were to pay a variety of other taxes and tolls (*abwābs*) which, like, forest and fishery tolls, were either consolidated with the whole sum of rent due from a given village community, or were appropriated by the land revenue administration as a form of their state salary. All these taxes and tolls (*sā'ir jihāt*) increased the norm of feudal exploitation of the peasants but, as concerned their volume, bore no comparison with the major agricultural rent-tax (*māl-o jihāt*). The additional taxes, even if legalised by the state, could have been collected either partially or not collected at all if it was so ordered by the *amīns* – officers responsible for the assessment of taxes.[21] But land tax (*māl*) was to be collected without any excuse.

Revenue collection was the duty of special fiscal officers subordinate to the capital-based central revenue office (*dīwānī*). The most important link of this network was the administrative apparatus of a district (*pargana*), the core territorial unit of the Mughal empire. The very process of revenue collection included two successive stages each requiring major roles from various office bearers of the *pargana* administration. This to a certain extent facilitated a kind of mutual control aimed at a full and timely appropriation of land revenue by the imperial treasury.

At the first stage the *amīns* and their agents, *mutaṣaddīs*, measured the fields allotted for various crops and assessed the total sum of revenue (*jama'*) for every village of the *pargana* under their jurisdiction. With the help of the village headmen (*muqaddams*) and scribes (*paṭwārīs*) the revenue was further assessed and distributed among the tax-paying agriculturists (*ra'īyats*). Information concerning the area allotted for various crops as well as the amount of land revenue (in kind or cash, as depended upon the crops) in each village was collected by the head scribe of *pargana* administration (*qānūngo*) and forwarded to the central revenue office – *dīwānī*. In the latter a whole army of scribes reviewed the information preparing condensed reports of the full amount of revenue (*jama'*) from the *parganas*, *sarkārs* (provinces) and *ṣūbas* (viceroyalties) – three successive layers of the Mughal administrative system. The thus collected data was utilised by the *dīwānī* office that operated through the *dīwāns* of the *ṣūba*s and their agents in the *sarkārs*, to control the regular collection of land revenue as well as to determine the areas granted by the emperor to various feudals.

Collection of revenue (*jama' bandī*) was the responsibility of the following office bearers: on the village community level it was its headman the *muqaddam*, on the *pargana* level it was *caudhurī*, the head of its revenue administration. But the key figures in revenue collection were *zamīndārs* whose duties and privileges will be discussed further on.

The collected revenue was forwarded to the local treasury department – *foṭah khānā* managed by the *karoṛī* and then either to the *jāgīrdār* within whose jurisdiction the *pargana* or its part was, or directly to the imperial centre.

The revenue apparatus of the Mughal empire that exacted rent from the peasant households based its activities, much like in any other feudal society, upon methods of non-economic coercion and was assisted by military forces commanded by the head officers of local garrisons (*faujdārs*) and military posts (*thānādārs*). *Chaudhurīs* and *zamīndārs* too had at their disposal some groups of foot soldiers (*piyādā*) and horsemen (*sawār*). Military forces commanded by the *jāgīrdārs*, including the *faujdārs*, were used to exert pressure on not only the tax-paying peasants but to an equal extent the lower ranks of administration, *zamīndārs*, *caudhurīs*, *muqaddams*, in order to facilitate revenue collection.

The three relatively autonomous and mutually controlling administrative systems (the one assessing revenue amount, the one collecting revenue and the one executing the non-economic coercion for the extortion of agricultural surplus) constituted in their totality a whole mechanism of feudal rent exaction from peasant households and its further distribution within the feudal class. The functioning of this mechanism was facilitated by the interest of every individual feudal who was legally supposed to offer either civil or military service to the Mughal throne, in exacting his share of the conglomerate feudal rent collected in the form of the state land revenue (*māl*) by the state from the rural taxpayers (*ra'īyats*). The share of each feudal depended upon the territory he had under his jurisdiction as a representative of civil or military administration.

The totality of duties and privileges pertaining to this or that post in the civil administration (revenue-administrative apparatus) was rather comprehensively and clearly determined by the central revenue office *dīwānī* under a respective title like *qānūngoī* for the *qānūngo, caudhurāī* for the *caudhurī, muqaddamī* for the *muqaddam*, etc. Same terms were applied to signify the titles enabling their holders to get a share of land revenue from a given territory. These privileges or titles were realised in two ways.

Firstly, the office bearers of village community or *pargana* were entitled to receive certain shares from the total sum of land revenue due from the villages under their jurisdiction. Secondly, they were entitled to collect the whole sum of revenue due from a certain part of territory (a village or some villages) under their jurisdiction. Land grant of this kind was known as *nānkār*. It is important to note that taxation of the *nānkār* lands was carried on by the same system and same apparatus (the *amīns* and so on) as that of the lands from which revenue was transmitted to the higher-ranked feudal lords.

It is well known that the lands (to be more precise – villages) from which land revenue was forwarded to the central revenue office constituted the so called *khāliṣa* domain. The income from these lands was used for the maintenance of the imperial court and other state expenditures. From the *khāliṣa* land fund, in which the conquered territories were included, various land grants including the conditional ones (*jāgīr*) and non-conditional (*suyūrghāl, madad-i ma'āsh*) were distributed. Since the *jāgīrs* could, after the end of the grant period or due to some other reasons, be confiscated by the treasury, a fixed and clearly cut border between the *khāliṣa* land fund and the *jāgīr* fund never existed. It was noteworthy that in the *dīwānī* the calculations of the assessed land revenue from both types of lands was carried on jointly, not separately.

One can agree with K.A. Antonova who described *khāliṣa* and *jāgīr* as two forms of the state feudal land property.[22] However the differences between these two forms of feudal land property relations are traceable only in the final phase of rent distribution within the ruling class.

I will repeat here that in a feudal society land property was "split" between peasants who controlled land as means of production and therefore possessed the rights to inherit and transfer the plots that belonged to them; and the feudals who controlled produce generated by peasants and determined its division into "surplus" and "necessary" products. Medieval India was not an exception here.

Nevertheless the basic distinction from the West was in the system by which not individual feudals but the state through its agents executed this control. Both the government land tax and the land rent were not levied separately but were combined in land revenue. Hence, in our understanding, the dominant form of feudal relations in late medieval India was state feudalism.

In this connection it is difficult to agree with Irfan Habib's assessment that ". . . while *māl*, the Mughal tax occupied an important position in Indian economy as rent in any feudal economy, it was not, properly speaking, rent or even a land tax. It was a tax on the crop".[23] It appears that in this passage socio-economic nature of the exaction from primary producers has been confused with the methods of calculating the exaction.

At the same time it has to be clarified in which forms and to what degree the tendency of development of private feudalism manifested itself throughout the evolution of the *jāgīr* as a form of feudal land ownership.

The scholars have taken note of the numerous references to hereditary *jāgīrs* (*jāgīr-i waṭan*) in the sixteenth-eighteenth century sources. Genetically, hereditary *jāgīrs* were of two kinds. The first type was service-bound *jāgīrs* which gradually, with the weakening of the central power and strengthening of that of the *jāgīrdārs* (especially big ones or situated on the periphery of the empire) were transformed in the sixteenth-seventeenth century from conditional to life grants and further on fixed as a possession of a certain family or clan. The sanctioning of these changes by the central power (through special documents or *sanads*) was either forced on the Mughals or was a testimony of their aspiration to win the support of the *jāgīrdārs* by bringing stability to the land grants system.

The second type of hereditary *jāgīrs* was the holdings of either the erstwhile independent Rajas or their vassals whose lands after the Mughal conquest were assimilated into the imperial domain. The Mughals usually took into consideration the hereditary character and alienability of the property rights (*milkiyat*) that existed prior to the Mughal conquest of a given territory.

The *milkiyat* land holding which is more often than not incorrectly denoted as "ownership" or "proprietary rights" was expressed in the hereditary and alienable entitlement of revenue collection on a certain territory. In the sixteenth-eighteenth century the land rights of this type were usually styled as *zamīndārī* and its holder as *zamīndār*. Therefore the holding of the *jāgīr-i waṭan* due to the *milkiyat* rights was also called in late medieval sources *zamīndārī* and the holder *zamīndār*. Since similar term was applied to the most widely spread strata of lower feudals the *jāgīr* holding *zamīndārs* were sometimes denoted by a special collective term *zamīndārān-i 'umda*.[24] On the basis of S. Nurul Hasan's and B.R. Grover's research into the ownership rights of the *zamīndārs* the latter may be divided into three groups: *peshkash*-paying vassal chieftains; former Rajas and their vassals who were holding their lands as hereditary *jāgīrs*; feudals of the lower ranks who owned and used village community lands.[25] The *jāgīrdar zamīndārs*, mainly Hindus, were part of the upper layer of the Mughal ruling class and even belonged to the ranks of the higher *manṣabdārs*.[26] As calculated by M. Athar Ali, at the end of the seventeenth-beginning of the eighteenth century 15 per cent of the higher *manṣabdārs* (i.e. whose *manṣabs* equalled 1000 or more horsemen) were Hindu *zamīndārs*.[27]

Hereditary character of the *jāgīrs* as well as the alienability of property rights of some *jāgīrdār* groups testified to the tendency of the development of certain elements of private property relations within the framework of state feudal property. At the same time for a decisive criterion, allowing to determine the ripening level of private feudal relations, we have to evaluate the subjugation of the state administrative revenue apparatus by the *jāgīrdār* within the limits of his *jāgīr*.

Already in the seventeenth century and especially in the eighteenth the *jāgīrdārs* were usually unable to fully collect the total sum fixed by a given land grant. Satish Chandra has rightfully seen it as a reason for the so-called *jāgīrdārī* crisis.[28] Perhaps the *jāgīrdārs*' aspiration to somehow compensate for the revenue losses made the system of "illegal" – from the viewpoint of the revenue administration – taxes and tolls, widely spread in the eighteenth century inevitable. With the help of their military units the *jāgīrdārs* collected these "illegal" taxes from the populations of the villages under their jurisdiction.[29] The decrease in the *jāgīrdārs*' income was brought about mainly by the growing resistance of the lower feudals (*zamīndārs*). They constituted the major link of the "rent-transmitting" chain and, taking advantage of the weakening of central power and feuds in the Mughal empire, spared no efforts to strengthen their proprietary rights. This layer of the feudal class just appropriated a considerable part of the *jāgīrdārs*' share off the aggregate rent.

The *jāgīrdārs* regularly sought help from the *faujdārs* who seized the castles, cattle and other movable property of some *zamīndārs* and handed the booty to the *jāgīrdārs* as a redemption of the *zamīndārs*' debt in revenue collection.[30] However the *faujdārs* could not always or would not assist the *jāgīrdārs* in collecting revenue.

It appears that, despite the development of hereditary *jāgīr*, this type of feudal land ownership never transformed itself into a transitional form from the state to private feudal property. This may explain why in the history of the Mughal empire the periods of consolidation of the *jāgīrdārs*' ownership rights were followed by the periods of curtailing the *jāgīr* fund by confiscating the *jāgīrs* into the *khāliṣa* domain (for instance, under Aurangzeb in the seventeenth century and Bengali ruler Murshid Quli Khan in the eighteenth) and frequent change of *jāgīr* holders.[31]

The *jāgīr* holders, though several thousand in number,[32] constituted a minority in the ruling class of the Mughal empire. The latter, as was rightly observed by S. Nurul Hasan, consisted of two main layers.[33] A majority of the Indian feudals were "primary *zamīndārs*" of S. Nurul Hasan who thus distinguished them from the *zamīndārs* who were holders of hereditary *jāgīrs*. [34] Taken together, these "primary *zamīndārs*" genetically constituted the feudalised elite of village community.

The most important feature of the "primary *zamīndārs*" as a layer of the Indian feudal class was that they enjoyed not only land ownership rights that legitimized their claims to surplus product, but the rights to use land as an object of economic activity. The latter rights (along with the lands they pertained to) were known by the special term *khūdkāsht*, were hereditary and alienable and were realised in the holder's choice of the way of cultivation: using one's own labour and that of the family, employing bonded labour of the low-caste members of the village community, leasing the land out. Like all rights in feudal society, the *khūdkāsht* rights were related to certain duties as concerned other property subjects. The landowners were obliged to ensure cultivation (by any of the above-mentioned ways) as well as payment of land revenue. Therefore a *zamīndār* was treated as *mālguzār*, i.e. a revenue payer. *Zamīndārs*' rights and duties were similar to those of other full-right members of village community, *ri'āyā* taxpayers. The *zamīndārs*' legally belonging to the ranks of the tax paying villagers was even sanctioned by a special term –

zamīndārān-ira'īyatī. The *khūdkāhst* lands of the *zamīndārs* were taxed like those of the other village community members.[35]

At the same time, the *zamīndārs*' place in the village community was special both in fact and by law: they constituted the feudalising elite of the village.

Firstly, during the period under review the *zamīndārs* either leased their *khūdkāsht* lands out or employed low-caste bonded labourers to cultivate them. Since the revenue due from the *khūdkāsht* lands was paid by the *zamīndārs* on reduced rates, the feudal character of their rights was determined by the fact that they appropriated a part of surplus exacted from the immediate cultivators of the *khūdkāsht* lands – in the form of difference between normal and reduced rates of the revenue.

Secondly, the *zamīndārs* enjoyed seigniorial rights to a certain territory (a village, its part, a group of villages, a *pargana*, etc.) which were realized by their appropriation of a part of feudal rent from the tax-paying residents under their jurisdiction. These rights (*zamīndāri*) were hereditary and alienable, representing, according to Irfan Habib's rightful observation, a form of the *milkiyat* rights. Emphasising the exploitatory character of the *zamīndārs* as a social group, Irfan Habib was right in observing that the *zamīndāri* rights were enjoyed by the representatives of the rural clans who were different from the peasants and dominated over them.[36]

The *zamīndars* as holders of various land ownership rights occupied a double position within the system of relations pertaining to feudal land property. On the one hand, as has already been mentioned, the ownership of the *khūdkāsht* lands reflected their genetic and economic links with the village community, including their position as tax-paying villagers, and therefore they were at par with other feudals who enjoyed no cultivation rights. The fact that the *zamīndārs* not only appropriated agricultural product but disposed of its major means, i.e. land, resulted in the emergence in medieval India of a peculiar social group which enjoyed ownership rights both as consumers and as producers of land rent.

On the other hand the *zamīndārs*' ownership rights to appropriate rent in their totality included the elements of both state feudal and private feudal land property. The reality was that the *zamīndārs*' seigniorial rights (*huqūq-i zamīndāri*) were of two types.

The first type of the *zamīndāri* rights was determined by the place of the *zamīndārs* within the structure of the Indian feudal class. The aggregate rights and duties of the *zamīndārs* pertaining to revenue collection within the area of their jurisdiction was termed as *khidmat-i zamīndārī*. The *zamīndārs* appropriated their share of feudal rent in three forms: (1) appropriation of a certain part of the total sum of revenue collected from the tax-paying residents of the area under their jurisdiction; (2) appropriation of the total sum of rent due from their service-grants (*nānkār*)[37]; (3) reduced taxation of their *khūdkāsht* lands. According to calculations by Shireen Moosvi, the *zamīndārs*' share in gross agricultural surplus was about 20 per cent.[38]

As mentioned above, the assessment of the form (kind or cash) and amount of land revenue due from the lands under the jurisdiction of a certain office bearer *zamīndār*, including the *nānkār* and *khūdkāsht* lands was made by the state independently from the landholder. The decisive role of the state in the realisation by the *zamīndārs* of their ownership rights (albeit hereditary and alienable) is conspicuous in the available data on the two types of the land revenue administration in the Mughal empire.

All villages in which the arable lands were taxed by the state and constituted the imperial domain (including the *khāliṣā* and the *jāgīr* lands) were divided into two groups. The first one comprised the villages to which the *zamīndārs*' seigniorial rights were relevant (*dehāt-i ta' alluqā*). The second group comprised the villages free from those rights (*dehāt-i ra'īyatī*). Since the villages of both types within a *pargana* limits were frequently located side by side, revenue collection was more often than not carried on by the same officers. However their ownership rights as relevant to the villages of different types varied to a certain extent. For example, a *zamīndār* who held the post of *pargana caudhurī* received his share of the total sum of revenue due from the *ra'īyatī* villages in the form of *rusūm-i caudhuraī* deductions, while from the villages under his seigniorial jurisdiction his share was *rusūm-i zamīndārī*; both shares were approximately equal (2–2,5 per cent in North India by the end of the seventeenth – beginning of the eighteenth century).[39] B.R. Grover has made a special mention of the impossibility of receiving both types of share (*rusūm*) from the revenue collected from the same territory.[40]

The analysis of the rights and duties of the *zamīndārs* as relevant to revenue collection (*khidmat-i zamīndārī*) demonstrates that the latter determined the place of the *zamīndārs* as allotted to them by the joint feudal, i.e. the state, within the system of collective appropriation of feudal rent. And this is, to our mind, the essence of state feudal land property.

Nevertheless the *zamīndārs* enjoyed seigniorial rights of a different kind that pertained to the same lands which the *zamīndār* held under his jurisdiction as a hereditary tax collector. These rights (*haqq-i zamīndārī*) were not connected with any form of service grants but expressed the *zamīndār*'s status as a feudal seignior, so to say, in its pure type. They were realised in the form of a special cess (*mālikānā*) which in the North India of the seventeenth-eighteenth century was, according to various sources, 1.25 per cent, 1.75 per cent, 2.17 per cent of the gross product and was collected from the tax-paying villagers by the *zamīndār* himself without any help from the revenue officers. A *zamīndār* retained his *mālikānā* rights even in cases when he lost his *khidmat-i zamīndārī* rights (i.e. ceased to act as revenue collector) or when his *zamīndārī* or its part was transferred to another person as an *a'imma*, a tax-free land grant fully excluded from the jurisdiction of the revenue administration.

The *mālikānā* rights of the *zamīndārs* are to be evaluated as a manifestation of private feudal property relations since in this case the appropriation of surplus product in the form of rent was separated from land revenue (it was realised by determining the amount and form of the exacted part of the product) and the very process of its exaction from the peasant households was carried on by an individual feudal independently of the state.

Therefore the *zamīndārs* constituted a special group of the Indian feudal class. They, firstly, personified both the state and private feudal land property relations and, secondly, enjoyed land ownership rights that expressed their command over not just the agricultural product but land as an object of economic activity.

In their totality the ownership rights of the "primary *zamīndārs*" which were a legal reflection of the place occupied by this group of the feudal class within the system of production and distribution of agricultural surplus (feudal rent) represented a mixed, transitory form of the state towards private feudal property relations.

Apart from the state and mixed (state-private) forms of feudal land property in India on the eve of the colonial era, there existed private feudal land property in two major forms.

The first type of private feudal land ownership relations comprised the holdings of the *a'imma* type (*madad-i ma'āsh, suyūrghāl,* etc.) granted by the emperor either to various religious establishments (Muslim or Hindu) or to individual canonical or lay feudals for their personal services to the state, or to those who brought virgin lands under cultivation. These grants were of various sizes – from a plot of land to a whole village or even a number of villages. The *a'imma* type of holdings belonged both to the *khāliṣa* and the *jāgīr* funds.

The land was granted to private persons for life or on hereditary basis and could be alienable too. Both groups of the *a'imma* type of holdings might include either the cultivated lands owned by the tax-paying villagers (including *zamīndārs*) or the virgin lands.

A somewhat special group of the *a'imma* type of holdings were the grants of virgin lands. Such lands were granted for a certain period of time after which the lands brought under cultivation were returned to the *khāliṣa* fund.

Common features of all land grants of the *a'imma* type were the following: firstly, they were not conditional on military or civil service and, secondly, they were fully excluded from the jurisdiction of the state revenue administration. The latter aspect fully testifies to the fact that the appropriation of the surplus product by the *a'imma* holder (including the revenue assessment and its exaction) was executed independently of the state administration. Therefore, the scholars would be fully justified judging the *a'imma* landholdings as private feudal property relations.

The second form of private property relations was represented by the ownership rights of those feudals who retained full autonomy in managing their lands (mainly as concerned feudal rent collection) as conditioned by payment of a certain tribute (*peshkash*) to the imperial treasury and, as a rule, military service. This group, first and foremost comprised a part of the upper layer of the Mughal *zamīndārs* (known as *peshkashī zamīndārī*). Certain theoretical and empirical difficulties crop up if we try to distinguish the private feudal landholdings of this type from the semi-autonomous principalities that acknowledged the Mughal suzerainty. In the latter case within a principality which was related to the Mughal empire as a "private feudal landholding" both the state feudal and private feudal land relations existing in the Mughal empire were as if reproduced.

The analysis of various land ownership rights as existed in the seventeenth-eighteenth century India allows us to arrive at the following conclusions:

Firstly, all forms of feudal landholding are classified by us as expressive of either state feudal or private feudal relations of land property. Concentration of the ownership rights of the above-mentioned two types in the hands of the same legal (and physical) persons, i.e. "primary *zamīndārs*" constituted a somewhat transitory form of the state-cum-private feudal land property relations

Secondly, the feudal class may be divided into two structural groups:

(1) Holders of ownership rights formally conditional on civil or military service to the emperor or a private feudal potentate, as distinct from the ownership rights that were not bound to such kind of service. The first category comprised all groups of *zamīndārs*, including *peshkashī zamīndārs*, *jāgīrdārs*, etc.; the second consisted mainly of the holders of the *a'imma* type of rights, in most cases not laymen, but people of religion.

(2) Feudals who directly participated in the process of rent extraction from peasants and were as a rule connected with communal land-owning, as distinct from those who realised their proprietary rights only during re-distribution of the agricultural surplus

extracted from the immediate producers. The first category included "primary *zamīndārs*" of the Mughal state and similar groups in other feudal states (including the vassal principalities of the empire) and huge feudal landholdings of *a'imma* type, the second one included the "feudal nobility" such as *jāgīrdārs*, *zamīndārān-i 'umda* and so on.

The division of the Indian feudal class into different structural groups does not mean that there was no overlapping and mutual penetration between them. On the contrary, one and the same person could enjoy ownership rights of various kinds.[41] This was facilitated both by the very essence of the feudal land ownership right, as realised by the appropriation of a fixed share of agricultural surplus extracted from the households of the immediate producers,[42] and by the fact that many ownership rights (like those of the *zamīndārs* or the *a'imma* holders) were of the *milkiyat* type and, what was more important, alienable ones. One may agree with Irfan Habib that "in the confusion which characterised the last phase of the empire, the tendency to convert claims to a share of produce into an absolute proprietary right over land appears to have been general".[43] But the final transformation of the state feudal relations into the private-feudal ones took place in British India only.

Between various groups of the feudal class a kind of interdependence existed as their proprietary rights in totality expressed the functioning of the general mechanism of exacting rent from the peasant households and further distributing it between the feudals. The very moment of distribution of this revenue rent determined the character of this interdependence: its essence was in each feudal's endless struggle for a bigger share in the agglomerated rent, and that in the form of widening his ownership rights. However the interlinks within feudal class were not at all limited by this struggle for distribution and re-distribution of agricultural surplus. They emerged in relation with the commonality of interests that were aimed against the peasantry, the feudal society's second major class which possessed the ownership rights on land as an object of economic activity.

Notes and References

1. S. Nurul Hasan, 'The Position of the Zamindars in Mughal Empire', *The Indian Economic and Social History Review*, Vol. I, No. 4 (1964); 'Three Studies of the Zamindari System', *Medieval India: A Miscellany*, Vol. I, Bombay, 1968; 'Zamindars Under the Mughals', *Land Control and Social Structure in Indian History*, Ed. by R.E. Frykenberg. Madison, 1969; 'Aspects of Zamindari System in Deccan (1695–1707)', *Indian History Congress, Proceedings of the 31st Session*, Varanasi,

1969, Patna, 1970; *Thoughts on Agrarian Relations in Mughal India,* New Delhi, 1973.

2. Irfan Habib, *Agrarian System of Mughal India,* Bombay, 1963; 'Evidence of 16th Century Agrarian Conditions in the Guru Granth Sahib', *The Indian Economic and Social History Review,* Vol. I, No. 3 (1964); 'The Agrarian System of Mughal India', *Enquiry,* New Series, Vol. II, No. 1 (1965) (ibidem in: Indian Society. Historical Probings. In Memory of D.D. Kosambi, New Delhi, 1974); 'The Mansab System, 1595–1637', *Indian History Congress. Proceedings of the 29th Session,* Patiala, 1967. Pt. I. Patna, 1968; 'Chapter VII (1), Chapter 8 (1), Chapter 9 (1)', *The Cambridge Economic History of India,* Ed. by Tapan Raychaudhuri and Irfan Habib, Vol. I. Cambridge, 1982; *Essays in Indian History: Towards a Marxist Perception,* Delhi, 1995. Unfortunately, the present author has got hold of a new edition of Irfan Habib's *Agrarian System of Mughal India* (Delhi, 2001) only after this article was sent to the publisher.
3. Satish Chandra, *Parties and Politics at the Mughal Court, 1707–1740,* New Delhi, 1959 (second ed. 1972); 'A Few Documents Pertaining to Zamindari From Thikana Records in the Former Jaipur State' *Indian History Congress, Proceedings of the 29th Session,* Patiala, 1967, Pt. I, Patna, 1968; 'Presidential Address', *Indian History Congress, 38th Session,* Bhubaneshwar, 1977 (off-print); 'Some Aspects of the Indian Village Society in Northern India during the 18th Century: the Position and Role of the Khud-kasht and Pahi-kasht', *The Indian Historical Review,* Vol. I, No. 2 (1974); *Medieval India: Society, the Jagirdari Crisis and the Village,* Delhi, 1982.
4. B.R. Grover, 'Nature of Land Grants in Mughal India', *The Indian Economic and Social History Review,* Vol. I, No. 1 (1963); 'Nature of *dehat-i taaluqa* (Zamindari Villages) and the Evolution of the *Taaluqdari* System During the Mughal Age', *The Indian Economic and Social History Review,* Vol. II, No. 2, 3 (1965); 'Elements of Continuity and Change in Land Ownership and Rights from the Mughal Age to the Early British Administration in India. Presidential Address. Medieval India Section', *Indian History Congress, 37th Session,* Calcutta, 1976 (off-print).
5. Shireen Moosvi, *The Economy of the Mughal Empire, A Statistical Study,* Delhi, 1987.
6. M. Athar Ali, *Bengal Under Akbar and Jehangir,* Calcutta, 1953 (2nd ed. Delhi, 1969); 'The Agrarian System of Mughal India', *Enquiry,* New Series, Vol. II, No.1 (1965); *The Mughal Nobility under Aurangzeb,* Delhi, 1966.
7. N.A. Siddiqi, *Land Revenue Administration under the Mughals,* Bombay, 1973.
8. I.H. Qureshi, *The Administration of the Mughal Empire,* Patna, 1969.
9. A.R. Khan, *Chieftains of the Mughal Empire during the Reign of Akbar,* Simla, s/a.
10. A.D. Khan, *Diplomatics of the Soyurghal Farman of the Great Moghuls (1556–1707)* Allahabad, 1994.
11. Muzaffar Alam, *The Crisis of Empire in Mughal North India: Awadh and the Punjab, 1707–1748,* Delhi, 1986.
12. Satish Chandra, 'Writings on Social History of Medieval India: Trends and Prospects', *Survey of Research in Economic and Social History of India,* Ed. by R. S. Sharma, Delhi, 1986; *Essays in Medieval Indian Economic History,* Ed. by Satish Chandra. Delhi, 1987.
13. I.M. Reisner, *Narodniye Dvizeniya v Indii v XVII–XVIII vv. (Popular Movements in India in the XVIIth-XVIIIth Century),* Moscow, 1961; 'Vosstaniye jatov oblasti Agra-Deli v kontse XVII-nachale XVIII v (The Jat Uprising in the Agra-Delhi

Region in the Late XVIIth-Early XVIIIth Century)', *Ucheniye zapiski Instituta vostokovedeniya (Proceedings of the Oriental Institute)*, Vol. XVIII (1957).

14. K.A. Antonova, *Ocherki Obshcestvennykh otnosheniy i politicheskogo stroya Mogolskoi Indii vremen Akbara (1556–1605)* (Essays on Social Relations and Political System of the Mughal India of Akbar's Epoch (1556–1605), Moscow, 1952; 'Obrazovaniye i rastsvet Mogolskoi imperii v XVI veke (Establishing and Flourishing of the Mughal Empire in the XVIth Century)', *Istoriya Indii v sredniye veka (Medieval History of India)*, Moscow, 1968.
15. C.Z. Ashrafyan, *Deliiski Sultanat (The Delhi Sultanate)*, Moscow, 1960; *Agrarni Stroi Severnoi Indii (XIII-seredina XVIII v.) (The Agrarian System of Northern India* (XIII-mid XVIIIth Century), Moscow, 1965; *Feodalism v Indii (Feudalism in India)*, Moscow, 1977.
16. Cf. *Land Control and Social Structure in Indian History*, Ed. by R. E. Frykenberg. Madison, 1969.
17. Similar processes took place in other feudal states of India, both in those which co-existed with the Mughal empire and those which succeeded it.
18. S. Nurul Hasan, *Zamindars Under the Mughals*, pp. 20–22. Following W.H. Moreland (*The Agrarian System of Moslem India*, Cambridge, 1929), who, as Satish Chandra has rightfully observed (Satish Chandra, *Writings in Social History of Medieval India*, p. 265), played an important role at the initial phase of the researches in economic history of medieval India, Irfan Habib suggests that collection of tribute (*peshkash*) from the vanquished feudals was the main form of land revenue (*kharāj*) in the Delhi sultanate upto the end of the XIIIth century (I. Habib, *The Social Distribution of Landed Property*, pp. 227–228).
19. The system of realisation of feudal rent in the XVIth-XVIIIth century India has been reconstructed on the basis of the above-mentioned works by Irfan Habib, B.R. Grover, M. Athar Ali and I.H. Qureshi.
20. This regulation had a meaning of rather a basis principle related to the assessment of revenue rates that varied depending upon the crops and other empirical factors; among the latter the villagers' ability to withstand the pressure from their superior feudals played a significant role.
21. S. Nurul Hasan, *Thoughts on Agrarian Relations*, p. 34.
22. K.A. Antonova, *Obrazovaniye i rastsvet Mogolskoi imperii v XVI veke*, pp. 398–400.
23. Irfan Habib, 'Chapter 9 (1)', *The Cambridge Economic History of India*, Vol. I, p. 235.
24. S. Nurul Hasan's classification of the *zamīndārs* is slightly different from ours. The first two groups he combined together as "chieftains"; however he demarcated "primary *zamīndārs*" who comprised only tax-paying villagers, from the lower rank of the feudals (S. Nurul Hasan, *Zamindars Under the Mughals*, pp. 18, 26, 27). Nevertheless in the earlier variant of this work he seemed to be more correct in including the lower rank of the feudals who dominated upon village community, into the "primary *zamīndārs*" group (S. Nurul Hasan, *Thoughts on Agrarian Relations*, pp. 30–33).
25. B.R. Grover, *Elements of Continuity and Change in Land Ownership and Rights*, p. 8.
26. A detailed study of the *manṣabdārī* system at the beginning and middle of the XVIIth century was made by Irfan Habib (Irfan Habib, *The Mansab System 1595–1637*).
27. M. Athar Ali, *The Mughal Nobility Under Aurangzeb*, p. 13.

28. Satish Chandra, *Presidential Address*, p. 12.
29. B.R. Grover, *Nature of dehat-i taaluqa*, p. 261.
30. Zahir ud-din Malik, 'Problems of Faujdari jurisdiction in Baiswara', *Indian History Congress. Proceedings of the 34th Session*, Chandigarh, 1973, Vol. I, Delhi, 1975, pp. 212–13.
31. Satish Chandra, *Presidential Address*, p. 11.
32. At the time of Akbar the number of *manṣabdārs* was 1671 persons out of total population circa one hundred million (Shireen Moosvi, *The Economy of the Mughal Empire*, p. 221).
33. S. Nurul Hasan, *Thoughts on Agrarian Relations*, p. 3.
34. Ibid., p. 30.
35. B.R. Grover, *Nature of dehat-i taaluqa*, p. 171.
36. Irfan Habib, *Agrarian System of Mughal India*, p. 141.
37. *Nankar* of the *zamīndārs* was equal to 10 per cent of the total *jama*' (Irfan Habib in *The Cambridge Economic History of India*, Vol. I, p. 240).
38. Shireen Moosvi, *The Economy of the Mughal Empire*, Chapter 7.
39. B.R. Grover, *Nature of dehat-i taaluqa*, p.171.
40. Ibid., pp. 171–72.
41. Interesting examples of the combination of the *jāgīr* holding and *zamīndārī* rights have been cited by S. Nurul Hasan (Aspects of *Zamindari System in the Deccan*) and Satish Chandra *(A Few Documents Pertaining to Zamindari)*.
42. This practically meant that the same land was an object of various ownership rights. The latter's transition from one hands to the other brought about a double result: on one hand, a feudal might concentrate in his hands different ownership rights pertaining to one and the same area and therefore claim a bigger part of surplus (for instance, if one person held the rights of *muqaddamī*, *caudhurāī* and *jāgīrdārī* on one village community; on another hand, one and the same feudal could possess various ownership rights relevant to various land areas.
43. Irfan Habib, 'Chapter VII (1)', *The Cambridge Economic History of India*, Vol. I, p. 177.

EIGHT

❖ Traditional Social Structure of Indian Village – The Case of Rural Bengal in the Late Eighteenth and Early Nineteenth Centuries

E. N. KOMAROV

THIS ARTICLE IS MAINLY to discuss the issue: Who was really the peasant and who was not in traditional Indian village. Consequently it will also deal with the differentiation of peasantry and respective differences in farming organisation. In conclusion it submits a hypothesis on the significance of traditional social structure in India for her history in modern times. The scope of the paper does not allow review of tenurial forms "above" the village, the place of artisans in its social structure, and village administration.

Some Historiographical Remarks

"The upper classes were not small limited groups but large in numbers and there was a diffusion of power, authority and influence", as Jawaharlal Nehru said regarding India's traditional social structure. He also pointed out that ultimately the "failing" of caste system and this structure "degraded a mass of human beings".[1]

Some quantitative substantiation of the caste composition of Indian population (naturally of the Hindus) is revealed by the National Sample Survey of 1952. The proportions of the upper, middle and low castes were 9.1 per cent, 25.1 per cent and 45.4 per cent respectively and scheduled castes and tribes comprised 20.3 per cent.[2] Arguably, despite some changes during the colonial period these proportions could hardly change very materially. In this case even 9.1 per cent made by high castes only look quite impressive, when compared, for example, with 1–1.5 per cent proportion of *dvoryanstvo* (the nobility) in the late nineteenth century Russia, notwithstanding the possible reservations about such a comparison. Meanwhile high and middle castes taken together as a certain traditionally (even if differently) privileged section, exceeded one third of the Hindu population.

Obviously, an exceptional numerical strength of the socially privileged groups had to be reflected in the social composition of the villagers. Early British administrators and subsequently researchers like W.W. Hunter, B.H. Baden-Powell as well as the Russian scholar M.M. Kovalevsky and German researcher Max Weber took notice of numerous socially privileged, land-holding but non-cultivating groups who were wholly or partly debarred by caste rules from performing agricultural operations. "Communal land ownership is often reconciled with the actual tillage of land not by owners but by non-free residents depending on them", as Kovalevsky wrote in 1879 quoting the example of the Rajput villages in Northern India.[3]

These observations were rather forgotten in the first half of the twentieth century, when traditional Indian village communities were idealistically viewed as egalitarian republics. Even Nehru called them "primitive republics" and "a kind of primitive communism".[4]

Marx pointed out in 1853 that "these little communities were contaminated by distinctions of caste and by slavery".[5] But he did not elaborate on that. In the description of the Indian village community which he quoted, only individual communal "officers and servants" were mentioned.

Taking cue from Marx's denial of egalitarian nature of Indian village community, I.M. Reisner in his studies on this subject in the late 1940s and early 1950s (first published in 1953), based primarily on the early nineteenth century Maharashtrian records, referred only to a few communal office bearers with the headman (*paṭil*) on top along with artisans as well as low caste or untouchable servants or bonded labourers under *baluta* system. But the latter were mentioned only briefly. Reisner noted that village administrative offices could be bought and sold and held by co-partners.

The principal position enjoyed by a few communal officers (especially the *paṭil*) but not a whole stratum was interpreted by Reisner as reflecting the process of "feudalisation" which meant the decline of primordial village community. He viewed the *paṭil* as "a kind of landlord" and stated that the village community "resembled an estate" while the *mīrāṣdār* was "a typical feudal peasant whose farming was based on his own labour".[6] In a sense Reisner's concept of "feudalisation" of communal officers was close to D.D. Kosambi's theory of Indian feudalism rising "from below" along with its emergence "from above" (1956).[7] However, since Reisner had in mind only communal administrative officers as such, and since the number of the latter was small, the number of his "feudals" rising from below was small, too. Meanwhile Reisner himself cited the case of a Maharashtrian village which had only 15 *mīrāṣdārs* as against 27 "bearers of hereditary village offices".[8] But he mentioned it only in a foot note and did not comment.

Nevertheless, it was Reisner who revived in the Soviet Union the studies on India of medieval and early modern times and that too in the years when it was rather risky to say on this subject something not exactly echoing what Marx had said on it.

Reisner's pupils in medieval India studies, particularly K.A. Antonova, C.Z. Ashrafyan as well as initially L.B. Alayev and myself took notice only of a few communal officers but not the whole privileged, mostly non-cultivating upper stratum within Indian village. In 1953 the present author went to the extent of saying that he was not interested in a category of villagers in Bengal who had "agriculture performed by their servants or by hired labourers" because they were "restrained by prejudice from personal labour" as Colebrooke put it relying upon his experience in Bengal in the 1790s. What I was interested in were two other categories one of which Colebrooke defined as "men of other tribes whose circumstances admit to their contending themselves with superintending the management of their land". And another one were "less opulent persons" who hired labourers for help "to their own labour".[9]* Quite a bit of evidence of the employment of hired labour (usually bonded to some or other extent) by the latter two categories inspired the present author to concentrate upon the differences among peasantry in farming and consequently on disintegration of the village community in Bengal.[10] All that was something familiar and distinct from the employment of "hired labour" by those who were debarred by caste rules from "performing agriculture" and whom Colebrooke nevertheless placed under the general caption of "peasants".

In the middle of the 1950s, A.M. Osipov[11] and myself in our studies on the then North Western Provinces of Bengal Presidency (later on United Provinces and now Uttar Pradesh) in connection with the 1857 Rebellion could not miss numerous privileged landholders, the village owners such as the *paṭṭīdārs* and "village *zamīndārs*" on the one hand and their subordinate *asāmīs* with certain traditional occupancy rights on the other hand. It was from among the former that the *sepoys* of the then Bengal Army were recruited and it were they who rebelled in 1857.

According to statistical accounts of the districts of Eta and Etawah

* Further references to his work (numbers of pages) are given in the text in brackets.

quoted by the present author but pertaining mostly to the 1870s, the owners of the *sīr* lands (i.e. *paṭṭīdārs* and "village *zamīndārs*") made about 10–12 per cent of all landholders while *sīr* lands comprised about 16–18 per cent of arable land. The average *sīr* plot was rather small – about 7–8 acres. It was bigger, but not so much, than the average *asāmī* holding (4–5 acres). The latter however exceeded the average holding of a still lower grade of tenants (3–4 acres). But the *sīrs* were either revenue-free or assessed at concession rates and the *paṭṭīdārs* and village *zamīndārs* were entitled to a share (usually about 5 per cent) of the revenue from the entire village.

Taking into account the modest average size of the *sīr* and the similarity of material conditions of its holders and of *asāmīs* as repeatedly referred to in contemporary accounts, the present author stated that "the majority of *paṭṭīdārs*, were peasants although they enjoyed a privileged position in the village community". Yet "a part" of the *paṭṭīdārs* was viewed as "petty feudal landholders" and so were village *zamīndārs*, especially when the number of partners was small.[12] However, both Osipov and this author did not elaborate upon what the "privileged position" meant and observing a certain discrepancy preferred to refer to the *paṭṭīdārs* as simply the *obshchinniki* (an old Russian word meaning "members of (village) community").

Meanwhile by the 1970s L.B. Alayev presented a different view and largely succeeded in substantiating it in his comprehensive studies on Indian village community based mostly on the nineteenth century statistical and other accounts relating also to the then North Western and later United Provinces.

Among his findings is the result of his calculations which demonstrated that in the district of Aligarh in the 1870s 2/3 of the *sīr* land were rented out in the case of small *sīrs* (average size 5.5 acres) and in the case of bigger *sīrs* this part varied from 4/5 to 9/10. It can be added that a holding of 5.5 acres was approximately what could be tilled with one plough. Alayev concluded that the poverty of small holders of *sīr* lands was prevalent notwithstanding the fact that "socially and politico-economically they formed a largely specific but undoubtedly feudal stratum".[13] When by the end of the 1960s Alayev shared his understanding with the colleagues it convinced me, more so because by that time I had read Sarat Chandra Chatterji's story *Pallī Samāj* (*The Village Commune*, 1916). Writing an introduction to the Russian edition of his works (1971) gave me an opportunity to correlate this concept with the brilliant narration of social relationships in rural Bengal by a classic of Bengali literature.[14]

The question may be asked whether these findings reflect also the conditions prevalent on the eve of British colonial conquest, i.e. some

70 years back in case of the then North-Western Provinces of Bengal Presidency. It can well be argued that basically they do as far as the proportions are concerned. For example if the number of *sīrs* increased and their average size decreased which was rather likely (but one cannot be sure), the same could be expected in the case of subordinate holdings too. Be what it may, the nineteenth century and even later source material gives an opportunity to study these problems as relevant also to pre-colonial times which otherwise cannot be studied in the same depth.

For the Soviet scholars the general Marxist notion of the peasant was a matter of course and they would not define it themselves. In India Irfan Habib ventured to present a definition which would be acceptable to Marxists and Chayanov, as he said. In his seminal essay on the history of Indian peasantry (1983) Irfan Habib defined the peasant as "a person who undertakes agriculture on his own, working with his own implements and using the labour of his family". He further pointed out that as soon as the use of hired labour and control of land are taken into consideration "the peasants seem to fall apart into different strata".[15]

However the case of Indian peasant appears to be even more or rather much more complicated.

According to common sense a person who is barred by the established social rules from performing agricultural operations cannot be regarded a peasant. It does not matter here whether a peasant actually performs them himself or supervises their performance by members of his family and/or by labourers in his farm. It is the absence of the ban that matters. The ban on performing agricultural operations could be fixed by caste rules as in India or by norms of conduct of the nobility and some other social groups as in medieval Europe. However in Europe in case of the nobility it was essentially a ban on manual labour in general. This ban appears essentially similar to the ban on performing agricultural operations in India. However in India some people were debarred from not all but certain operations or from ploughing only. Consequently in such cases the socio-historical identification cannot but depend on concrete social existence and occupation of the given group in the given locality.

Meanwhile the respective caste rules were not mentioned by Irfan Habib at all. Although he is cautious in his treatment of the "stratification" in medieval Indian village yet he views the latter's higher strata as "peasants" too but "upper peasants" in distinction from "ordinary peasants". He referred to caste only to argue that in multi-caste villages, caste would reinforce stratification", at least implicitly as that of the peasantry.[16]

N.A. Siddiqi, as early as in 1970 opposed the applicability of the term "peasant" insisting that that it obliterates the basic social and economic differences between the two major strata of the village community. Siddiqi not only regarded the village *zamīndār* primarily as a landowner entitled to a part of the produce, but also as a "peasant" in the sense that he "hired labourers" for ploughing his fields.[17] By itself the employment of "labourers", more so in medieval times, is hardly enough for such an identification. Feudal landholders in a very proper sense of the term ("above" the village) could do the same whether they were Russian *pomeshchiki* or Bengali *zamīndārs* and *ta'aluqdārs* (on their *nijjots*).

S. Nurul Hasan in the 1970s viewed landholding villagers as "peasant proprietors" or "free peasants" on the one hand and "tenant-cultivators" on the other. However he stated that "no substantial percentage of these peasant proprietors was engaged in the actual cultivation almost entirely with their own labour, though the available evidence on this point is totally inadequate".[18] It appears that later evidence shed some light on this point too. S. Nurul Hasan seemed to have modified his view as in a lecture delivered by him in 1985 in the Institute of Oriental Studies, Moscow. In any case he enumerated five "major" operations which the medieval "landholders" did not perform, namely ploughing, sowing, irrigating, weeding and harvesting. Yet it is also clear enough, especially from the later evidence, that not all the privileged land-holders abstained from performing all these operations.

Satish Chandra (1974) in his study comprehensive despite its article form, of the Indian village society in the eighteenth century made a point of major significance. It reads: "Absence of a rigid demarcation among different classes of peasants as among the zamindars imparted a great flexibility to the feudal system in India without, however, modifying it in essence".[19]

To sum up this very brief review of some of the studies which the Indian scholars have made on the subject one more is to be referred to. It is a very interesting and informative work by Arvind N. Das who traced the history of a Bihari village from its foundation in the beginning of the eighteenth century by an affluent *kāyastha.* In the 1770s there were 15 big *kāyastha* families, who were the *māliks* (owners) of the village and its *girhatta* (respectable men as *gṛhastha* in Bengal), the lands of the village were cultivated by husbandmen of *dhanuk* caste (traditional/professional cultivators) settled under *kāyastha māliks* and by local tribals as "labourers". Artisans were also "invited" who worked under *jajmānī* system. *Dhanuks* "developed feudal loyalties toward their respective householders and the relationship lasted in this fashion for nearly two hundred years".[20] The study shows in full light of history how a village community could be formed in late medieval India and what it actually was.

The Case of Bengal

The notion that the villagers enjoying upper tenurial status as the "petty" *zamīndārs* etc. were essentially "peasants" is present in the studies on rural Bengal as well. Sirajul Islam, in his otherwise highly informative work on Bengal land tenure in the nineteenth century (1985), stated that "a great majority" of 25000 petty *zamīndārs* who controlled 7327 villages in Sylhet in 1790 were mere "peasant proprietors".[21] However it is not difficult to calculate that there were only three such *zamīndārs* per village. In a village described by Sarat Chandra's story mentioned above there were some 20 *brāhmaṇ* and *kāyastha* families who would call themselves *zamīndārs* although only two of them could claim that status. They were not peasants like some 15 *kāyastha* families who by 1770 had owned a village in Bihar the history of which was traced by Arvind Das.

Sirajul Islam analysed the data of household census of a *mauẓa* (village) in the district of Bakarganj in 1859. Out of a total of 150 households only 30 were recorded as agriculturists (*kṛṣikārak*) and the rest as non-agriculturists (*akṛṣikārak*). To my humble knowledge of Bengali these terms appear artificial. Meanwhile, out of 120 "non-agriculturists" only 16 households were recorded as maliks, i.e. proprietary households whom or most of whom the author appears to take for real land-owning non-cultivators, whereas a majority of the apparent non-agriculturists actually were cultivators, as he says, "in the proper sense of the term". According to him they acquired some tenurial rights (*haqiyat*) and reported themselves as non-agriculturists for the sake of distinction from "ordinary cultivators" (*karṣas*), who "had no social status".[22] In any case one cannot but note the prevailing mentality obviously connected with the actual social structure in this case when those who, according to the author, were in fact cultivators would not call themselves *kṛṣikāraks*, i.e. literally, makers of agriculture (*kṛsi*).

The word *kṛṣak* was and still is a simpler and more general term meaning "peasant". It was used in the nineteenth century Bengali literature particularly by its great writer Bankim Chandra Chatterji one of whose essays was entitled *Bangādeśer Kṛṣak* (*The Peasant of Bengal*, 1873). Again with my poor knowledge of Bengali I wonder if there was ony difference in the meaning of the words *kṛṣak* and *kṛṣikāraks*, the latter perhaps implied more action and actor and hence possibly actual performance of agricultural operations.

Anyway, there are Bengali terms that clearly define distinct social and socio-professional affiliations in the village. They are different from names of castes as well as from numerous terms for tenure holders, which may not have similarly clear social connotations.

The most general social division appears as that between *bhadralok* (respectable person, gentleman) and *abhadra* (opposite attribute). The juxtaposition of *bhadra-abhadra* prevails throughout Sarat Chandra's *Pallī Samāj,* despite the fact that some *bhadraloks* lived in abject poverty ("Brahmin children are starving"). It is noteworthy that in the 1870s W.W. Hunter styled the *khūdkāsht* rayats ("resident cultivators" in his words) as "*bhadralok,* or respectable class", who formed "the governing body of the village commune".[23] How far they or many of them were actual cultivators is a different matter.

There was another pair of opposite social or socio-professional terms. One of them, *gṛhastha* implied a respectable (usually high caste) householder. The other, *cāśī* (*cāśā*), derived from the word *cāś* (ploughing, tillage; husbandry; cultivation) meant exactly a ploughman as a person performing ploughing in general but not necessarily as the agricultural labourer defined by another term which will be referred to elsewhere below. The word *cāśā* also meant precisely a husbandman as such. Colloquially *cāṣā* (not *cāṣi*) also implies "rustic", "uncultured".

We have a well-formulated description of both the *gṛhasthas* and the *cāśīs* presented by Rajendra Mitra, a prominent figure of the nineteenth century Bengal. In 1846 he wrote:

> "There are two classes of people who compose the agricultural community, viz. Grihasthas and Chasis. Grihasthas let their lands to husbandmen, receive a certain rent or portion of the produce, or hire labour to cultivate them, *confining themselves to mere direction and supervision.* This class consists of Brahmans, Baiddas, Kayasthas, Kaziz, Maulevis, Khankars etc., who *however humble in circumstances, consider it derogatory to their honour to handle agricultural implements.*
>
> Chasis are *real agriculturists.* They *either cultivate for themselves, or for others, or superintend their own cultivation.* Men of low castes such as Pods, Tiaris, Sadgops, Kaibarats, Goahlas, Jolahs etc. constitute the chasi class. And their proportion is generally greater and varies in different districts".[24]

Incidentally, in this description a purely Hindu term *gṛhastha* covers Muslim gentry too. As for *cāṣīs,* perceptive witneses pointed out the divergent roles in farming played by peasants proper under the process of differentiation.

In a short story by Rabindranath Tagore, *Śubhadṛṣṭi* ("Auspicious Look", 1894) one finds a description of a "prosperous *gṛhastha* household" (*satchal gṛhastha ghar*) with "rows of granaries and a big clean cattle-shed". The *gṛhastha* was a Brahman and his household was obviously not a peasant farm but a kind of a small manor. Incidentally, a young rich *zamīndār* having caught sight of a girl therein whom he mistook for the *gṛhastha*'s daughter decided there and then to marry her. No idea of any misalliance whatsoever would occur to him.[25]

It is also known that there were high ranking landholders who did "every kind of work with their own hands except holding the plough", as Francis Buchanan wrote about the *ashrāfs* ("Muslim high ranks") in his description of Patna district (about 1807). In the same description he mentioned *bepāris* (traders) who were considered as "ploughmen and had large farms". Incidentally, he included *gṛhastha Bepāris* into "chasas" as a class.[26]* Another contemporary author (1858) described the *cāsī* of *sadgop* caste as a husbandmen only who would not take any other trade and would do nothing else but look after their mango trees, weed their rice fields or grow indigo.[27] Notably ploughing is conspicuous by its absence in this list of operations.

The above evidence shows the existence of two major groups of villagers engaged in farming as well as the absence of a rigid demarcation between them. Each major group had its marginal subgroups, the margins varying regionally. Obviously the growth of commodity production as observed from the sixteenth century played its role.

The socio-economic organisation of farming in India in the very beginning of the nineteenth century is known in its major features mainly thanks to enquiries, surveys and studies by Francis Buchanan. Colebrooke's study of husbandry of Bengal was also a major contribution.

Buchanan's classification of farmers by the size of average holding in a class (group) and the respective distribution of land in the district of Dinajpur in 1807 (Vol II, p.906) are presented with some added calculations in the table.

Most probably these statistical data are in the nature of an estimate. Besides, neither tenurial status nor caste composition of Buchanan's "farmers" are referred to. Hence it fails to tell us what the minimal tenurial status of the accounted holdings was.

The major emphasis in Buchanan's account is on a rather detailed description of conditions and activities of main groups of farmers. For example, Buchanan provides information as to who were the *halmīrs* (owners of many ploughs) mentioned in pre-colonial sources and how they operated.

Along with distribution of farmers by size of holding he roughly estimated their distribution by number of ploughs (vol. II, p. 904):

above 5 ploughs – "one farmer in 16" (about 6–7%).
3–5 ploughs – "perhaps 7/16" (about 40–50%)
1–2 ploughs – obviously about a half

---

* Further references to his work (numbers of pages) are given in the text in brackets.

TABLE: CATEGORIES OF FARMERS AND DISTRIBUTION OF LAND IN THE DISTRICT OF DINAJPUR (1807)

Category of farmers as defined by Buchanan	Average size of holding		Number	%	Area† (%)
	Bīghās	Acres‡ (approx.)			
1. Principal	165	85–100	6600	1,7	7,4
2. Great	75	40–45	8800	2,3	4,5
3. Comfortable	60	30–35	11000	2,8	4,5
1–3. (Upper group)			26400	6,8	16,4
4. Easy (middle group)	45	23–28	198000	50,9	60,9
5. Poor	30	15–18	55000	14,1	11,3
6. Needy	15	7–9	110000	28,3	11,3
5–6. (Low group)			165000	42,3	22,6

† Buchanan gives the size in *bīghās*. Conversion into acres is at 0.5–0.6 *bīghā* per acre as reported by him (about 0.5) in Dinajpur and by Colebrooke (0.6) in Calcutta.

‡ Total area — 14619000 *bīghās* calculated on the average sizes of holding and numbers of frarmers in of the respective categories. But this figure does not correspond to the total of 14619000 *bīghās* of arable land referred to by Buchanan elsewhere.

Since according to Buchanan one plough was "usually" required to cultivate "10 large *bīghās*" the owners of more than 5 ploughs belonged to two upper groups of farmers and perhaps partly to the 3rd group classified by Buchanan by average size of their holdings. This is clearly the upper crust. Owners of 3–5 ploughs can be viewed as "upper-middle" group by the size of holding. The rest are "lower-middle" and low groups.

Farms which had 5 or more ploughs can well be regarded as "large establishments" in the then Bengal under its agricultural conditions. Since 2–3 pairs of bullocks were required for one plough such farms held at least 10 to 15 bullocks beside cows and calves. According to Colebrooke, big farmers "entertained" a herdsman who tended up to "50 oxen and cows" (p. 98). "Rich" farmers had "higher priced cattle" (Buchanan, vol. II, p. 906). Leading farmers known as *maṇḍals* (and by other terms), probably those whom Buchanan called "principal" and "great", employed a markedly better agricultural know-how as compared with the ordinary ones.[28] Thus richer farms had a certain superiority in terms of equipment and technique.

Although Buchanan does not give any information on caste composition of "farmers" it can be presumed from his account that a majority of those who had up to 5 ploughs were socially (and also "operationally") peasants, albeit some could be small feudal landholders like a *gṛhastha* in Tagore's short story. About farmers with 3–5 ploughs Buchanan states: "These are not exempt from holding the plough, but hire in servants to make up the deficiencies on the number of labourers that may be in their families". It was also noted that rich farmers "seldom labour with their own hands, but keep as many ploughs as they have dependent relations (elsewhere: "sons and brothers") or hire 2 or 3 additional men" (vol. II, p. 905).

The differences in size of holding and number of ploughs were clearly interconnected with differences within the peasantry in terms of employment (occupation). The farmers having at least 3 ploughs "never hired themselves as labourers". In slack season (on clay lands) they "purchase rice and carry it to the markets by which they have considerable profit", whereas poor farmers (1–2 ploughs) "hire themselves as day labourers to those who cultivate free soils, or as porters to merchants and manufacturers of sugar and indigo" (vol. II, p. 904).

A tenant holding 15 *bīghās* on share (half of grain produce) worked four months a year as a labourer. His wife also worked for others. The wages of both of them together (about Rs 14) made 2/5 of the family income (about Rs 37) of which 1/15 was from spinning. "Probably" more than 150 thousand families were employed "entirely in this manner". The number is close to the number of "farmers" whom Buchanan classified as "poor" and "needy" (taken together). It means that the majority of small peasants doing their own farming but mostly as sharecroppers could not exist without employment as hired labourers, actually medieval kinds. It is also obvious that bigger farmers and even middle ones who or whose relations tilled the land but never hired themselves as labourers could not dispense with employing permanent farm hands let alone day labourers. Even if there was some sort of mutual exchange of labour by ordinary farmers, Buchanan's detailed descriptions show that typical employers were better-off as well as high caste. In Bihar "no man in tolerably easy circumstances performs any part of this labour (reaping and threshing) further than to watch" (vol. III, p. 225). People of high caste would not work as day labourers (vol. III, p. 309).

Thus it appears that the employment of "hired labour", widespread as it was despite its medieval character, reflected both a certain economic differentiation of the peasantry and the age-long social stratification fixed by caste system.

Bonded Labourers

The traditional stratification was first and foremost reflected in the case of permanent labourers, mostly ploughmen but was less pronounced in the case of day labourers. The former were clearly distinguished from the latter by the term *kṛṣan* dating from pre-colonial times. The latter were called *majūr.* This term is used up to now also for factory workers, which is noteworthy. Early British observers in Bengal called permanent labourers "farm servants" and others just "labourers".

Kṛṣans were doubtlessly of very low castes. However no separate caste of *kṛṣans* is known in Bengal. This may be an indication along with some other ones that *kṛṣans* as such might appear or at least blow up in number in later pre-colonial times. In the enumeration of various social groups and occupations in Mukundoram's *Caṇḍīmaṅgala* (the late fifteenth or early sixteenth century) as quoted by Tapan Raychaudhury, *kṛṣans* were not mentioned.[29] It is different in Rameshvara's *Śivāyaṇa* (the middle of the eighteenth century). The poet tells how *īśān* (master) siting in a field sets task to *kṛṣan.* It appears that *īśān* did some operations himself but mainly watched the work "like a tiger" and would not permit a respite.[30] Another indication of the growth of medieval-type wage employment is presented in a study by Benedicte Hjejie, one of the first studies in the history of agricultural bonded labour in early colonial India. The author quoted a Tamil document (written not later than 1815–1819) where it was stated that the *pallans* were an original caste of agricultural labourers, whereas the *pariyans* had only been employed in the same task from much later day, and that this accounted for the sharp rivalry between the two.[31]

In Bengal of the early nineteenth century *kṛṣans*, at least many of them, were undoubtedly bonded labourers. But certainly they were not slaves. Their state looked better in terms of lesser bondage and depression than that of their counterparts in adjacent Bihar or in certain areas of South India, where the relics of ancient slavery were preserved. As Buchanan and Colebrooke reported, *kṛṣans* were hired, at least formally, for a definite period of 6 months or a year. They were usually paid in cash, and were also given food and clothing. However, there was a practice of *kṛṣans* mortgaging their labour without a real hope of redemption. Plots of 2–3 *bīghās* were customarily allotted to *kṛṣans* but often on a share of produce.

There was a certain element of agricultural corvee in the exploitation of *kṛṣans* as well as some sharecroppers by their masters in some areas or cases. In my 1957 article[32] I quoted the narrations by Colebrooke and Buchanan which can be construed as presenting a kind of corvee with an exceptionally high rate of exploitation. Studies on other regions revealed similar facts. For example, there were "labourers" in Bihar called *jirātiyās* who in many cases received land "rent-free and worked for the landowner without remuneration in agricultural season",[33] as Arvind Das put it. I allude to these facts without details, for which there is no place here, to draw attention to the existence of a sort of corvee for agricultural operations in India because of a widespread notion that nothing of the kind was there in the East.

There was no rigid demarcation between *adhiyārs* and *kṛṣans* at least in their material conditions. Yet according to Buchanan the conditions of former were somewhat better than of the latter. The comparison of two sample budgets quoted by him showed that the annual income of a sharecropper's household with 7 *bīghās* (Rs 36–14–0) could exceed that of a *kṛṣan* family by some 4 rupees (1/8). But the gap was probably greater because I doubt the income calculated by Buchanan for a *kṛṣan* hired for 6 months (Vol. II, pp. 912, 913).

On the contrary, according to a calculation by Colebrooke "a hired labourer" earned more than "a peasant cultivating for a half of produce" (p. 102). Obviously the difference between the two was precarious.

The estimated number of *kṛṣans* in Dinajpur was 80,000 families (Vol. II, p. 912) against an estimated 3,89,000 of "farmers". Thus the proportion of *kṛṣans* could be about 17 per cent of agricultural population. It may coincide with the proportion of landless agricultural labour in Madras Presidency in the early nineteenth century estimated by Dharma Kumar as 17–25 per cent.[34]

The presence of "a class" of landless labourers in traditional Indian village is some times viewed as a specific feature of the latter.[35] Meanwhile hired labourers existed in the medieval European villages too. In his reference to rural population in England of the fifteenth and early sixteenth centuries Marx took note of the peasants who in their spare time worked for big landowners as well as "a separate class of labourers in proper sense of the word, although small in number, both absolute and relative". Along with their wages they were granted a cottage and four or more acres of land. Elsewhere, Marx also pointed out that in medieval Europe more substantial dependent peasants had in their turn their own serfs.[36]

Incidentally in the climatic conditions of England 4 acres meant at that time hardly more than 2–3 *bīghās* customarily allotted to *kṛṣans* in Bengal. But a *kṛṣan* was also customarily charged half of produce from these *bīghās*. Hence the difference was not so much in the supposed greater number of such agricultural labourers in India (actual comparison is yet to be made) but first and foremost in that they were much more depressed under caste system and obviously most brutally exploited. In this respect they really were a specific feature of the Indian social order.

The "peasant sorely exploited himself, joined in practising the severest repression of the menial labourer. This has surely been one of the fatal tragedies in Indian social history",[37] as Irfan Habib put it.

Share-crop System

Under the then conditions including traditional agricultural technology (according to the nineteenth century European experts it was of a high level in terms of know-how but not of implements) the expansion of operational holding of a rich farmer appears to have reached its limits. In Buchanan's account, farmers holding from 30 to 100 acres hired only 2–3 ploughmen in addition to their dependent relations, and the remainder of their land was given to "people who cultivated it on share" (Vol. II, p. 905). There are enough indications that poor peasants who had about 1/4 of land in Dinajpur cultivated it wholly or partly on share. According to various contemporary sources share-cropping did not prevail in Bengal while it was prevalent in Bihar.

One can see a certain historically conditioned duality in share-cropping system in India. In a number of cases it was a form of primitive rent in kind and reflected a relatively primitive farming which produced simply cultivable crops (coarse cereals etc.) mostly for immediate consumption of both a small owner (obviously a poor *gṛhastha* and the like) and his tenant. However, coarse grain was a commodity too and in many, perhaps even in most cases share-cropping system was a certain form of commodity production. In the conditions limiting the employment of hired labour, irrespective of how much it was bonded, the share-cropping system was a substitute to it while providing for dependence and enhanced exploitation of the peasant something like that of the bonded labourer. British administrators and observers in Bengal repeatedly claimed from the second half of the eighteenth century onwards that it were various landowning "monied men" who lent to the cultivators the cattle and implements and charged usually up to a half of produce as well as the interest. As Colebrooke put it "whatever be proportion (of division), it is mostly nominal" (p. 53), i.e. the landowner charged as much as he could.

The production of more valuable commercial crops including fine rice required a more sophisticated agriculture and hence a relatively more independent farmer paying money rent which at least customarily was equal to about one quarter of produce as against up to a half of it in cases when a peasant held one part of land on money rent and another one on share. It was the former where he cultivated more valuable crops and it was this part to which he paid "all his attention", used fertilisers, did multiple ploughing and weeding (Vol. II, p. 908).

In this connection it is noteworthy that the level of agriculture on *sir* lands of numerous small *paṭṭīdārs* and village *zamīndārs* in the North-Western Provinces who did not cultivate themselves but employed "servants" or share-croppers was often lower than its level on the lands held by *asāmī* peasants. This can be regarded as an evidence of depressive impact of the multiplicity of traditionally non-cultivating upper stratum of the village in agriculture.

The situation in Bengal appears to be somewhat different. It were often rich peasants of medieval type who dominated within the village, primarily not as big producers (although they had larger operational holdings too) but rather as "monied men" – peasants turned traders-cum-money lenders.

The stock of "principal" and "great" farmers varied from Rs 1000 to Rs 5000 and sometimes reached Rs 20000 (Vol. II, p. 907). It can be calculated that Rs 5000 were equal to the price to some 250–300 ploughs with three pairs of bullocks for a plough or to the costs of annual maintenance of at least 300 permanent labourers (prices quoted by Colebrooke, p. 36). Buchanan reported:

> "It may indeed be said that their stock carries on at least one half of the cultivation of the country. Most of the adhiyars and small peasants are more indebted to them than the whole value of their stock, and for six months in the year would starve, did not the wealthy farmers advance them grain to eat". The zamindars (landholders usually "above" the village in Bengal) had but to reckon with the principal farmers (Vol. II, p. 905).

The strikingly wide and massive spread of usury exploitation in traditional Indian village is yet to be explained. Perhaps it was somehow connected with the combination of the impressive scope of simple commodity production (Bengal was called by Colebrooke "a commercial country") on the one hand and severe traditional depression of a large mass of population under caste-system on the other.

Thus the upper section of the villagers consisted of two major socially different groups.

One of them comprised traditionally privileged (high caste) landholders who were in fact small feudals or at least more feudals than peasants, their farms (if not too small) being of manorial nature. It is also known that at least some of them were not strangers to commerce and usury. This group appears to have largely provided for the multitude of upper classes in general and for intellectual section of the latter in particular, a section which was in pre-colonial India markedly developed but within the scope of traditional society.

Another group was formed by substantial farmers who were actual peasants or men of peasant origin turned traders operating also as money lenders. Probably they formed a big chunk of Indian traditional mercantile capital, hardly limited to "professional" (by caste) merchants who caught the eye more often than others.

The upper and middle strata of medieval India gave rise to intellectual and commercial groups that were able to modernise by nineteenth century. A majority, however, remained essentially medieval folks till the 1920s and a significant proportion, even until Independence. The traditional social structure of Indian village appears to have played its role in what I have called "elitist modernisation"[38] in India under colonial rule and consequently in her socio-political development before and to decreasing extent also after Independence.

Notes and References

1. Jawaharlal Nehru, *The Discovery of India*, Bombay, Reprint; 1969, p. 257.
2. National Sample Survey, No. 14. Report on Some Characteristics of the Economically Active Population. Government of India: Dehli, 1959.
3. M.M. Kovalevsky, *Obshchinnoye zemlevladeniye, prichiny, khod i posledstviyya yego razlozheniya.* (Communal Landholding. The Causes, Process and Consequences of its Disintegration.) Moscow, 1879, Vol. 1, p. 47.
4. Jawaharlal Nehru, op. cit., p. 248.
5. K. Marx, 'The British Rule in India', Karl Marx and Frederick Engels. *Articles on Britain*, Moscow, 1971, p. 172.
6. I. M. Reisner, 'Nekotoriye danniiye o razilozhenii derevenskoy obshchiny u marrathov v XVII – nachale XIX v. (Data on Disintegration of Village Community of the Marathas in the 17th through the Early XIXth Centuries)', *Ucheniye zapiski Instituta vostokovedeniya* (Memoirs of the Institute of Oriental Studies), Vol. V, Moscow, 1953.
7. D. D. Kosambi, *An Introduction to the Study of Indian History*, Bombay, 1956.
8. I. M. Reisner, *Narodniye dvizheniye v Indii. XVI–XVIII vv.* (Popular Movements in India in the XVIIth and XVIIIth Centuries), Moscow, 1961, pp. 73–74.
9. H. T. Colebrooke, *Remarks on the Husbandry and Internal Commerce of Bengal*, London, 1806, pp. 96–97, (Colebrooke's Original Thesis, 1794).
10. E. N. Komarov, *Agrarniye otnosheniya i zemelno-nalogovaya politika angliyskikh kolonizatorov v Bengalii v seredine – vtoroj polovine XVIII veka. Kandidatskaya dissertatsiya. Institut vostokovedeniya AN SSSR.* (Agrarian Relations and Land Revenue Policy of British Colonial Rulers in the Second Half of the XVIIIth Century. Candidate (Ph.D) Thesis Presented to Institute of Oriental Studies, USSR Academy of Sciences.), Moscow, 1953. Also: 'Bengalskaya derevnya i krestyanskoe khozyaistvo vo vtoroi polovine XVIII veka. (The Village and Peasant Farming in Bengal in the Late XVIIIth and Early XIXth Centuries)', *Ucheniye zapiski Instituta vostokovedeniya* (Memoirs of the Institute of Oriental Studies), Vol. XVIII, Moscow, 1957, pp. 33–96.
11. A. M. Osipov, 'Krestyanstvo Severo-zapadnykh provintsiy nakanune vosstaniya v Indii 1857–1859 gg. (The Peasantry of the North-Western Provinces on the Eve

of the 1857–1859 Rebellion)', *Narodnoe vosstaniye v Indii 1857–1859 gg* (The People's Rebellion in India in 1857–1859), Moscow, 1957.

12. E. N. Komarov, 'Zemelno-nalogovaya politika kolonialnykh vlasteji i razvitiye agrarnykh otnosheniy v Severo-zapadnykh provintsiyakh Indii v pervoi polovine XIX v. (Land Revenue Policy of Colonial Administration in the North Western Provinces of India in the First Half at the XIXth Century)' *Indiya. Statyi po istorii* (India: Essays in History), Moscow, 1959, pp. 56, 58.
13. L. V. Alayev, *Sotsialnaya struktura indiyskoy derevni (Territoriya Uttar Pradesha XIX veka)* (The Social structure of Indian Village. The XIXth Century Territory of Uttar Pradesh), Moscow, 1976, p. 223; Also by the same author: *Selskaya obsjchina v Severnoy Indii'. Osnovniye etapy evolutsii.* (Village Community in Northern India. The Main Stages of Evolution), Moscow, 1981.
14. E. N. Komarov, 'Predisloviye (Preface)', Shorotchondro Chottopaddhay. *Sozhzhennyi dom. Povesti i romany.* (Home Burnt Down. Stories and Novels.), Moscow, 1971.
15. I. Habib, 'The Peasant in Indian History', *Social Scientist.* Marx Centenary Nomber, 1983, N. 3, pp. 56, 57.
16. Ibid., p. 57.
17. N. A. Siddiqi, *Land Revenue Administration under the Mughals (1700–1750)*, New York, 1970, p. 11, 21.
18. S. N. Hasan, *Thoughts on Agrarian Relations in Mughal India*, New Delhi, 1973, pp. 18, 22, 23.
19. Satish Chandra, 'Some Aspects of Indian Village Society in Northern India during the XVIIIth Century. The Position and Role of the *khud—kasht* and *pahi—kasht*', *The Indian Historial Review.* 1974, N 1, p. 61.
20. A. N. Das, *The "Long Duree". Continuity and Change in Changel.* CASP 14. Rotterdam: Erasmus University. 1986, p. 13.
21. S. Islam, Bengal Land Tenure. The Origin and Growth of Intermediate interests in the XIXth Century. *CASP 13.* Erasmus University: Rotterdam, 1985, p. 4.
22. Ibid., pp. 98–101.
23. W. W. Hunter, *The Annals of Rural Bengal*, Vol. II, London, 1972, p. 52.
24. Rajendralal Mitra, 'The Zamindar and the Ryot', *The Calcutta Review*, Vol. VI, 1846, p. 325.
25. Rabindranath Thakur, *Galpaguccha*, Kalikatta, 1363 (Bengali era), p. 438.
26. R. Montgomery Martin, *The History, Antiquities, Topography and Statistics of Eastern India*, London, 1838, Vol. I, pp. 299, 300.
27. 'Bengal Village Biographies', *The Calcutta Review*, 1858, No. 51, p. 209.
28. *Report from the Bengal Government on the Bengal Tenancy Bill*, Calcutta, 1883, Vol. II, p. 467.
29. T. Raychaudhury, *Bengal under Akbar and Jahangir*, Calcutta, 1953, p. 173.
30. D. Sen, *Banga Shahitya Parichaya*, Kalikata, 1914, pr. 563.
31. B. Hjejle, *Slavery and Agricultural Bondage in South India in the Nineteenth Century*, The Scandinavian Institute of Asian Studies Joint Reprint Series No. 1. Copenhagen 1967, p. 82.
32. See note 10.
33. A. N. Das, op. cit., pp. 13, 85.
34. D. Kumar, *Land and Caste in South India: Agricultural Labour in Madras Presidency during the Nineteenth Century*, Cambridge,1965, p. 181.

35. U. Patnaik, 'On Evolution of the Class of Agricultural Labourers in India', *Social Scientist,* No. 7, July, 1983, p. 4.
36. Karl Marx. *Das Kapital.* Vol. I, Chapter 24; Vol. III, Part II, Chapter 47. Russian edition. The imperfect English rendering has been done by me.
37. I. Habib, op. cit., pp. 32, 38.
38. E. Komarov. 'Elitist Modernization in Colonial India: Some Specificities of Generation and Concentration of Power Resources', Democracy in the Modern World. Essays for Tatu Vanhanen, University of Tampere. Tampere, 1989.

PART III

Texts and Ideas

NINE ❖

The Ancient Map of South Asia

A. A. VIGASIN

THE INDIAN CHAPTER (VI.56–106) OF *Natural History* by Pliny the Elder[1] is not so popular in Indological studies as Arrian's *Indica* or Strabo's *Geography*. It does not contain any picturesque scenes, any vivid descriptions of exotic animals or peculiar customs of the Indians. The Roman geographer gives mainly the dry lists of countries and peoples (*locorum nuda nomina* – III.1). It is not easy to find any system in these endless enumerations – and modern scholars even think that there is no such system at all. Pliny's geography is regarded as a chaotic and uncritical compilation from various sources. According to the late Prof. P.H.L. Eggermont[2], it is possible to speak only about "pseudo-geography". We shall try here to disprove this statement and to show that *Natural History* is a valuable source to reconstruct the map of ancient India.

It is important to take two points into consideration: (1) Pliny used the works of Hellenistic authors (*auctoribus Graecis* – VI. 58); (2) the Greeks had at their disposal some Indian oral sources of information. So it is necessary to reconstruct the Greek original of the Latin toponymic or ethnic names. And the latter is to be compared with the forms met in vernacular languages of ancient India, i.e. in local (Prakrit) dialects.

The composition of the chapter is not a bit chaotic one: the first part (VI. 61–63) contains itinerary from the Punjab to the mouth of the Ganges, the second one (VI. 64–78) – the above mentioned lists of the Indian peoples, the third one (VI. 80–106) is devoted to the description of Taprobana (Lanka) and navigation in Indian Ocean between South India and the Mediterranean area. The sources of information used for every part were different ones. Up to the river Sutlej the way was measured by the companions of Alexander the Great (*Alexandri Magni comites, itinerum eius mensores* – VI. 59, 61). The measurements from that point and up to the mouth of the Ganges were made for his successor Seleucus Nicator by the ambassadors (e.g. the famous Megasthenes) sent to the city of Pataliputra (*reliqua inde Seleuco Nicatori peragrata sunt* – VI.63). The maritime trade with South Indian rulers Keralaputra and Pandya (Pliny's *Caelobothras, Pandion* – VI.105) flourished from the Augustan times – Pliny used here quite recent information, acquired through some merchants and navigators. The central part of the chapter is especially interesting for Indological studies. Its sources are not clear, but A. Dihle[3] was sure that they belonged to the early Hellenistic period.

The starting point for Pliny's enumeration of the Indian peoples is again the North-West frontiers of the country, the mountains of Hindukush (Hemodus), inhabited by the tribes of Isari, Cosiri and Izi (VI.64). Cosiri (Casiri) were mentioned earlier (VI.55) as the people of Central Asia, neighbouring to Phocari (Tokharians, *Τόχαροι*, Sanskrit – *Tukhara*) and Thuni (Chinese, *Θῖναι*, Sanskrit – Cīna). Casiri were regarded as "Indians" (*iam Indorum*), but not civilised ones, because they practised cannibalism (*humanis corporibus vescuntur*). This tribe occupied the central part of Hindukush, near the pass between India and "Scythia" – the nomads went regularly through this pass (*nomades quoque Indiae vagantur huc* – VI.55). Identification of Casiri/Cosiri is uncertain, but they are to be compared with Prakrit *Kasīra* (Sanskrit – *Khaśīra* – Mahabharata[4], VI.10.66: *khaśīrāśca tukharāśca*; *Mārkandeya-purāna*[5] 57.34: *cīnāścaiva tuṣarāśca bahulā bāhyato narāḥ*). The tribe is to be located near the modern Nuristan (Kafiristan), where even today the nomads cross Hindukush on their way to India.

The next name Izi may be compared with Yidga-speaking population of Chitral. So the tribes are enumerated in the direction of Himalayas (Imaus) – i.e. to the North-East. We can only guess that the unidentified tribe of Isari occupied the Southern part of Hindukush.

To the tribes of Himalayas Pliny gives the name Chiratosagi. Without any doubt *Chirato* here corresponds to the Indian name Kirāta, denoting Himalayan mountaineers. In the eastern part of Himalayas, where the Blessed One Śakyamuni was born, lived the famous clan of the Śākyas (Pali – *Sakya*, Prakrit – *Sakkia*), corresponding to Latin – *sagi*.

Then follows the region bordered by the Eastern Himalayas, the Bay of Bengal and the Gangetic delta. According to Pliny, it was inhabited by Maccocalingae, "nearest to the Ocean" (*mari proximi*). To the North from them the tribe of Malli was situated – close to the "mountain Mallus". This tribe (Malla) and the mountain of that name (Mallagiri) are frequently met in the legends about the life and *nirvāṇa* of the Lord Buddha Sakyamuni (*Jataka* IV.438, 439[6]). In any case, the territory of Maccocalingae is identical with modern Bangladesh (ancient Baṅgo or Vaṅga). But the interpretation of the name is uncertain. In the MSS of

Natural History "C" is often confused with "G" (e.g. *Calinga/Galinga, bragmanae/bracmanae* etc). Perhaps in this case too we may assume Maggo (Greek *Μάγγο*). But double γ in Greek is pronounced as "ng". In the ancient dialects of Eastern India the sounds "b" and "v" were confused with "m" and we'll see further on that an anonymous Indian informant pronounced Pulinda as Molinda. If this reasoning is acceptable, Pliny's *Maccocalingae* represents Sanskrit *Vaṅgakaliṅga* which occurs several times in *Mahābhārata* (e.g. VII.10.15; VI.10.46, cf. VIII. 12.59; 49.79). The Roman geographer gives precise description of this locality: "the river Ganges is the boundary of this region" (VI.64: *finisque tractus eius Ganges*).

Immediately after, his itinerary transcends this limit, turning to the South. On the coast of the Bay of Bengal was situated the country of Kalingas. According to Pliny, the king of this race (*Calingarum* – VI.65) has 60,000 infantry, 1,000 cavalry and 700 elephants. But the next monarch is even mightier, he has 4,000 cavalry, 4,000 elephants and 50,000 infantry. He rules over the "spacious island" in the river (*insula . . . magnae amplitudinis*), containing a single race named the Modogalinga (*gentem continens unam nomine Modogalinga*). The term "insula" is misleading – it is difficult to imagine an island in the river so densely populated. Perhaps it was the result of interpreters' mistake: Sanskrit *dvīpa* (Prakrit *dīpa*) denotes not only "island", but also a country between two rivers (e.g. *Kurudvīpa* – "the land of the Kurus", cf. *Brahmāṇḍa-purāṇa*[7] 53.140: *dvirapastvāt smṛto dvīpaḥ*). The second element of the ethnic name – Galinga is obviously identical with Kalinga. The first element (Modo) is more difficult to interpret. Latin "o" quite often stands for Indian "u" (e.g. in the words: *Pāṭaliputra – Παλιβόθρα*, Candragupta – *Σανδροκό ττος, pulinda – molinda* etc.). So Indian original for *modo* must be *mudu.* I agree with J. Filliozat[8], that Latin form *Modogalinga* may be reconstructed as *Muḍukaliṅga.* The word *muḍu* in Telugu language means "three". Muḍukaliṅga is nothing but Sanskrit – Trikaliṅga, i.e. Telugu-speaking population of Andhra Pradesh, or Telingana. So the "spacious island" of Modogalinga race is the Andhra kingdom between Godavari and Krishna rivers.

Next follows (VI.67) the long list of the peoples: "beyond it are situated the Modubae, the Molindae . . . the Modressae, . . . the Calissae, Sasuri, Passalae, Colobae, Orumcolae, Abali and Thalutae". The first two names are identical with Sanskrit – Mutiba and Pulinda, the neighbours of Andhra (cf. Aitareya Brāhmana VII.18: *andhrāḥ pulindā mutibāḥ* and also *andhrapalida* in Aśokan XIII Rock Edict)[9]. The series goes on from Andhra to the North, after Molindae follow Modressae. They are not to be identified with Madra – the famous tribe of the Punjab. There was another tribe – Madraka, mentioned in *Mahābhārata* (XII.200.39) among the races of Deccan: *dakṣiṇāpathajanmānaḥ sarve . . . andhrakāḥ . . . pulindāḥ . . . madrakaiḥ saha.*

The next pair in the given list are Calissae and Sasuri. If the source of information was connected with the Eastern regions of India (like Andhra, forming the starting point of this series), we must take into consideration some phonetic peculiarities of the local dialects. Pillar Edicts of Asoka contain the form *pulisa*, corresponding to Sanskrit *puruṣa.*[10] By analogy we can expect Prakrit *kalisa* (Latin *Calissa*) from Sanskrit *Karuṣa.* Karuṣa (or Kāruṣa) is the tribe well attested in *Mahābhārata* and located[11] in the modern district Rewa, to the South of Prayāga. Their neighbours were Śūrasena (Prakrit Sūrasena) with the capital in the city of Mathura. They are to be compared with Sasuri, mentioned by Pliny (cf. transposition of the syllables in Prakrit: Varanasi/ Vanarasi etc).

In the next pair – Passalae and Colobae – the first one is identical with the Pañcālas in the Ganga – Yamuna Doab. Pañcālas are usually associated with the Kurus. The Prakrit form of the word "Kuru race" (*Kauravya*) is Korabbo. Since we must expect the peculiar features of the Eastern dialects, it would be pronounced as Kolabbo (= *Colobae* of Pliny the Elder). But if these Colobae = Sanskrit *Kauravya*, the next name of Orumcolae is to be compared with Sanskrit – Uttarakuru. We see the same transformations in Greek *Παλιμβόθρα*, Latin *Palibothri* from Sanskrit *Pāṭaliputra*: dropping of the syllable "ta" (cf. Ardha-Magadhi: *bori=badari*), nasalisation of the vowel, "o" instead of "u". It is a well known fact that the word *Uttarakuru* has two meanings: (1) the mythical people of Trans-Himalayan region, (2) the Northern branch of the Kurus. Orumcolae is a real tribe, situated in the Northern part of the Ganga-Yamuna Doab. But the mythical people were also mentioned by the Roman scholar. He cited (VI.55) a certain Amometus, who composed a book about these "Attacores", comparing them with the Hyperborei of the Greek mythology.

We can not identify the last pair – Abali and Thalutae – with any degree of certainty. But their location must be somewhere to the North from the Ganga-Yamuna Doab. Abali may be compared with Ambara (modern Ambala? – one more instance of dialectal confusion between "r" and "l").

After this long list of the peoples Pliny comes back to the king of Andhra (Modogalinga) and his enormous army. This passage has an interesting continuation: "But the tribe of Andarae (*gens Andarae*) is even more powerful (*validior*), with a great many villages and thirty towns fortified with walls and towers; they furnish their king with 100,000 infantry, 2,000 cavalry and 1,000 elephants, the people of Dardae is very rich in gold". Andara is usually identified with Andhra Pradesh, but we have arguments to challenge this identification: (1) Andhra was already mentioned under the name Modogalinga (= Trikaliṅga), (2) It is not easy to deduce Andara from the Prakrit Amdha (i.e. Andhra), (3) It would be absurd to mention Dardae – the famous people of Dardistan (North-Western India) as a part of Andhra kingdom, situated in the South-Eastern India. I agree with P.H.L. Eggermont,[12] that Pliny's Andara corresponds to Gandara (Sanskrit–Gandhara) in NW India and E Afghanistan. The first letter was dropped out of MSS in the same manner, as in the name of Candragupta, preserved by Plutarch – *Ανδροκόττος*, instead of *Σανδροκόττος*. Gandhara included Dardistan and was famous for fortified towns and a lot of villages.

In the Greek literature the kingdoms of the Punjab, visited by the troops of Alexander, traditionally were compared with an Empire in the Gangetic basin (*Prasii*, i.e. Sanskrit – *Prācya*, the "Eastern peoples", or *Palibothri* – from Sanskrit – *Pāṭaliputra*, the capital of Magadha). Pliny also asserts, that "almost the whole of the peoples of India are surpassed in power and glory by the Prasii"(VI.68). He gives a short description of "their very large and wealthy city of Palibothra" and the army of their king with 600,000 infantry, 30,000 cavalry and 9,000 elephants.

Then follows (VI.69) an additional remark: "Further up country from these (*ab his in interiore situ*) are . . . the Suari, in whose dominion is Mount Maleus upon which shadows fall towards the north in winter and towards the south in summer, for periods of six months alternatively". The last detail shows, that the point in question lies in the South of India, near the equator (only at the equator do shadows fall towards the south just six months). Mount Maleus is to be identified with Sanskrit Malaya (Southern part of the Western Ghats, Kerala – cf. Mahāmayūri[13] 40: *malaye . . . Keraleṣu*; the name – from Dravidian "Malai", i.e. "mountain"). In the second book of *Natural History* (II.184) Pliny wrote: "There is Mount Maleus in the country of the Indian tribe Oretes (*gens Oretum*), where the shadows fall towards the north in winter and towards the south in summer". More than hundred years ago Christian Lassen[14] formed a pretty good idea, that Latin expression *gens Oretum* reflects the Greek *'έθνος 'ορειτῶν*, i.e. "the people of mountaineers". And we should only add, that the last one seems to be a translation of the Indian word Malayalam – designation of the inhabitants of Kerala region.

The eastern part of Far South (modern Tamilnadu) is the land of Colas. This name was reproduced by Claudius Ptolemaeus[15] (VII.1.68) as *Σῶραι* – without any doubt an original form for Pliny's Suari (cf. Pliny VI.75 *Suaratta* from Prakrit *Soraṭṭha*).

After the excursus about the southern regions of Kerala and Tamilnadu the author comes back to the Magadhan empire. He says (VI.70) that the river Yamuna flows through the territory of this country

(Palibothri) between two towns of Methora (Mathura) and Chrisobora. The second element of the last word represents apparently Sanskrit – *pura* ("town", cf. *putra* – *βόθρα* in the name of Pataliputra). The first one may be identified with the ethnicon occurred before: *karisa* – karuṣa (cf. pulisa*puriṣa* – *puruṣa* in the Aśokan inscriptions[16]). Pliny used here the source with western dialectal features (in contrast with the previous case: *Calissae*, cf. *Κλεισοβόρα*, Arrian's *Indica* VIII.5). I suppose as Sanskrit original *Karuṣapura* (Prakrit *Karisapura* and *Kalisapura*), i.e. "the town of the Karuṣas", moulded upon such known names as Kaliṅganagarī or Pulindanagara.

This passage was important for Pliny to determine the frontiers of Magadha. The tribe of the Karusas lived at the confluence of the rivers Yamuna and Ganges. So if the Yamuna basin between the towns of Methora and Chrisobora belonged to the Palibothri, their kings' dominions did not overlap Mathura. In any case the Indus river was just outside this empire (VI.70 – *Indus statim a Prasiorum gente*).

Drifting from the Eastern to the Western part of India, the Latin geographer draws a diagram of the country as a whole. He reckons the distance between the (mouths of) the rivers Indus and Ganges as comprising 2,100 Roman miles (VI.70). The maritime route is sketched from the delta of the Ganges by navigation up to the mouth of the Indus and noting all the distances between the sea-ports (in all about 3,220 miles).

The series on the races of Western India (VI.73) starts with the same point where the author had stopped before; i.e. from the northern region between the rivers Indus and Ganges, in the foothills of the Himalayas, near the Kulu valley. The list contains Caesi, Caetriboni, Siluestres, Megallae, Chrysei, Parasangae and Asmagi. After Latin word Caesi the Greek *καῖσοι* can be reconstructed; it is to be identified with Sanskrit *Khaśa* (Prakrit *Khasa*), the people of Himachal Pradesh. *Caetri* may be compared with *Catriei* in the Latin MSS of Claudius Ptolemaeus (VII.1.64). The Greek original of the latter has *Χατριαῖοι*, located in the region of Kuruksetra. *Siluestres* (lit. "the tribes of the jungles", *jāṅgala* in *Bhiṣmaparva* 10.3; *aṭavi* in *Bṛhatsaṃhitā* XIV.29 = *boni*, Sanskrit – *vana*, *vanarāṣṭra*?) must be placed farther to the south.

We are on a firmer ground with *Megallae* and *Asmagi* – Sanskrit Mekala and Aśmaka (with characteristic vocalisation in both cases: k – g). Mekala was a country near the source of the Narmada river, Aśmaka was lying on the banks of Godavari. Pliny (VI.73) says that the region of Asmagi is abundant in the wild beast – tiger (*tigri fera scatentes*). This detail is very suitable for Aśmakas. Their lineage was even deduced from a certain Kalmāṣapada (lit. "one with spotted feet"), a cannibal, searching the jungles for human flesh "like tiger for cattle" (*vyaghraḥ paśum iva* – Mahābhārata I.166.36).

Just as it was for the grammarian Panini, the land of Aśmakas forms a southern limit of Pliny's geographical horizon. From this point he starts going to the West and North-West. In the middle of the great desert (Thar) is located the tribe of Suri. It is identical with Sanskrit Śūra (Prakrit Sūra). According to *Mahābhārata* (IX.36.1) Śūra lived in the region of Vinaśana, in the vicinity of Abhiras (*tato vinaśanaṃ rājanājagāma halāyudhaḥ śūrābhirān prati dveṣād yatra naṣṭā sarasvatī*). The tribe of Abhiras (*'Aβεριά* in Periplus of Erythrean Sea,[17] 41) occupied the area near the Great Rann of Kutch, Śūras inhabited some place to the North, in western part of Rajasthan.

Brahma-*purāṇa*[18] (XIX.17) gives enumeration of some "Western peoples": *surāṣṭra, śūra, abhira, arbuda, māruka, mālava.* Some of them are present also in the *Natural History*, Pliny tells: "below these deserts are the Maltaecorae, Singae, Maroae, Rarungae, Masugae (MS versions: *Morum, Moruni*). These peoples are the inhabitants of the mountains that stretch in a continuous range on the coast of the ocean; they are free people having no kings, and they occupy the mountain slopes with a number of cities". This colourful description looks like the picture of Rajasthan in the early medieval times. It is sure that Malwa and the neighbouring regions are meant here.

In the Western dialects "l" was pronounced as "r" (e.g. in Asoka's XIII Rock Edict from Girnar: *pariṃda* instead of *palida/pulinda*). The ethnic name of Mālava could be transformed into *Mārava* – the people of Maroae in *Natural History*. It is a well known fact that this tribe was actually "free people having no kings" – in ancient Indian texts it was called *Mālavagaṇa.* The coins of this clan and republic are discovered mostly in the region of Jaipur.

The name of *Masugae* (*Moruni*) can be compared with *Māruka* in the above mentioned list from Brahma-*purāṇa.* Rarungae corresponds to *Roruka* – the capital of the Sauvīra tribe, inhabitants of the Southern part of Sind.

One of the famous races of Rajasthan were the people of *Śālva* (Mahabharata V.54.18). According to Kāśika on Panini (IV.I.173), this union included six tribes: Udumbara, Tilakhala, Madrakara, Yugandhara, Bhuliṅga and Saradatta. Two of them, Pliny enumerates here (VI.75 and VI.77): *Bolingae* = *Bhuliṅga* and *Odonbeorae* = *Udumbara.* It is possible also to identify *Madrakara* with the above-mentioned people of *Malthaecorae.*

Pliny mentions also in this region "Capitalia – the highest of the mountains of India". This *Capitalia* is identical with the Mount Abu (=*Arbuda,* cf. *Brahma-purāṇa* about the tribe of *Arbuda* between Abhira and Māruka). Mount Abu is actually not the highest mountain in India, some mountains in the South are higher, but Greek authors give the name of "India" to the North only, not to the extreme South, or *Limyrike* (the country of Dravidas).

The route continues farther to the West, where little kingdoms of Oratae and Suarattaratae are located. The latter one is Surāṣṭra on Kathiawar peninsula. Pliny says that local king does not use war elephants (VI.75) In the corresponding passage of *Arthaśāstra* it is mentioned that war elephants in Surāṣṭra are of bad quality (II.5.15–16). Northern Kathiawar was occupied by the people of Ānarta – may be it is identical with Pliny's Oratae.

But especially interesting in this context seems to be "the fine city of Thorax", "guarded by marshy canals which crocodiles, creatures with an insatiable appetite for human flesh, render impassable save by way of a bridge". The name of Thorax (Greek *Θόρακ-* or *Θωρακ-*) may be compared with Sanskrit *Dvārakā* (i.e. Dwarka in the NW part of Surāṣṭra). Dvaraka was the capital of Kṛṣṇa. It was described in Mahabharata (III.16) as a fine city surrounded by canals. Historical Dwarka was situated on the ways to Arabia Felix and its richness was caused by the flourishing maritime trade in the last decades BC.

The mention of "Thorax" reminds Pliny about another "fine city". The Roman geographer reproduces its name as *Automula.* Its description makes it impossible to localize this town in the region of Gujarat (Surāṣṭra): "Another town in their country is also highly spoken of, Automula, which is situated on the coast, at the point of confluence of five rivers and has a celebrated market".

There is no confluence of the five rivers in Surāṣṭra, there is no big river there at all. The author has in mind not Gujarat, but the region of the Punjab (literally "the country of five rivers"). The town situated there, at the confluence of five rivers, and famous as a centre of international trade is Multan (Sanskrit Mūlasthāna). We can presume only, that there was a mistake in the Greek text used by Pliny the Elder: the name of the town Mula was amalgamated with the word *α'υτό.*

Then follows a long list of the Indian peoples (VI.76): Derangae, Posingae, Butae, Gogoraei, Umbrae, Nereae, Brangosi, Nobundae, Cocondae, Nesei, Palatitae, Salobriasae, Orostrae, "the last people being adjacent to the island of Patala". This remark makes it evident that the enumeration moves from Multan towards upto the mouth of the Indus.

The second list includes the peoples: Mathoae, Bolingae, Gallitalutae, Dimuri, Megari, Ardabae, Mesae, Abisari, Silae. This time direction is given by Pliny himself: "from the same point onward the tribes dwelling on the Indus – our enumeration proceeding upstream". Some of the names can be identified: *Mathoae* – *Mᾶθαι* (Arrian[20], *Indica,* 4) – Prakrit *Maccha* – Sanskrit *Matsya, Bolingae* = *Bhuliṅga* etc. At the end of the list we find the tribe of Abisari (Sanskrit *Abhisāra*). They were inhabitants of Kashmir region and their king Abisares was mentioned many times by the Greek writers in connection with Indian expedition of Alexander the Great.

The last list of the peoples includes the well-known names of the towns: Taxila, Peucolitae (*Puṣkalavatī*), the capital of the tribe of Asini named by Alexander "Bucephala", the burial-place of his horse etc. So the Roman geographer comes back to the point he started his description of India with.

The next passage about the island of Taprobana begins with the information derived from the works by Megasthenes and Alexander's companion Onesicrites. And Pliny adds an interesting remark: "so far the facts stated have been recorded by the early writers" (*hactenus a priscis memorata*). Thereafter he continues with the recent information, quoting one of his contemporaries who visited Ceylon "during the principate of Claudius". "The facts recorded by the early writers" were not improved upon by later travellers or mixed with the reports made by the latter. Contemporaries could make only some additions to the established tradition set by earlier scholars.

This distinctive feature of the *Natural History* is to be demonstrated in the description of India too. In the last part of the Indian Chapter (VI.104–105) Pliny reproduces the facts acquired by navigators of the first century AD, at the peak of the Indo-Roman trade. But such an information was not included in the core of his Indian Chapter – Pliny used there quite different sources: the works written by the companions of Alexander the Great and by the Greek ambassadors sent to the Indian court in the early Hellenistic period.

The core of the Indian Chapter (VI.64–78) seems to be homogeneous. Its distinctive features are the lists of Indian tribes and also pieces of information about military forces of the local kings (every time following one and the same scheme: the number of infantry, cavalry and elephants). This information is one-sided: the author shows no interest in Indian strategy or customs, military equipment or fortifications.

The lists of the peoples are present also in other chapters of *Natural History*. But these statistics of Indian armies are unique. Such a characteristic detail makes it possible to suppose that the whole passage was composed on the basis of a single source.

At the very beginning of his book on Geography (III.1) Pliny himself tells us about his manner of writing a scholarly work. He made a selection from various books on a particular topic and based his own research on the work he considered especially reliable one. Some details only were added from other sources.

The geography of India is described by Pliny with remarkable accuracy. The German philologists of the last century tried to find in this text the traces of many sources, but without any success. If Pliny himself could compose it as a kind of mosaic, we must presume, that he was an excellent specialist on India. But he was not!

Pliny (VII. 58) names two Greek writers, which were for him the best authorities on India: Megasthenes and a certain Dionysius, "sent by Philadelphus". Some scholars[21] supposed that Pliny's description of India was based mainly upon Megasthenes' *Indica.* We cannot agree with this hypothesis. The Roman scholar does have some short quotations from Megasthenes – and every time we can find corresponding passages in the works of other ancient writers, by whom Megasthenes was cited: Strabo, Arrian, Diodorus. But the main part of Pliny's chapter on India with the above mentioned lists of peoples and enumeration of military forces is unique.

Some peoples of India were mentioned by both: Megasthenes and Pliny the Elder. And we can note, that they give different spellings of their names. Quoting from Megasthenes, Pliny would give the name of Himalayan mountaineers (*kirāta*) as Sciritas.[22] But he uses quite different form – Chirato. So he gives the outline of on Indian map following some other work, not Megasthenes.

We may suppose that this source of information could be the above-mentioned Dionysius. The official character of the latter's diplomatic mission to India can explain the distinctive features of the text. The author's attention was focussed on ethnic and political geography of India – not on physical one. The work by Dionysius was more an official report than a literary production.

We do have information on Dionysius' career. The famous astronomer Claudius Ptolemy[23] cites his book and his observations on planets many times (Ptol. Synt. IX.168, 169, 170, 187, X.236, XI.263). These astronomical observations were made between 272 and 240 BC. So his scholarly activity coincides with the reign of Ptolemy Philadelphus and his son. Dionysius was a court astronomer and introduced a new era, starting from 285 BC (date of Philadelphus' coronation).

The last date cited from Dionysius by Claudius Ptolemy, is 240 BC. So the work by Dionysius was published in the 30s of the third c. BC. If he was active as a scholar from the 70s of the same century, we can give approximate dates of his life as 300 – 230 BC. It is more likely, that he was sent as ambassador to the court of Aśoka Maurya, because during the reign of the latter's father, Bindusara, he must have been too young.

But the diplomatic contacts between India and the Ptolemaic Egypt could be established only after the II Syrian war had ended (253 BC). Philadelphus died in 246 BC. So the date of his embassy to India may be established around 250 BC. Maybe it was Ptolemy's answer to the Aśokan mission, mentioned in his edicts and dated by the same period.

An official report by Dionysius was preserved in Alexandria and used by Pliny. Perhaps it was the main source for the Roman scholar to compose the Indian chapter of his *Natural History.*

In the middle of the third century BC an Egyptian ambassador had more reliable sources of information than Megasthenes or the companions of Alexander the Great. Two generations of the Greeks had already lived in the dominions of the Indian king. Dionysius could meet Greek merchants, who had information about the real geography of the country, not about fabulous creatures.

So Pliny gives us a rare chance to reconstruct the political situation in India in the third century BC. The political map was marked by the incontestable hegemony of the Magadhan king, whose dominions were the whole Ganga basin. But the Greek writer of the early Hellenistic age mentions also some other mighty kings: those of Kalinga and Trikalinga (Andhra), Mekala and Aśmaka, Gandhara and Punjab (Mulasthana), Suraṣṭra etc., as well as autonomous tribes inhabiting the lands of modern Rajasthan. This information preserved by the Latin geographer, makes it possible to reconsider the nature of the so-called all-Indian empire. Pliny knows Magadhan hegemony, but he has no idea about any "Imperial unity".

Notes and References

1. Pline l'Ancien, *Histoire Naturelle,* Livre VI, 2 partie. Texte établi, traduit et commenté par J. André et J. Filliozat. P. 1980.
2. P. H. L. Eggermont, *Alexander's Campaign in Sind and Baluchistan and the Siege of the Brahmin Town of Harmatelia.* Leuven, 1975, p. 164.
3. A. Dihle, *Die entdeckungsgeschichtlichen Voraussetzungen des Indienhandels der rőmischen Kaiserzeit \\ Aufstieg und Niedergang der rőmischen Welt,* II.9.2. 1978, p. 556.
4. *The Mahābhārata. Text as constituted in its critical edition,* Vol. II, Poona, 1972 (cf. *Bhiṣmaparva* ed. by R. Kinjawadekar, Poona, 1931, 9.68).
5. *Mārkaṇḍeya-purāna,* ed. J. Vidyasagar, Calcutta, 1879.
6. G. P. Malalasekara, *Dictionary of Pali Proper Names,* Delhi, 1995, Vol. II, pp. 453–54.
7. *Brahmāṇḍa-purāṇa,* ed. by J. L. Shastri, Delhi, 1973.
8. Pline l'Ancien, op. cit. (Commentary by J. Filliozat), p. 97.
9. U. Schneider, *Die grossen Felsenedikte Aśokas,* Wiesbaden, 1978, S. 77.
10. J. Bloch, *Les inscriptions d'Asoka,* Paris, 1950, pp. 161, 164, 169.
11. B. Ch. Law, *Tribes in Ancient India,* Poona, 1973, p. 88.
12. P. H. L. Eggermont, op. cit., p.181.
13. S. Levi, 'Le Catalogue geographique des Yakṣa dans la Mahāmayūri', *Journal Asiatique,* 1915.

14. Ch. Lassen, *Indische Altertumskunde*, Bd. 2, Bonn, 1852, S. 667.
15. L. Renou, *La Geographie de Ptolemee, L'Inde* (VII.1–4). Texte établi par L. Renou. Paris, 1925.
16. J. Bloch, op. cit., pp. 161, 164.
17. *Periplus Maris Erythraei.* Text with introduction, translation and commentary by L. Casson, Princeton, 1989.
18. *Brahmapurāṇa*, Bombay, 1963.
19. *The Kauṭilīya Arthaśāstra*, Vol.1, Ed. by R.P. Kangle, Bombay, 1969.
20. *Arrianus. Scripta Minora.* Lipsiae, 1967.
21. E. G. C. Mullerus, *Fragmenta Historicorum Graecorum*, Vol. II, p. 397 f, J. McCrindle. *Ancient India as Described by Megasthenes and Arrian*, Calcutta, 1960.
22. Cf. quotation from Megasthenes in Aelian 16.22 (Aelian. *On the Characteristics of Animals*, London, 1958).
23. *Ptolemy's Almagest.* Ed. by G. Toomer, London, 1984.

TEN

On the Authenticity of the *Āpastambadharmasūtra* Text

A. M. SAMOZVANTSEV

THE ĀPASTAMBADHARMASŪTRA IS ONE of the early prosaic *dharmaśāstras*, i.e. the *dharmasūtras* which belong to the tradition of the *gṛhyasūtras* or the collections of domestic rites. As is well known, the *dharmasūtras* of Āpastamba, Baudhāyana and Hiraṇyakeśin together with the *gṛhya* and other *sūtras* dealing with the interpretation of traditional fields of ritual practice (*gṛhya, śrauta* etc.), were a part of the ancient collections of ritual books (*kalpas*), composed in the Vedic schools. It has often been proved that the text of a number of the *dharmaśāstras*, was in this or that way reworked, at times to a very large extent, and the extensive textual fragments were thereby incorporated into the compilation (as an example the text of the *Baudhāyanadharmasūtra* may be mentioned here). However, the *Āpastambadharmasūtra* itself presumably belonged to the *dharmaśāstras* whose textual entity hardly left the Sanskritologists any grounds for doubt. P. V. Kane, in particular, cited the evidence from the written sources in favour of the authenticity of the present *Āpastambadharmasūtra* text as the one which, at least beginning from AD 400, had been free from the later insertions.[1] We may to a certain extent ascertain what the original text of the *Āpastambadharmasūtra* looked like with the help of the *sūtra* of Hiraṇyakeśin, which, being composed on the base of the former, had borrowed many *sūtras* from it. Although the *dharmasūtra* of Hiraṇyakeśin is the earliest text throwing light upon the composition of the *Āpastambadharmasūtra*, which is of great value for the verification of the authenticity of the latter text, its data is not known for sure.[2] Yet, G. Bühler insisted that some 100–150 years might have separated the *dharmasūtras* of Āpastamba and Hiraṇyakeśin from each other.[3]

Yet, the compiler of the *sūtra* of Hiraṇyakeśin could have based himself upon the already reworked version of one of the more ancient *dharmasūtras*.

However the question arises: is it possible by analysing the text of the *Āpastambadharmasūtra*, by revealing its features and principles of composition to ascertain its primordial contents? And in general too: is it possible to reconstruct the contents of any standard (complete) *dharmaśāstra*, on condition that the text should have certainly developed according to its own laws?

The answer, in our opinion, is positive. The standard (complete) *dharmaśāstra*s are those in which the adaptation of *dharmic* contents was a two-dimensional process: on one hand, as the formation of the traditional rubrics and sub-rubrics (*dharmic* themes) with the subsequent joining of the large sections of the text on the basis of the former into huge thematic blocks. On the other hand, it was a sort of "filling" the *dharmic* themes, the adaptation of the contents within them with the possible moving of material from one rubric to another.

The *dharmic* themes organised by the prescriptions peculiar to the *āśramas* (prescribing the relevant *ācāras* or behavioural norms with ritual playing the regulatory role) appear to a considerable extent as completed ones already in the *dharmasūtra*s (the reader should be reminded that this material had been actively elaborated in the *gṛhyasūtra*s).

Hence the material adaptation by the *dharmic* themes is connected in the *dharmasūtra*s and more so in the *dharmaśāstra*s mainly with the formation of the two large thematic sections, namely, of *prāyaścitta* (religious law) and of *rājadharma*. The content of the latter is much broader than that of the civil law (royal justice) proper, but it is the notion of the royal justice that gradually emerges as semantic equivalent for the *rājadharma* (especially in the *Yājñavalkyasmṛti* and the *Nāradasmṛti*). The adaptation of the legal material by the *dharmaśāstra*s was going on until the stage of the exhaustive elucidation of the full set of law-connected rubrics, first and foremost the *rājadharma* ones, was achieved. This process is especially observable in the *Manusmṛti* and the *Yājñavalkyasmṛti*, and with the composition of the latter two *dharmaśāstra*s the development of the genre in the two above-mentioned spheres came to an end.[4]

It appears that the standard *dharmaśāstra*s beginning with the *Āpastambadharmasūtra* and including the *Yājñavalkyasmṛti* (unlike the late ones in which separate *dharmic* themes or thematic blocks were included and the textual development was of a different character), may, as a rule, be regarded as self-sufficient ones, and it is only whether one or another *dharmic* rubric is developed/undeveloped and also filled/unfilled with material that may be discussed here.

As for the late diversified *dharmaśāstra*s, if one attempts to restore their primary text (in case it was distorted, reworked, augmented, etc.), this would, at least in a majority of cases, hardly yield positive results.

However, the case is somewhat different with the standard *dharmaśāstras*. On the basis of these texts we may trace a certain evolution of the thematic rubrics of the *dharmaśāstra*, the place of which in text and also specific features relevant to this or that text and distinct stage of the genre development were fixed and changed from time to time and from one text to another. In other words, the peculiarities, say, of the *Āpastambadharmasūtra* text are quite distinct from those of the *Manusmṛti* and the *Yājñavalkyasmṛti* texts and vice versa. Let us examine the main composition principles of text of the standard *dharmaśāstras* and especially of the *dharmasūtras*.

It is well known that the *dharmaśāstras* describe the behaviour rules of a devoted Hindu, first and foremost the twice-born. In the initial phase both the text and its contents were organised according to the *āśrama* or temporal principle, i.e. according to the prescriptions peculiar to the *āśramas* or stages of life like the Brahmana pupil, the householder, the forest hermit and the ascetic. The Vedic *saṃhitās* and the literature of the *brāhmaṇas* and the *upaniṣadas* do not dwell upon the *āśramas*. It appears from the *Gautamadharmasūtra*[5] I.3.35 which quotes from the preceptors, that the Vedas had prescribed the only one *āśrama*, namely, that of the householder. As one ensuring the birth of offspring and the life cycle itself it is regarded as the principal one, at times the only one (the *Baudhāyanadharmasūtra*[6] II.6.11.29). Yet, the elements of the *āśrama* order may be found as referred to in the late Vedic literature, for example, in the *Bṛhadaraṇyakopaniṣad* II.4.1, VI.2, where the householder is juxtaposed with the forest hermit. The names of separate *āśramas* which were later on established are absent here.[7] The concept acquires its shape in the late *upaniṣads*: hence, four sections of the *Āśramopaniṣad* are devoted to the description of the four *āśramas*. The *āśrama*-wise principle of the composition of material describing domestic rites was applied in the *gṛhyasūtras* and slightly later in the *dharmasūtras* of Āpastamba, Baudhāyana etc.

If we mark out, following the *sūtrakāras*' example, the life norms prescribed for a *snātaka* (a pupil who has completed his education), we may present the composition of the text as follows. The text of the *dharmasūtras* could be composed in accordance with stages of life as it is done by the *Āpastambadharmasūtra*,[8] which describes the *dharmas* of the four *āśramas*, including those of pupil (I.1.9–I.29), of *snātaka* (I.30–32), of householder (II.1–20), of ascetic (II.21.7–17) and forest hermit (II.2.18–23.3); the *rājadharma* (II.25–29.10) appears here as a supplement (to be discussed below). Sometimes only a part of the *dharmasūtra* prescriptions was narrated as the *dharmas* of the four *āśramas*, which may be seen in the text of the *Vasiṣṭhadharmasūtra*:[9] the *dharmas* of pupil (VII), of householder (VIII), of forest hermit (IX), of ascetic (X), of *snātaka* (XII). There are similarly composed texts of the *Gautamadharmasūtra* (the *dharmas* of pupil – I.1.6–I.2, of ascetic – I.3.10–24, of forest hermit – I.3.25–34, of householder – I.4–8, of *snātaka* – I.9) and of the *Baudhāyanadharmasūtra* (the *dharmas* of pupil – I.2.3–4, of householder – I.3.5.–II.9.16, of ascetic – II.10.17–18, of forest hermit – III.3.3., of *snātaka* – I.3.5.f., II.3.5.10–3.6.). A part of the prescriptions peculiar to the *āśramas* could be treated separately from the *dharma* of the *āśramas* as this happened with the rules of a pupil's initiation in the *Vasiṣṭhadharmasūtra* XI.49–79. The complicated compound text of the *Baudhāyanadharmasūtra* has one small additional block wherein the *dharmas* of the four *āśramas* are mentioned: that of pupil (I.6.11.15), of forest hermit (I.6.11.16–17), of ascetic (I.6.11.18–28), of householder (I.6.11.29 ff.). The *dharmas* common for all the *āśramas* are in the foundation of the small fragment from the *Āpastambadharmasūtra* II.21.1–6. As this text is in the focus of our attention, it has to be noted that the prescriptions to the four *varṇas* comprise the fragments I.1.4–8 and II.10.5–8, the latter is of especial significance. Following the ideal pattern of the four *āśramas* order, i.e. beginning with the *āśrama* of pupil and including the one of ascetic, the *dharmas* of the four *āśramas* are first narrated in a particular sequence in the *Vasiṣṭhadharmasūtra* and, then, in the *Manusmṛti* and the *Yājñavalkyasmṛti*.

Given all the possible inconsistency in the organisation of material and the description of the *āśrama dharmas*, the *sūtrakāras* usually perceive the logic in the textual evolution and note the beginning and the end of both the smaller topics and the bigger ones, pertaining to the *āśrama* prescriptions. With this purpose they use the conjunction *atha* meaning "now" (sometimes the conjunction combination *athātas*), as this appears from the texts of the *Āpastambadharmasūtra* II.21.7 (*atha parivrājakaḥ* – now [follow the duties] of a wondering ascetic), II. 21. 18 (*atha vanaprasthaḥ* – now [follow the rules pertaining to] a forest hermit); likewise in the *Baudhāyanadharmasūtra* I.3.5.1, 10, II.10.17.1, III.3.3.1., the *Vasiṣṭhadharmasūtra* XII.1 etc. In other cases the text also formulates an important prescription for one's admission into an *āśrama*. The most significant example of such prescriptions is the one pertaining to the householder's marriage in the *Āpastambadharmasūtra* II.1.1, the *Gautamadharmasūtra* I.4.1 and the *Vasiṣṭhadharmasūtra* VIII.1. Prescriptions to a pupil are of the same meaning (the *Baudhāyanadharmasūtra* I.2.3.1, the *Gautamadharmasūtra* I.1.6, the *Āpastambadharmasūtra* I.1.9 etc.). In other cases the text may mention a norm of behaviour which would symbolise one's admission into an *āśrama* (the *Gautamadharmasūtra* I.3.10, 25, the *Vasiṣṭhadharmasūtra* IX.1, X.1). Moreover, at least the *Baudhāyanadharmasūtra* III.10.10.1 and the Gautamadharmasūtra III.1.1 define their own composition as the *āśrama* – *varṇa* one.

If the *āśrama*-wise and temporal composition of material appears in the texts more ancient that the *dharmasūtras*, the one relevant to the *dharmas* of the four *varṇas* is not so significant. However we should clarify here that the *dharmaśāstra* text may be either organised by describing the *dharmas* of the four *varṇas* or may contain a group of prescriptions treating separately the duties of the members of each *varṇa*. As far as the texts of the *Āpastambadharmasūtra* and the *Baudhāyanadharmasūtra* are considered, they feature just the groups of prescriptions formulating the duties of the four *varṇas*, i.e. their *dharmas* in the narrow sense of the word (the *Āpastambadharmasūtra* I.1.4–8, II.10.5–8, the *Baudhāyanadharmasūtra* I.10.18.2–6). It is remarkable that in both *dharmasūtras* the theme of the king, *rājadharma*, appears as linked to the statements on the above *dharmas*: in the *Baudhāyanadharmasūtra* the *rājadharma* includes the *dharmas* of members of the four *varṇas* (I.10.18.1–2 = 6–7 ff) whereas in the *Āpastambadharmasūtra* it is developed from them (II.10.5 = 8–9 = 11.4). The same semantic connection, albeit in a much more developed shape, may be seen in the *Gautamadharmasūtra* (duties of the four *varṇas* – II.1, *rājadharma* – II.2–4). At any rate, it seems strange that in the *Āpastambadharmasūtra*, in contrast with the other *dharmasūtras*, the duties of the *varṇas* are partly discussed in the beginning (I.1.4–8) as well as in the main part of the text (II.10.5–8) while the extensive fragment on the *rājadharma* (II.25–29) is in the concluding part.

The *Vasiṣthadharmasutra* (II, see especially II. 13–50) deals with the *dharmas* of the four *varṇas* too, though the *rājadharma* is placed outside both the *dharmas* of *varṇas* and *dharmas* of *āśramas* (XVI, XIX). We also may note that, unlike the texts of the *Āpastambadharmasūtra* and the *Baudhāyanadharmasūtra*, a large part of the *Vasiṣthadharmasūtra* and the *Gautamadharmasūtra* texts is arranged in accordance with prescriptions addressed to the members of the *varṇas* (the *Vasiṣthadharmasūtra* II–IV – *dharmas* of the *varṇas*, VII–X – those of *āśramas*; the *Gautamadharmasūtra* I.1.6–1.9 – *dharmas* of *āśramas*, II.1–9 – of *varṇas*).

The arrangement of text of the *Viṣṇusmṛti*[10] is similar to that of the *Gautamadharmasūtra* (II – duties of members of the four *varṇas*, III–XIV – *rājadharma*, XV–XCV – *dharma* of *āśramas*).

As for the *Manusmṛti*[11], the *dharmas* of the *āśramas* are stated within the limits of the *dharma* of Brāhmaṇa here (II.27–VI) while the further contents follow the pattern of the Gautamadharmasūtra II.1 (VII–IX.324), then, those of *Vaiśya* (IX.326–333) and of *Śūdra* (IX.334–335) are featured. The duties of the four *varṇas* are discussed in the *Manustmṛti* I.88–91. As it turns out, a part of text of the *Gautamadharmasūtra* (II.1) is similar in meaning to that of the *Manusmṛti* (II–IX). While using the "*dharmas* of *varṇas*" expression for the of the *Āpastambadharmasūtra* and the *Baudhāyanadharmasūtra* texts, the above-mentioned consideration has to be borne in mind.

The end of the *Gautamadharmasūtra* text (III.1.1) which does not look as a compound one runs as follows: "Both *dharma* of *varṇas* and *dharma* of *āśramas* have been declared" (*ukto varṇadharmaśca' 'śramadharmaśca*), and appears natural as sections of this text really deal with expounding the *dharmas* of these two kinds. G. Buhler expressed the opinion that the analogous *sūtra* III.10.10.1 of the *Baudhāyanadharmasūtra* was borrowed with the whole chapter III.10.10 from the text of the *Gautamadharmasūtra*.[12] From the standpoint of composition the *sūtra* evidently plays in the *Baudhāyanadharmasūtra* text the same part as in the *Gautamadharmasūtra* one and the compiler's motives are also similar. However the *sūtra* creates a strange impression here just because the *varṇa dharmas* and the text organisation corresponding to them are of much less importance in the *Baudhāyanadharmasūtra* than in the *Gautamadharmasūtra*. The inserted fragment containing the *sūtra* III.10.10.1 looks as if renewing, according to the later pattern, the ancient and loose text of the *Baudhāyanadharmasūtra*.

If we neglect the small introductory fragment I.1.4–8, in the *Āpastambadharmasūtra*, the *dharmas* of the *varṇas* appear to be discussed in several *sūtras* only (II.10.5–8). Strangely enough, the compiler proclaims in sūtra II.25.1: "The general and special *dharmas* of all *varṇas* have been declared. But we shalll now declare (those) of the king in particular" (*vyākhyātāssarvavarṇānāṃ sādhāraṇavaiśeṣikā dharmā rājñastu viśeṣādvakṣyāmaḥ*). The text reads so not only regardless of its own *āśrama*-temporal composition but also of what is said in previous *sūtra* II.24.14, the closing in chatter II.24, which unambiguously points out that up to this very place the text has discussed the conduct relevant to the *āśramas* and not the *varṇas*. Indeed, the elaboration upon the *dharma* of a forest hermit and of all *āśramas* taken together is concluded in the *Āpastambadharmasūtra* II.23.2. The characteristic features of adjacent *sūtras*, II.24.14–25.1, to our mind, can stimulate the understanding of the transformation which has been undergone by the text of the *Āpastambadharmasūtra*.

To begin with, in the *Āpastambadharmasūtra* the *rājadharma* topic is treated in two parts: firstly it is formulated within the limits of the householder *dharma*, wherein *rājadharma* adjoins the *dharmas* of the *varṇas* (II.10.5=8–9=11.4). Then, secondly, the prescriptions addressed to the king are shaped as a certain kind of appendix to the principal *dharmasūtra* text, which is preceded by the well-known description of "general and special *dharmas* of all *varṇas*" (II.25–29.10).

In the *dharmaśāstras* the two-part composition of the *rājadharma* material may be seen, apart from the *Āpastambadharmasūtra*, in the

Vasiṣṭhadharmasūtra (XVI, XIX), but, in contrast with the former, both parts of *rājadharma* look in the latter as counterbalancing and supplementing each other. The analysis of the *rājadharma* as treated in the *dharmasūtras* from the viewpoint of its contents organisation shows that chapter XIX of the *Vasiṣṭhadharmasūtra* is closer to the composition which is traditional for the *dharmasūtra* texts. The contumely and the assault and battery are described there among the typical delicts that appear in the *Āpastambadharmasūtra* and in the *Baudhāyanadharmasūtra* as the most frequent element in the description of legal cases. On the contrary, chapter XVI refers to the legal cases that were not a feature of the early *dharmasūtras* and concerned mainly the property relations. These are the two traditions (the earlier and the later one) in the description of legal cases, and, as a matter of fact, the subjects of chapters XVI and XIX of the *Vasiṣṭhadharmasūtra* look deliberately delimited while contents are relevantly distributed among them. As it follows from the text, the contents of chapter XIX are confined to the topic of the establishment of *dharmas* by the king and their violation by the subjects, and also to those of war and taxation, i.e. to the subject of chapter VII of the Manusmṛti and of the end of the book II of the *Yājñavalkyasmṛti*. In both cases we deal with the part of text of *rājadharma* which describes the ideal conduct of the king in his own country and is now and then called *rājadharma* as such, unlike chapter VIII of the *Manusmṛti* and book II of the *Yājñavalkyasmṛti*, dedicated to the *vyavahāra* or legal proceedings, i.e. to the subject of chapter XVI of the *Vasiṣṭhadharmasūtra*.[13] Thus, chapters XVI, XIX of the *Vasiṣṭhadharmasūtra*, given their own characteristic features, are interconnected, and what we have here is the transformation of the *rājadharma* of the *dharmasūtras* into that of the *dharmaśāstras*.

This very case indicates the essential difference between the texts of the *Vasiṣṭhadharmasūtra* and the *Āpastambadharmasūtra* as the latter features the two *rājadharma* sections both of which are different in their nature and obviously composed in different times.

The *rājadharma* section in the *Āpastambadharmasūtra* II.10.9–11.4 obviously presents its earliest form, while the method of adjoining the *rājadharma* text with that pertaining to the *dharmas* of *varṇas*, which, in their turn, concretise the *dharmic* occupations of a householder, has first been utilised by the *Āpastambadharmasūtra* (II.10.5=8–9=11.4) and, then, by the *Baudhāyanadharmasūtra*, taken in its present form (I.10.18.1–2=6–7=19.19), by the *Gautamadharmasūtra* (II.1–2=4), the *Manusmṛti* (II.26–VII=IX.324–335) and the *Viṣṇusmṛti* (II–III=XIV).

This archaic and, probably, unaltered *rājadharma* of the *Āpastambadharmasūtra* could have even been regarded as the earliest text of its kind, but for the supposition founded on the analysis of the *rājadharma* contents development, that the hitherto available compound text of the *Baudhāyanadharmasūtra* I.10.18, being, evidently, a relatively late version of *rājadharma*, contains several *sūtras* which belong to its ancient nucleus. This nucleus consists of the *sūtras* I.10.18.7–10 (comp. *Āpastambadharmasūtra* I.10.11 ff.). It is apparently the most ancient text of *rājadharma* among other similar ones from the available *dharmaśāstras*. Proceeding from these *sūtras*, we may draw the conclusion that the functional nucleus around which the notions of archaic *rājadharma* were grouped is dominated by the motive of appointment of domestic priest and of waging war by the king. It is the projection of the main special *dharmas* of the *kṣatriya* king, i.e. waging war (getting king's livelihood by force of arms) and imposition of order-maintaining punishment upon the offenders (by the appointment of domestic priest), that makes the *rājadharma* text two-part and also facilitates uncorporation of the contents into the *rājadharma* section.[14]

The archaic character of the above-mentioned *rājadharma* fragment from the *Āpastambadharmasūtra* is as observable as the relatively late character of its 11.25–29.10 fragment. Judging both by its style and also by its development, we may note its striking difference from the *rājadharma* of II.10.9 ff., and, on the contrary, at least the legal sections of the 11.25–29 fragment reveal the striking similarity with those of the *Gautamabharmasūtra*. It is illustrated by the following table which helps to compare the composition of the legal themes of both the *dharmasūtras*.

The *Āpastambadharmasūtra*	The *Gautamadharmasūtra*
Adultery: II.26.18–27.13	Contumely, assault and battery, adultery: II.3.1–3
Contumely, assault and battery: II.27.14–15	Assault and battery, contumely: II.3.4–11
Stealing: II.27.16–17	Stealing: II.3.12–15
Field: II.28	Field: II.3.16–25.
Trial: II.29.5–10	Trial: II.4

It seems plausible that the *Gautamadharmasūtra* text had been composed approximately in 1st century AD. Its legal topics, as stated above, are probably based upon those of the *Āpastambadharmasūtra* text, but not vice versa. Besides, it appears that the former text is more developed than the latter.[15] Consequently, we may suggest that the II.25–29 fragment of the *Āpastambadharmasūtra* must have been composed somewhat earlier than its *Gautamadharmasūtra* counterpart, namely, about first century BC or a little later.

One detail testifies to the relatively late character of the fragment

II.25–29. We should focus on the concept of the king as the founder of the stronghold town and the kingdom as elaborated upon in the *Āpastambadharmasūtra* II.25.2 ff. This concept would afterwards manifest itself in the *Manusmṛti* VII.69 ff., the *Yājñavalkyasmṛti* I.321, the *Viṣṇusmṛti* III.4 ff. It is also available in a much more developed form in the *Kauṭilīya Arthaśāstra*[16] II.1 ff., wherein king plays the role of the organiser and builder of his kingdom. This important motive of king's behaviour and of organisation of the *rājadharma* contents is known neither to the *Baudhāyanadharmasūtra*, the *Vasiṣṭhadharmasūtra*, nor even to the *Gautamadharmasūtra*.

However, there is another noteworthy detail in the same chapter II.25 of the *Āpastambadharmasūtra*, which displays the very ancient tradition and, besides, unknown to any other *dharmaśāstra*. Here we should refer to fragment II.25.12–14 and especially to *sūtra* II.25.12 which runs as follows: "Having built a place for dice-playing in the midst of the assembly-house (and) sprinkled (it) with water, (he who manages the play) should put on (it) the dice in even numbers, made of *vibhitaka* (wood), as many as are needed" (*sabhāyā madhye' dhivedanamuddhatyā' vokṣyā' kṣānnivapedyugmān vaibhītakān yatharthān*). A little carlier the building of the assembly-house by the king is included by the compiler into a much more capacious topic of the foundation of stronghold town and the kingdom by the king (II.25.5), which looks exceptional within the tradition of the *dharmaśāstra*; therefore, the *sūtra* II.25.5, as it appears from the text finds its development in the *sūtras* II.25.12–13.

In his commentaries upon the *sūtras* II.25.5, 12–13 Haradatta naturally interprets them within the framework of the tradition known to him, i.e. as a description of a gambling-house bringing income to king. The gambling-house organisation, as it is known, was regulated, for example, by the *Yājñavalkyasmṛti* II.199–203 and by the more ancient text of the Kauṭilīya *Arthaśāstra* III.20.1–13. Therefore Haradatta in his commentary upon *sūtra* II.25.13 refers to the *Yājñavalkyasmṛti* II.199–200 (see also his commentaries on *sūtras* II.25.5, 12). Yet, we think that the compiler hardly meant the gambling-house, but rather the organisation of the assembly-house of the *kṣatriyas*, where dice-playing had a ritual meaning. Apart from other considerations in of our supposition,[17] we may only stress that the place for dice as mentioned in the *Āpastambadharmasūtra* is term *adhivedana* which occurs in some late Vedic sources (the *Maitrāyaṇi Saṃhita* I.6.11, the *Śatapatha Brāhmaṇa* 5.3.1.10, the *Kāthaka* 8.7) and signified earthen floor uncovered with wooden flooring, as a place for dice in the *sabhā* (assembly-house).[18]

The *Āpastambadharmasūtra* fragment II.25.12–14 seems to be developed enough, and, in our mind, only transmits a far more ancient tradition, appearing, evidently, as a reminiscence in the present case.

Given the rare character of this case, it seems possible for the text like the *Āpastambadharmasūtra*, which has some archaic features.[19]

It should be observed in this connection that the *Āpastanbadharmasūtra* does not strictly distinguish between the subjects of *rājadharma* and *prāyaścitta*; this is more noticeable in it than in other *dharmasūtras* not to mention the metric *dharmaśāstras*.[20] Thus the topic concerned with the avakīrṇin or a pupil who has violated his vow of chastity, is featured both in the section on *rājadharma* (II.26.18 ff.) and in the one on *prāyaścitta* (I.26.8); in both of them the same delict is differently pictured, and in the two corresponding sections either the civil punishment or the expiation are prescribed for the same delict. It should be kept in mind that other *dharmaśāstras* discuss this topic solely in the *prāyaścitta* section (*Baudhāyanadharmasūtra* II.1.1.29–31, *Vasiṣṭhadharmasūtra* XXIII.1–3, the *Gautamadharmasūtra* III.5.17–19, the *Manusmṛti* XI.119, the *Yājñavalkyasmṛti* III.280). In addition, we should notice that, unlike other *dharmasūtras*, the *Manusmṛti* and the *Yājñavalkyasmṛti* the text of the *Āpastambadharmasūtra* is not completed with a section on *prāyaścitta*, as it happened with the *dharmaśāstra* at a later stage of its evolution. As regards the contents of chapter II.25 of the *Āpastambadharmasūtra* with which the *rājadharma* section opens, they must be regarded as unique and deserve a special research.[19]

Let us now discuss the formula of the *Āpastambadharmasūtra* II.25.1 "the general and special *dharmas* of all *varṇas* have been declared" again. As itself it testifies to the relatively late composition of the fragment, in comparison with the main *dharmasūtra* text. This formula presupposes that by the time the above-mentioned fragment II.25–29 appeared the principle of the organisation of the *dharmic* contents according to the occupations prescribed for the members of the four *varṇas* could have already formed. As it has been observed earlier, this principle does not seem to be a characteristic feature of the *Āpastambadharmasūtra* and the *Baudhāyanadharmasūtra* texts, both of which follow the more ancient *āśrama*-temporal arrangement of contents. In the second place, the formula involved in the *sūtra* II.25.1 was oriented towards the text which to a considerable extent was to be founded upon the description of the *varṇa* occupations, i.e. a text typologically similar to that either of the *Gautamadharmasūtra* or of the *Manusmṛti*.

When we look at the stylistic features of the *sūtra* II.25.1 of the *Āpastambadharmasūtra* we may notice that the usage of the verb *vyākhyā* by the compiler in the form of the participle *vyākhyāta* is natural enough for the *dharmasūtras*, including the *Āpastambadharmasūtra* (I.4.7, II.21.17 etc.; comp. also the *Āpastambadharmasūtra* I.1.1 and the *Baudhāyanadharmasūtra* I.1.1.2). However question arises: what does the compiler mean by his statement "dharmas of all varṇas have been declared"?

Should we suppose that he was to some extent guided by the previous text of the *dharmasūtra* (it must be recalled that only a few *sūtras*, I.1.4–8, II.10.5–8, are therein dedicated to the description of the *dharmas* of the *varṇas*)? Or did he open the text II.25–29 with a stereotyped formula which by no means correlated with the previous contents and, rather, followed a text of another *dharmaśāstra* or, in a wider sense, of another tradition in the organisation of the *dharmic* contents, accepted by the *dharmaśāstra* and different from the one peculiar to the *Āpastambadharmasūtra*? We would prefer the letter whereas the former seems unlikely. Having composed the II.25.1 formula, the compiler seems to have rather followed a stereotyped text which had been the basis of the fragment II.25–29.

If we assume that text of the *Āpastambadharmasūtra* was amplified (we have a reason to think so), a natural question arises: was the conclusion to the text an integral part of the whole fragment? There is no reason to believe that this conclusion on the essence of *dharma* and of the four *varṇa* order in fragment II.29.11–16, on one hand, and fragment II.25–29 itself, on the other, were not composed at the same time. The scholars in this case usually pay attention to the *sūtras* II.29.11–12. Some of them are of the opinion that in the *sūtra* II.29.12 the compiler referred to the *arthaśātra* which had by tradition been considered the *upaveda* of the *Atharvaveda*.[21] Although the compiler mentions the *arthaśāstra* in the main part of text (II.10.15), the above *sūtra* may point out that the conclusion to the text of the *Āpastambadharmasūtra* might have been composed relatively later.

Moreover, it is obvious from the *dharmasūtra* text that while the first eight *sūtras* form the introduction elaborating upon the essence of *dharma* and of the four *varṇas* order, the last six ones likewise form the conclusion dedicated to the same topic.[22] Hence the compiler introduced the so-called frame construction, thus organising the text accordingly, following the frame of the four *varṇa* order. Meanwhile, the usage of such frame construction may be rarely found in the text of the *dharmasūtras*. The frame construction appears in the *Manusmṛti* (I.1–4 ff., XII.126) and in the *Yājñavalkyasmṛti* (I.1–2, III.328, 334), though both of them fill it with the contents different from those included into the frame of the *Āpastambadharmasūtra* text. And, as far as we know, such frame is not used by the compilers of the later *śāstras*.

Anyhow, there can be no doubt that the introduction on the essence of *dharma* and of the four *varṇa* order had been supplemented in the *Āpastambadharmasūtra* by the corresponding conclusion on the same theme, while the frame construction was composed in the way similar to that of the *Manusmṛti*, and the *Yājñavalkyamṛti*, provided no innovations were included into the introduction itself at the same time. At any rate, one may see that the *Āpastambadharmasūtra* text proved to be completed under this very pattern and, accordingly, this offered the appropriate conception of contents organisation.

The introduction to the *Āpastambadharmasūtra* text is clearly divided into two parts. The first one contains the definition of the essence of *dharma* (I.1.1–3) while the second one defines the four *varṇa* order (I.1.5–8). Thereupon the compiler discussed the prescriptions addressed to different *āśramas* and began with the description of a Brāhmaṇa pupil's initiation (I.1.9 ff.). Other *dharmasūtras* equally begin with denoting the essence of *dharma* (the *Baudhāyanadharmasūtra* I.1.1.1–4, the *Vasiṣṭhadharmasūtra* I.1–4, the *Gautamadharmasūtra* I.1.1–5), but the subsequent text varies in different sources as the *Baudhāyanadharmasūtra* and the *Vasiṣṭhadharmasūtra* describe the *śiṣṭas* – those who are learned in the Veda as well as *dharmic*/non-*dharmic* acts, whereas the *Gautamadharmasūtra* mentions prescription addressed to different *āśramas* and elaborates upon a pupil's initiation. None of them, after the essence of *dharma* had been defined, busied himself with the description of the four *varṇa* order. It was the *Āpastambadharmasūtra* alone that formulated the *dharmas* of the *varṇas* in two places: I.1.4–8 and II.10.5–8. One would describe that style of the *sūtras* like the I.1.5, 8 as somewhat artificial, unusual for this context. It would be more beneficial for our study, however, to limit ourselves to this statement alone and to avoid too far – reaching conclusions on this subject. There is no ground to suppose that the introduction to the *Āpastambadharmasūtra* text is a compound one.

As for the conclusion to the primary text of the *dharmasūtra*, we believe that this might have been different from the presently existing one. It would not be out of place here to consider the religious-philosophical concept of the *dharmaśāstra* in this connection.

Up to the time of the composition of the primary text of the *Āpastambadharmasūtra*, the religious-philosophical concept of the *Ātman*, the Absolute, the comprehension of which was regarded as the highest and final purpose of life of every twice-born, especially a Brāhmaṇa and led to the attainment of heavenly bliss and freedom from further rebirths, had already been formed. There are relevant places in the *Āpastambadharmasūtra* text (I.22.2, 4, 23.2 etc.). Besides, in the standard *dharmaśāstras*, including the *dharmasūtras*, purification is described as a natural and necessary precondition of salvation, i.e. the liberation of an individual soul from the bonds of further rebirths (in the late *dharmaśāstras*, in most cases composed by joining together separate *dharmic* themes, the traditional religious-philosophical concept of the *dharmaśāstra* may not be expressed textually). Thus, the *Vasiṣṭhadharmasūtra* postulates at I.1 "salvation (liberation) of people" (*puruṣaniḥśreyasa*) as the aim of one's cognition of *dharma*, and, describing the means of its achievement, points out at the end of text (XXIX.21), that one who has purified himself from all sins would attain heavenly bliss (. . . *vihāya sarvapāpāni nākapṛṣṭhe mahīyata*). Similarly the *Baudhāyanadharmasūtra* IV.8.8.13 concludes that pure souls achieve liberation (. . . *siddihiṃ yānti śuddhaśarīriṇaḥ*). In *śloka* IV.8.8.15 the same *dharmasūtra* discusses one's release from the sins and one's being in the state of felicity in the world of Brahma (*mucyate sarvapāpebhyo brahmaloke mahīyate*). The *Gautamadharmasūtra* declares in the closing *sūtra* III.10.50 that of all the *dharma* followers it is a connoisseur of *dharma* (*dharmaśāstra*) who first reaches the heavenly world (*dharmīṇāṃ viśeṣeṇa svargaṃ lokam dharmavidāpnoti* . . .).

The leading idea of the ultimate liberation of a soul (*niśreyasakara*) and of the attainment of heaven (freedom from rebirths), appearing in the *Vasiṣṭhadharmasūtra*, passes as a leitmotif throughout the conclusive part of the *Manusmṛti* text, wherein the compiler denotes a Brāhmaṇa's conduct leading to the liberation (XII.82) and acts facilitating the release of his soul (XII.83–84) the highest of them being the cognisance of the *Ātman* (XII.85). The final liberation of the soul is elaborated upon in XII.104, 116, and, according to the closing verse of the *Manusmṛti* (XII.126), one reading the *śāstra* of Manu would obtain "the desired state" (. . . *yatheṣṭām. . . gatim*), i.e. the heavenly bliss, etc., as Kullūka explains in his commentary to this *śloka.*

Can we found somewhere in the *Āpastambadharmasūtra* text, immediately after the statement upon the *dharmas* of the four *āśramas* the abovementioned motif of attaining heaven and immortality, the one that would reproduce the religious-philosophical concept common for all the *dharmaśāstras*?

Let us apply here to the contents of chapters II.23–24 of the *dharmasūtra.* As it has been noticed earlier, the description of a forest hermit's *dharma* completes with the *sūtra* II.23.2. As for the subsequent text, we designate it with the dotted line.

In II.23.3–4 it is stated: "Now (the following) two *ślokas* from a purāṇa are quoted: "Those eighty thousand sages who desired to get an offspring (passed) to the south by Aryaman's road (and) obtained burial grounds. Those eighty thousand sages who desired no offspring (passed) to the north by Aryaman's road (and) obtained immortality" (*atha purāṇe ślokāvudāharanti – aṣṭāśītisahasrāṇi ye prajāmīṣira ṛṣayaḥ / dakṣiṇenā' ryamṇaḥ panthānaṃ te śmaśānāni bhejire // aṣṭāśītisahasrāṇi ye prajām neṣira ṛṣayaḥ / uttareṇār'yamṇaḥ panthānaṃ te'mṛtatvam hi kalpate //*). It should be noted that the same concept, though in a more developed form, in similar way appears after the description of *dharmas* of the four *āśramas* in the *Yājñavalkyasmṛti* III.184–188, 193–196.

Sūtra II.23.12 runs as follows: "After that (the burial) there (follows) a reward without end, (which) is designated by the term "heavenly" (*tataḥ paramanantyaṃ phalaṃ svargyaśabdaṃ śrūyate*). In chapter II.24 the compiler discusses the theme of the ancestors' rebirth in their posterity and of obtaining immortality by the mortals (II.24.1 ff.).

Text II.24.5–6 points out that "they (ancestors) live in heaven until the end of the world, (thereupon they) stay (in heaven), being the seed of the new creation of the world", the *Bhaviṣyatpurāṇa* says (*ābhūtasaṃplavātte svargajitaḥ / punassarge bījārthā bhavantīti bhaviṣyatpurāṇe*).

Sūtra II.24.8, in which Prajāpati is cited, reproduces, though not quite consistently, the whole of a twice-born's living cycle, according to which all the previous contents of the *dharmasūtra* are arranged, and approves of it and designates as the most important duties "(the study) of the trinity of the Vedas, the pupilage, the procreation of children, the faith, the asceticism, the sacrifices (and) donation of gifts" (*trayīṃ vidyāṃ brahmacaryaṃ prajātiṃ śraddhāṃ tapo yajñamanupradānam . . .*).

In the next *sūtras* II.24.9–13 the elaboration upon the theme of ancestors and of their offsprings is continued and the subsequent text discusses the creation of the world (*sarga*) by Prajāpati and the sages abiding in heaven due to the merits of their devotion; further goes the closing *sūtra* II.24.14 which precedes the *rājadharma.* As has already been mentioned above, this *sūtra* as if summed up the statement of *dharmas* of the four *āśramas* and designated the order of text of the *dharmasūtra* as the *āśrama*-temporal one.

In that way, in our opinion, the primary text of the *Āpastambadharmasūtra* was concluded just with chapters II.23–24 with their central idea of achievement of heaven and immortality, whereas chapters II.25–29 describing *rājadharma* and renewing both text and composition of the *dharmasūtra* after the pattern of a later *dharmaśāstra* were afterwards added to them.

Notes and References

1. P. V. Kane, *History of the Dharmaśāstra* (Ancient and Mediaeval Religious and Civil Law). Vol. I, Pt. I, Poona. 1968, p. 66.
2. P. V. Kane, *History of the Dharmaśāstra.* Vol. I, Pt. I, p. 91.
3. 'Āpastamba and Gautama. Transl. by G. Bühler', *Sacred Books of the East*, Vol. II, 1879, p. XXIV.
4. A. M. Samozvantsev, *Pravovoi tekst dharmashastry* (The Legal Text of the Dharmaśāstra), Moscow 1991 , p. 270.
5. *'Gautamapraṇītadharmasūtrāṇi', Ānandāśramasaṃskṛtagranthāvaliḥ.* 1966, No. 61.
6. *Baudhāyana-dharmasūtra* with the "Vivaraṇa" Comment. By Srī Govinda Swāmī and critical notes by M. M. A. Ch. Śāstri. Ed. by U. Ch. Paṇdaya. Varanasi, 1972.
7. A. Ya. Syrkin, *Nekotorye problemy izucheniya upanishad* (Some Problems of the Study of the Upaniṣads), Moscow, 1971, pp. 100–101.
8. *Āpastambadharmasūtra* with the Comment. Ujjwala by Srī Haridatta Miśra. Ed. by A. Ch. Śāstri and A. R. Śāstri, Benares, 1932.

9. [Vaviṣṭha] *Athorisms of the Sacred law of the Āryas, as Thought in the School of Vasiṣṭha,* Ed. by A.A. Führer. Bombay, 1883.
10. *Viṣṇu Smṛti (the Institutes of Viṣṇu).* Together with Extracts from the Sanskrit Commentary of Nanda Paṇḍit Called Vaijayanti. Ed. with Critical Notes, an Anukramanika, and Indexes of Words and Mantras by J. Jolly. Varanasi, 1962.
11. *The Manusmṛti with the Comment. Manvarthamuktāvali of Kullūka.* Ed. with Critical and Explanatory Notes a.o. by N. R. Acharya. Bombay, 1946.
12. 'Baudhāyana. Transl. By G. Buhler', *Sacred Books of the East,* 1882, Vol. I.14, p. 310.
13. A. M. Samozvantsev, *Pravovoi tekst dharmashastry,* pp. 197–99.
14. Ibid., p. 191f.
15. Ibid., p. 192.
16. *Kauṭalīyam Arthaśāstram.* 1–3. With the Commentary of T. Gaṇapati Śāstri. Trivandrum, 1924–1925.
17. Ibid., pp. 70–71; W. Rau. *Staat und Gesellschaft nach den Brāhmaṇa-Texten dargestellt.* Wiesbaden,1957, pp. 76–77.
18. W. Rau, *Staat und Gesellschaft,* pp. 76–77.
19. Regarding the above-described peculiarities of the *Āpastambadharmasūtra* text V.V. Vertogradova, a Russian Sanskritologist, has suggested in an oral communication that the text probably discloses the so-called lateral non-textual borrowing related to the public life realities of the Vedic India.
20. A. M. Samozvantsev, *Pravovoi tekst dharmashastry,* pp. 183–84.
21. P. V. Kane, *History of the Dharmaśāstra,* p. 63; 'Āpastamba and Gautama. Transl. by G. Bühler', p. XXX.
22. A. Vigasin, V. Romanoff. 'Iz nablyudeniy nad kompozitsiyey dharmashastr (From the Observations upon the Composition of the Dharmaśāstras)', *Drevniy vostok i antichniy mir* (Ancient Orient and Antiquity), Moscow, 1980, p. 85.

ELEVEN ❖ Man and Principles of the Universe as Described in the *Garuḍa-Purāṇa*

E. V. TYULINA

THE PECULIARITY OF ANCIENT and medieval cultures is manifested in the fact that their world outlook is based upon the conception of the anthropomorphous universe as one gigantic organism where human body and cosmos are both isomorphous. In India the idea of anthropomorphous universe was embodied in the image of cosmic giant *Puruṣa*, the first human being, from whose body the world and the human society were created. Moreover, this myth is of utmost importance for the Indian culture. Since ancient times up to our days this myth has been subject to numerous modifications. One of these is shown in the framework of this article. Though *puruṣa* means "Man", in reality it signifies a certain universal principle which is the foundation of the world. Sometimes it is called *Mahāpuruṣa* "Big Man", meaning that his dimensions are gigantic and all-embracing.

The basic chain, which bound up "Man" with "Cosmos" was sacrifice. Let us recall the myth of *Puruṣa.* In hymn RV.X.90[1] *Puruṣa* is a sacrifice, as a result of which there appeared the following things: Vedic hymns, animals, human *varṇas* and all cosmic elements. At the same time certain organs are associated with certain cosmic elements; for example, creation of the Moon is connected with the mind, the Sun with the eyes, the Fire (*Agni*) with the mouth, the Wind with the breathing, the Air with the navel, the Sky with the head, the Earth with the feet, the different directions with the ears (RV X.90.9–14). In the later tradition *Puruṣa* personifies *Yajña* – the Sacrifice. As a result of this sacrifice *Puruṣa* becomes the universal model of the world, society and human being. In the middle ages the image of *Puruṣa* together with the whole complex of traditional conceptions connected with him gave raise to special meditation practices, the aim of which was to realise oneself as *Puruṣa,* in order to merge with the Absolute. These practices are quite interesting as they demonstrate medieval understanding of the world universality principle.

For our research we have chosen a medieval source known as *Garuḍa-purāṇa* (further abbreviated as GP), one of the highest authority in the Hindu religious tradition. Due to the fact that the GP is a compilation of the texts which are different as concerns the content and the time of their creation, it is very difficult to date it even approximately. It is believed that the oldest parts were being formed in AD sixth to seventh centuries and finally it was formed in AD ninth to tenth centuries. There were, however, some further alterations still later. There are several editions of GP, which differ from each other. We used for our research the text of *Garuḍa-purāṇa* edited by Jivananda Vidyasagar, and published by Sarasvati Press, Calcutta, in 1890.

The choice of this source is inspired by the fact that in it anthropological theme is paid a lot of attention to. Even the traditional interpretation of the *purāṇa* bears the evidence of it. GP consists of two parts. The first is encyclopaedic part and deals with different aspects of human life and rules of behaviour. It is called *Ācāra* (*Karma*)-*kāṇḍa.* The second is devoted to the subject of death and after life. It is called *Preta* (*Dharma*)-*kāṇḍa,* or the book about the dead, their souls (*pretas*) and their posthumous fate. Another name of the book is connected with the fact that the book deals with *dharma.* The fulfilment of the *dharma* is the key point in the posthumous destiny of a man. There is a GP edition which consists of three parts. The *Brahma* (*Mokṣa*)-*kāṇḍa,* is added. It is devoted to Viṣṇu as supreme God and to *mokṣa,* or final liberation.[2]

We see that the basic principle of the text structure is connected with the cycle of human life: life, death and a certain highest aim, which is the possibility of liberation from the chain of rebirths. We might assume that the first book devoted to human behaviour during life shows us what is meant under the word "man" in the *purāṇa* content. Nevertheless if we look upon the real content of the book, we shall see that it includes the texts that are traditional for *purāṇas* (the myths of the world creation, history and final destruction of the world, genealogical records etc.), vast parts describing the ritual, astrological and fortune-telling texts, a temple construction guide, a treatise on precious stones, passages from the *dharmaśāstras*, grammar and metrics guides, medical and geographic treatises, etc. Why have all these topics been included in the book devoted to human life? It looks that the key to understanding of the meaning of the book is rather small but a very important text which could well be called "On The Birth of Man".

The structure of the chapter is dialogic, which is quite common for this kind of sources. It is the dialogue between god Viṣṇu and Garuḍa. Garuḍa asks: "How does life come into being in the four species of living beings?" and expounds his own understanding of the origin of human existence. He says that a human being is "skin, blood, flesh, fat, marrow, bone, the living nucleus, hands and feet, tongue, generative and excretory organs, hare, nails, joints, ducts and the different lines drawn over the body, lust and anger, fear and shame, mind, joy, skin of various colours punctured with holes and shrouded with a network of fatty matter" (GP.II.22.1–4).

In this description Man is pictured as a chaotic collection of organs and tissues, as something that can be described as the matter. Besides, it is also a combination of various emotions and passions. Everything taken together, according to the Hindu conception, belongs to the world of illusion and testifies to the imperfection of Man. Moreover, it is a hindrance to the process of his spiritual self-perfection. Garuḍa himself in his question makes an assumption that all these things are "the net of Indra in the valueless ocean of rebirths" (GP. II. 22.4.) The fact that the negativity of estimation is expressed with the help of the chaotic description is of great importance for us. As a rule, in the ritualistic literature all descriptions of Man are put in good order. It is exactly this structural order that the notions of sacredness are associated with, and, consequently, with perfection of any phenomenon, because a non-sacral thing cannot be perfect. Among these kinds of models the vertical one is spread most of all, where organs are described in sequence from feet to the top of the head. Human feelings always correspond to organs with which they are associated. In this text, however, the generally accepted rule of this relationship is not present, which means that Garuḍa's depth of knowledge is not sufficient. He knows only the basis of teaching about Man, namely, that his existence is illusory. To organise this chaos, to make the act of birth sacral, it is necessary to interpret it according to generally accepted models of the ritual. Answering Garuḍa's question Viṣṇu begins his teaching with the ritualistic description of conception. It should be performed in accordance with certain rules. If these rules are not observed the subsequent fate of man is negatively influenced and there is no possibility realising this life as a sacrifice. Secondly, there is a time factor, the sequence of formation of organs and tissues which transforms chaos into order. Creation of each organ corresponds to a certain month thus making their formation dependent upon the specific order (GP II.22.21–28). It is obvious that this scheme of putting the body into existence does not correspond to anatomical conformity. It evidently copies the traditional schemes of ritual actions. Funeral offerings can serve as an example. The offerings of so called *piṇḍas* (lumps of sacrifice food) symbolised the corresponding organs of a new human body which is formed after the death of the previous human body and, simultaneously, symbolised the time of their formation. "On the first day the head appears from the *piṇḍa*, on the second, the neck and the throat, on the third appears the heart. On the sixth and seventh days the waist and the sacred organs are created. On the eighth – the hips, on the ninth – knees and feet." (GP.II. 5.68–70). According to the GP the number of the days during which a new body is being formed corresponds to the nine lunar months of forming a human body. In the chapter "On the Birth of Man" this scheme of the ritual is used for the description of the "right" process of forming a human body. Together with this process there is merging of human image with the image of the Vedic first human being, the cosmic giant *Puruṣa* who is the first sacrifice. When he was dismembered there arose the world and the human society. The *Śatapatha-brāhmaṇa* says: "Human being is, undoubtedly, a sacrifice. A sacrifice is a human being because he who makes a sacrifice is a human being and each time when he makes a sacrifice it (the sacrifice) has the dimension of a man. That is why a man is a sacrifice (*yajña*)" (ŚBr. I.3.2.1.).[3]

The text "On the Birth of Man" is, no doubt, devoted to the merging of the image of oneself with the image of *Puruṣa*, which introduces a series of archaic features. The most important thing is that the body is perceived as a sum of discrete, a kind of independent from each other, parts; its development is pictured as mechanical collection of a certain quantity of organs and elements, with which the notion of integrity and perfection of the universe are associated. Vedic hymns are the prototypes of such notions (RV X.90 and AV X.2).[4] It is just in these hymns that we find the moment of the process of construction of the human organism, collecting it from a certain sum of body parts and cosmic categories.[5]

The birth of a new body after death as well as the development of human foetus are described in GP as "construction" of a human organism from the necessary set of organs and parts of the body. The notion that *Puruṣa* is a conglomerate of the world elements was also derived from the Vedic hymn (RV X.90). In GP five such elements are mentioned. The embryo is composed of "earth, water, fire, wind and ether. All of them, bound by muscles, make the embryo suffer" (GP.II.22.24–30). Such description is traditional and can be often met in many variants on the pages of religious literature. Particularly, it resembles the analogous description in *Yājñavalkya-smṛti*' (YS III.75–109).[6] This source tells about the birth of *Puruṣa – Ātman* in the human womb. GP borrowed this text for analytical meditation – an inner ritual, that makes it possible to sacralise human life. In GP which pays much attention to the symbolism of numbers there are five elements giving birth to another five components that form tissues and human properties. The parts predominant in the principle of earth are skin, bones, nerves, hair and flesh; the parts predominant in the principle of water are saliva, urine, semen, marrow and blood. Hunger, somnolence, thirst, lethargy and brilliance are the qualities of fire. Running, breathing, contracting, stretching and thwarting are the qualities of wind. And resonant sound, cavity, gravity, hearing and supporting everything are the qualities of ether (GP II.22.30–36). The number of five is connected with one of the notions of perfection such as completeness, the unity of the world and Man. If one of the elements is absent, or there is some disproportion it causes damage and leads to illness of a man. Death is viewed upon as consecutive breaking of the elements (GP II.21.26–27).

If we look upon the "preliminary" description of Man given by Garuḍa, we may notice that it mentioned the same organs and emotions as Viṣṇu's answer. But in this case they systematised, that is, each element of the human body is correlated to the system of the universe as well as to the sacred time and to the scheme of the sacrifice. Thus, Man is isomorphous to *Puruṣa.* The teaching of the five elements each having an analogy in the organs as well as in the manifestation of the vital functions of the organism was used for practical purposes as well; for example, for diagnostics and classification of diseases. In case of disproportion the necessary things were "completed" with the help of some artificial means like food, drink, and similar things which were considered to be the manifestation of necessary elements.

The presence of the five elements in human body was not considered something precious in itself. In Hinduism it is viewed as illusory like any kind of material manifestation. Of value here are just the above mentioned means of its realization. This is often underlined in the text (GP II.31; 32; 36). It is this knowledge that gives power over the microcosm of the human body and, in the long run, is a means of overcoming its materiality. It underlies the ability to control these elements and in case of disease to cure the organism. Consequently, the model created on the basis of sacrifice, that is, being a matrix facilitating the analysis and description of the processes in human organism is more perfect than the organism itself.

GP offers several schemes for realisation of man's essence. These schemes are derived from the sources belonging to different times and are rather artificially stuck together. They are united only as they deal with sacrifice. Thus, next to the description of arteries and winds in the organism there is a comparison of Man with vessel; description of his vital functions is next to process of making food. It should be noted, that in the Sanskrit language the word "vessel" (*pātra*) also signifies "a virtuous man". Such notion is likewise connected with sacrifice but in this case the sacrifice is secondary, where the object of sacrifice is substituted by the symbolic equivalent, in this case by food. In the *purāṇa* Man is a creature busy with food making. It is described as follows: in human body "the water is over the fire, the food is over the water. The *prāna* blows on the fire from below, over which food and water are brought by the wind. The fire thus blown separates the waste matter and the nutritive element" (GP.II.22.43–44).

The comparison of food and cooking with Man has been successfully interpreted by V.N. Romanov who analysed the *dharmasūtras* and *dharmaśāstras*.[7] He made it clear that food cooked on the fire of home hearth gets into man; the juice of the food made by the inner fire of digestion, becomes flesh, fat and bones, it forms the human body. This human body is therefore the object of life sacrifice, embodied in the performance of the rituals of the life cycle. Going through them, the man "prepares his body for the final sacrifice on the funeral pyre, where his own body is substituted for the food offered to gods. The whole sequence of the life cycle proves to be successive preparation of "juice" which is transformed due to the process into suitable sacrificial material (*dravya*)[8]. In the *dharmaśāstras* similar description of birth is available in the text from Yājñavalkýa (YS III 71–109), which was used by V.N. Romanov as an illustration of his arguments. This text appears to be one of the sources for the authors of GP. In *Yājñavalkya-smṛti* conception is described as one of the stages of the transformation cycle of the entity called "the supreme juice". In short, this cycle looks as follows: sacrifice is put into fire – there comes smoke which is transformed and returns to earth as rain – rain feeds the vegetation which is food – food is consumed to become male semen (YS III. 71–72). In GP when the process of conception is described this theme is also present to a certain extent. The mother of the child to be born is compared with a vessel, in which the sacrifice starts. Semen is compared to food similar to *amṛta* (GP II.22.15). Besides, recommendations are given to determine what sort of food should be eaten before conception and what must not be consumed if the aim of the conception is to give birth to a boy who will be a new sacrificer.

Another matrix of self-realisation is the comparison of Man with town. The authors of *purāṇa* managed to include the image of the Man-vessel into the general content of the chapter, nevertheless, the description of the Man as town is given in the previous chapter (GP II.21), where the discussion about the essence of life has already started. In accordance with the given explanation, human body is a single column made of sinews, decorated with two pegs and endowed with the sense-organs, with nine outlets. It is attacked by the objects, is full of lust and anger. It has both love and hatred, thirst and poverty, entrapped in the network of covetousness, shrouded in the cloth of greed, bound by illusion. It is a city ruled by consciousness, in six vestibules and inhabited by *Puruṣa* (GP.II.21.35–38). As it has already been mentioned, the birth of Man is often compared with the "construction" of his body. One of the earliest descriptions of building the human body is the *Atharvaveda* hymn (AV X.2). The body is described there as a successive joining of organs in the direction from below to above. In the middle ages the image of the Man-town or the Man-fortress sometimes transforms into a very detailed description of a man as an architectural ensemble having a lot of details.

It is known that according to Hindu notions a human body is just a temporal abode. Birth is just transmigration, moving to another habitation. Before inviting a man into this world it is necessary to provide him with a new house. The whole chapter "On the Birth of Man" is devoted to the creation of mental image of the body – the body of *Puruṣa*, which was the most perfect sacrifice and at the same time the most perfect principle of world establishment.

As far as the image of the Man-town is concerned, GP gives a very condensed variant. It depicts not a "stronghold with perfect qualities", but a rather unattractive "structure", a conglomerate of negative emotions. On the whole the description of the Man-town is a construction of the image predetermined by the folk etymology, where the word *Puruṣa* is derived from *pur* (town). Such description which precedes the chapter on birth (i. e. "construction" of Man) supposes that it will be followed by the recommendations how to build a "more perfect" dwelling place and how to control it. It is the knowledge of these principles that one should have in order to realise the main aim of human birth, that is, the sacrifice of life. It is particularly stressed in the phrase immediately following the description: "Those people who do not realise themselves this way are similar to cattle" (GP II.21.39).

The chapter on birth is interesting because it repeats in miniature the subjects of the first book. Among other things there is also a treatise concerning the basic principles of construction. According to it a so-called *vastu-puruṣa* should lie at the basis of a building. Translated literally, "*vastu-puruṣa*" is "Man-place (for a House)". "His head is worshipped in the north-east, his feet – in the south-west, his arms – in the south-east and in the north-west" (GP I.46–47). The procedure of place consecration for a future building (*vastu-pūjā*) consisted of the correct placing and worshipping the guardian deities; thus, the future dwellers were saved from forthcoming misfortunes and illnesses. The ritual is based on the same scheme – *Puruṣa*'s image.

We should also note the "anatomical part" of the chapter "On the Birth of Man". This description looks like real life: the main attention is paid to quantitative proportions of different tissues of the man: "The fleshy matter in the body is about a thousand *palas* in weight, . . . the blood is a hundred *palas* in weight, . . . the fat is about ten *palas* and the skin is about that much. The marrow is about twelve *palas*, the blood plasma is three *palas* . . . and so on (GP.II.22.47–51). It goes without saying that this optimal quantitative composition of human body is but numerical symbolism and not the real state of affairs.

The most important to us is that the above-mentioned description joins the theme of sacrifice. It rather looks like a guide on performing a ritual, with instructions on what quantity of what material should be sacrificed. A text, devoted to the so-called *Nārāyaṇa-bali* ritual can serve as an example. The ritual is performed in the case when it is impossible to cremate a dead man and thus to complete the ritual of his life. In this case it is recommended to make a puppet or effigy of sacred *kuśa* grass as a substitute of his body: " The blades of *kuśa* grass should be tied well to constitute the different limbs. Forty blades of *kuśa* grass at head and ten at the neck. Twenty in the region of heart, twenty in the belly, hundred in the thighs and twenty at the hips. Four for penis, six for the testicles, ten for the toes" and so on (GP.II.30. 46–48). If we look at the description of the Man once again, we see that it is a list of optimal composition of a body "being prepared" for life, the main sense of which is sacrifice. Thus, the anatomical description serves the same aims as we have in the description of Man as town and vessel – introducing Man into the context of sacrifice, of which *Puruṣa* is its oldest symbol.

The chain of similes as variants of Man-realisation created by the tradition in different times, testifies to the fact that the birth is described in the text not literally but as a stage by stage embodiment of traditional notions of Man-Sacrifice. Along with such texts there was a special meditative practice in which, while concentrating, the practitioners created a special set of images on the basis of certain matrices consecrated by the tradition. It is difficult to say what appears first: religious practice or a new stage of the text development activity. Apparently both the text and the ritual are the result of a certain type of culture, which V. N. Romanov called "ritualistic".[9]

The chapter "On the Birth of Man" allots most of its space to the description of Man as the Egg of Brahma. Here the birth of Man is compared with the primary creation of the Universe and is described with the help of the same images that are used in description of the Egg of Brahma, which is the foetus of the universe. In the *Viṣṇu-purāṇa* the creation of the Egg is described as follows: the five elements not yet connected between themselves could not create living beings. Therefore they joined and formed the Egg, that was floating like a bubble on the surface of the water. The Egg was a dwelling place for Viṣṇu in the form of Brahma. There were continents and oceans, mountains and planets, parts of the universe, gods, demons and humanity (VP I.2.50–65).[10]

Meditation about one's body as the Egg of Brahma makes it possible to include it into the common mythological context and to transform it from formless mass of bones, flesh, emotions, etc. to the dwelling place of gods. The main principle of the text construction is successive description of the body as a receptacle of continents, oceans, mountains, rivers, planets and other worlds, in other words as the embodiment of *maṇḍalas* of the above mentioned phenomena. The first *maṇḍala* is the *maṇḍala* of worlds which formed the Universe in its projection upon the body. At the same time each world (there are 14 in the chapter) has its analogy in the body. Man's skeleton is formed by the seven higher regions, most frequently mentioned in the text: the *Bhūr* (The Earth) – in the centre of the navel; the *Bhuvar* (the Atmosphere) is above it. The *Svar* (the Sky) is in the heart. The *Mahar* is in the throat. The *Janas* is in the mouth; the *Tapas* is on the forehead. The *Satya* is in the aperture of the head. (GP.II.22.53–56). There are also seven lower regions descending from the earth one below the other: the *Patala* is in the hips, the private parts are *Mahātala*, the thigh is *Rasatala*; the calf is *Talātala*; the knee is *Satala*; the upper surface of the foot is *Vitala*; the sole of the foot is *Atala*. Thus, there is a typical vertical model of the Universe, where the most sacral and important place is situated on the top, and the less important and the lowest are situated below. Next *maṇḍala* embodied in Man is the *maṇḍala* of continents. It is based on the geographical notion which is typical for the *purāṇas*. Like in other cases, the theme that had a detailed coverage in the first book of GP, here is given a projection upon Man. In the first book the Earth was described as floating upon water and consisting of seven continents. The word *dvīpa* is literally translated as "the land surrounded by two streams of water". *Jambu-dvīpa* is situated in the centre of the world, then there are other continents surrounded by "seven oceans". They are the following: *Lavaṇa* (the Salt ocean), *Ikṣu* (sweet), *Sura* (Wine), *Sarpis* (Butter), *Dadhi* (Curd), *Dugdha* (Milk) and *Jala* (Water) oceans" (GP.I.54.5). Moreover each continent is situated around the subsequent ocean. So we have a concentric structure of the world, which resembles to a certain extent the inner side of a half of an egg cut in two. Such concentric situation of the continents is too schematic and by no means testifies to the fact that medieval Hindus did have such a fareiful understanding of geography. Most likely it is a verbal description of *maṇḍala* which helps to construct a scheme summarising the already existing knowledge of the Earth. In our case the authors of the *purāṇa* needed such a compact scheme which like a sacrificial formula of a ritual makes it possible to link the reflections on human birth with the creation of the universe.

The *maṇḍala* of the continents is projected on the human body as follows: "The *Jambu-dvīpa* is stationed in the bones; the *Śāka-dvīpa* in the marrow; the *Kuṣa* in the flesh; the *Krauñca* in the head; the *Śālmali* in the skin; the *Gomeda* in the hair; the *Puṣkara* in the nails." (GP.II.22.59–60). The oceans are situated as follows: "The Salt ocean is stationed in the urine; the Milk ocean is stationed in the phlegm; the Butter ocean in the marrow, the *Rasa* ocean in the lymphatic secretion; the Curd ocean in the blood; the Water ocean in the region of excreta and the Ocean of sugar cane juice in semen". (GP.II.22.61–62). Though within the body the location of continents and oceans is not presented geometrically, it is of formal character as well. In the basis of it there is just an outer similarity of the tissues and secretions of the organism with the substances from which geographic objects got their names. There are also other analogies. For example, the ocean of sour milk is located in blood, which coagulates – "curdles"; the milk ocean is located, naturally, in milk; the Salt ocean – in urine, etc. The source of identifying bones with *Jambu-dvīpa* lies in its name. It is so called since in its centre there is the *jambu* tree, around which the whole world is situated. This tree was considered to be the foundation of the universe. In the human body it is the skeleton which plays the part of the foundation and which becomes the symbol of *Jambu-dvīpa*. Thus the source of the similes of this kind is associative principle which testifies to the fact that here we have a kind of purely mental theoretical activity, the aim of which is the realisation of oneself as not only an embodiment of the world but main image of culture as well.

Another "geographic" *maṇḍala* existing within the body is the *maṇḍala* of mountains. "The mount Meru is in (upper) triangle; the mount Mandara is in the lower triangle; the mount Kailāsa is in the right; the Himālaya is in the left; the mount Niṣadha is in the upper surface. The Gandhamādana is to the right and the Ramaṇa is in the linear sections in the left side" (GP.II.22.57–58).

The researches explain such localisation very differently. According to one explanation the upper triangle is projected upon the triangular shoulder-blade, the lower one is projected upon the thighs[11] (it looks like a description of a man in a sitting position with crossed legs). Another interpretation is given by E. Abegg, a distinguished researcher of GP. He links the mountain localisation with their location in *maṇḍala* based upon a twelve-petal lotus, in the centre of which there is the sacred syllable "Aum". Referring to the commentary, he gives one more explanation, according to which the upper triangle is placed in the region of heart.[12]

Both the mountains and the continents are seven in number. The sacred mountains are situated in man's energetic centres which the *yogins* viewed as most important. In this case, of importance for us is not the exact place of mountain localisation, but the main principles of description making it possible to understand the meaning and purpose of the text. The fact that the *maṇḍalas* of all the phenomena are of anthropomorphic form is very important. Due to it they are all as if dissolving in the image of *Puruṣa.* It should be noted that the description of the creation of Brahma's Egg ends with the conclusion that the world created in the above-described way and consisting of earth, water, fire, air and ether, all the organs of perception and inner beings is called *Puruṣa* (VP I.2.65).

Both geographical and celestial objects are associated with *cakras,* the energetic centres. The body is viewed upon as a peculiar star map: "The Sun is stationed in the sound-circle; the Moon in the spot-circle (on the forehead); the Mars in the eyes; Mercury in the heart; the Jupiter in the navel; the Venus in the semen; the Saturn in the umbilical region; Rahu in the mouth and Ketu in the feet (GP.II.22.63–65).

Thus the text depicts not a process of formation and development of a living animated organism, but a process of mental joining of various symbolic systems connected with the image of Man. The more such systems are projected upon the human body the greater the volume of traditional notions embodied in Man. In this embodied organism each organ may be the analogy of a certain star as well as of some world, of a mountain, an ocean, etc. Thus, the body is realised as an original clot of *maṇḍalas* where each element in its turn has a whole bundle of analogies with this or that manifestation of the material world.

Such mental operation corresponds to the medieval religious practice, which pursues the aim of mystical communion of follower with the primary Universe. Such unity became possible in the case when both Man and the Universe have similar structure. The chapter "On the Birth of Man" is a text where all the necessary knowledge is given in a very compact form. As a matter of fact it is just a hint that there must be a wider variety of texts. As it turns out all this variety is included into the first book, where necessary disciplines are set forth to a greater or lesser extent. They are as follows: astrology, geography, medicine, sacrifice, building. All of them are based on the anthropomorphous image of the Universe. This scheme is used even in the notion of God. The example of it is the meditation upon the imagined image of Viṣṇu. The model of this meditation is like this: "Viṣṇu is he, whose mouth is fire, crest the firmament, navel the horizon, feet the earth; eyes the sun and the moon . . ., whose breath is the wind, whose hair are clouds and whose joints are the rivers . . .; whose belly are the four oceans (GP.I.2.21–23). Accordingly, "the moon has come out of his mind and the sun out of his eyes. The fire has come out of his mouth. . . . The earth has come out of his feet, the quarters out of his ears. The heaven has come out of his head" (GP.I.2.25–26).

Thus, it is exactly *Puruṣa* who was associated in the middle ages with the conception of perfection, underlying all these phenomena. It has to be borne in mind that *Puruṣa* was the first sacrifice from which the Universe appeared. That is why the cognition of the world based upon the schemes discussed by the *purāṇa* is equalled to sacrifice. It also refers to the chapter "On the Birth of Man" which is included in the book devoted to the ritual of the last life cycle, connected with death and cremation. Here there is a continuation of the subject that can be traced from the *gṛhya-sūtras,* where the whole of a householder's life was included in the sphere of ritual.

It should also be noted that the chapter is devoted not merely to the ritual actions, but to the mental operation, which owed its existence to the interpretation of corresponding rituals. A special world outlook and a special psycho-technique enabling to reach it acquire the status of sacrifice . It becomes possible on a certain level of the development of consciousness, when the latter begin to operate the separate system groups of symbols which permits to create analogies between the dissimilar phenomena and to transfer them from one symbolic system to another. Such analogies make it possible to create an integral picture of the world and replace mythological universality, which united a part and a whole, microcosm and macrocosm, nature and society in the time when abstract thinking was absent.[13] In the GP text immediately after the description of world creation from the body of Viṣṇu, which surprisingly resembles the sacrifice of *Puruṣa,* there is an enumeration of the main topics, an obligatory one for *purāṇas* as a specific genre. The *purāṇa* itself views these topics as the manifestations of God and equates the meditation on them with the meditation upon embodiment of Viṣṇu. In another text on meditation Viṣṇu is called "an eternal subject of all the speeches". In consecutive order he is announced to be a single whole with the Moon, the Sun, the five elements of the world (earth, water, fire, air, ether), with emotions (feelings) and with organs of perception, to be a single whole with the universe and with inner essence of Man, who contains in himself the world along with the capacity of giving birth and the place of the end of the whole existence. The *purāṇa* contents in a sense bring these principles into life. Using one and the same scheme based upon the image of *Puruṣa*-sacrifice for a great variety of phenomena it makes them sacral and transforms them into the embodiment of Viṣṇu. To show the paths of the manifestation of Viṣṇu in the universe, the whole traditional spectrum is used: genealogy, history of gods and sages, myths of origin of living being and people, stones and mountains, etc.; that is a great variety of works, united by the fact that they are based on a single anthropomorphous structure.

The above-mentioned scheme of *Puruṣa*-sacrifice is used even in understanding and description of history. Right before the account of the history of the universe, it is stated that Viṣṇu being manifested in the world as *Puruṣa* is at the same time the embodiment of *Kala* (Time). The same can be said about *purāṇa:* "the embodiment of Viṣṇu". The *purāṇas* themselves while determining their contents mark out the following five topics: (1) Creation (*sarga*); (2) Dissolution and Re-creation (*pratisarga*); (3) Genealogy (*vaṁśa*); (4) Periods of time with Manu as the primal ancestor (*manvantara*); (5) History of royal dynasties – solar and lunar (*vaṁśānucarita*). All of them this way or another are connected with the history of universe and the living beings, inhabiting it. In the later *purāṇas* as well as in GP, all these historical themes "drowned" in the ocean of subjects, from mythology to "scientific" treatises, and this enables us to mark out the encyclopaedism as the most important feature of the *purāṇas*. In other genres of traditional literature, however, the *purāṇas* are invariably called "stories about the past times". What is the reason for it? The answer can be found in the idea of sacrifice, where two categories proved to be congruent – the categories of time and space.

The history of organism formation as we saw it in the chapter "On the Birth of Man" was presented as a successive combination of the parts of the anthropomorphous universe. According to the same scheme the history of the universe was presented as collecting and joining together of all kinds of phenomena. The process of development was substituted by the process of creation of analogies between different objects. The chapter "On the Birth of Man" is an example of it. Man's coming into life is comprehended as a creation of a series of analogies corresponding to the parts of his body: it is supposed to be achieved both with the help of mythological images and with the help of geographic and astronomical symbols, the symbols coding the basic knowledge about the arrangement of the universe. The possibility of analogising all the above-mentioned phenomena is facilitated by the very fact of their being projected upon human body. In such a text history is understood as the world description – the description of the universal body of Viṣṇu, who is the embodiment of *Puruṣa* and *Kala* (time).

To sum up, we should note that in GP we deal with a rather peculiar concept of perfection, i.e. the concept of perfect principles as the foundation of all the world phenomena. This principle is primordial and is traced back to the time of world creation. The greater is the number of phenomena realised with the help of traditional schemes, the more perfect and sacral the universe would be and closer to perfection would man become. The aim of human life, which embodies in itself both the idea and the ideal of sacrifice, is therefore established as the reaching of final liberation, putting an end to the cycle of rebirths. The latter means nothing but the confluence with the primordial sources of the universe, overcoming personal ego, communion with the Absolute, embodied in the image of Viṣṇu.

Notes and References

1. *Rigvedasaṁhitā*, With the commentary of Sayanacharya. Ed. by F. Max Muller. Vol. 1–4, -L., 1890–1982.
2. *Garuḍapurāṇa*, Bombay, 1906.
3. *Śatapatha-brāhmana in the Mādhyananna-śākhā with Extracts from the Commentaries of Śāyana, Harisvāmin and Dvivedagaṅga*. Ed. by A. Weber. Berlin, 1855.
4. *Atharvavedasaṁhitā. With the comm. of Sāyanachārya*. Vol. 1–4, Bombay,1898.
5. T. Y. Elizarenkova, V. N. Toporov, 'K strukture AV. X. 2: opyt tolkovaniya v svete indiiskoi antropologii (Towards the Structure of AV.X.2: An Experiment of Interpretation in the Light of the Vedic Anthropology') *Literatura i kultura drevnei i srednevekovoi Indii* (The Literature and Culture of Ancient and Medieval India), Moscow, 1987, pp. 43–73.
6. *Yājñavalkya or the Institutes of Yājñavalkya with the Commentary Mitākṣara of Vijñāneśvara*, Ed. by B. Sh. Moghe, Bombay, 1892.
7. V. N. Romanov, *Istoricheskoye razvitiye kultury. Problemy typologii.* (Historical Development of the Culture. The Problems of Typology), Moscow, 1985, p. 63.
8. Ibid., pp. 92–93.
9. Ibid., pp. 58–59.
10. *Viṣṇupurāṇam*. Bombay, 1896.
11. *The Garuḍa purāṇa. Trans. and. Annot. by a Board of Scholars*, Delhi, 1982, P. III, 884.
12. E. Abbeg, *Der Pretakalpa des Garuḍa-Purāṇa*. Berlin, 1956, s. 208.
13. I. M. Dyakonov, *Arkhaicheskiye mify Vostoka i Zapada* (Archaic myths of the Orient and the Occident), M. 1990, p. 12.

TWELVE ❖ # Devotion and Dissent: Urban Heterodoxies in Medieval India and Western Europe – A Comparative Study

E. YU. VANINA

THE VERY ATTEMPT TO compare pre-modern (or later medieval) cities of the West with those of India may be opposed by many colleagues engaged in historical, cultural, religious or allied studies. Scholars working in the field of West European history, culture and religion quite rarely come together with their "Orientalist" colleagues to share the results of their respective findings. In too many cases the "Occidentalists" view the Orient as a kind of abnormal deviation from the only true and "progressive" model of development. Orientalists also turn to the West only to stress the uniqueness of the Eastern civilisations. Sometimes the specific features of the Orient are being looked upon as a proof of the East's backwardness and stagnation, sometimes as an evidence of its chosen spirituality, harmony and loyalty to the centuries' old way of life.

The comparative study presented here is being undertaken with a different purpose in mind. Whatever the specific features of countries and regions may be, whatever the differences between civilisations, religions and cultures may exist, all of them have been and are inseparable parts of human history and world culture. Even in medieval times, when the peoples of the globe had in many cases no idea of each other, humanity was nevertheless diversified and unified at the same time. Unity never meant the subjection to a single "rightful" model, while diversity never supposed the negation of common socio-economic and cultural laws of evolution. These laws or tendencies have had and are having now innumerable manifestations in concrete life. Even the parts of Great Britain have had well-known peculiarities of historical and cultural development; it has been more so in Europe, a variety of models and even much more so in India, a subcontinent and rainbow of races, cultures and ways of life. But it was out of this endless diversity that the real unity emerged, making Britain a part of the West, India a part of the East and all of them parts of the world civilisation. Medieval period in the West and in the East had different points of beginning and completion, different cultural backgrounds and pace of development, but these dissimilar societies had much in common as concerned various spheres of life, including social relations, moral norms and values. The article presents just a small part of thought-provoking material which may be obtained by comparative studies of medieval societies in the East and in the West. The purpose is not to provide answers for all questions arising from such a comparison, but to provide stimuli for further discussions, for cooperative efforts of the "Occidentalists" and "Orientalists" in historical and socio-cultural research.

Given all dissimilarities between the Indian and Western models of urban life, we may note that social functions of medieval cities were nearly the same. In Europe and in India cities were, albeit in different forms, military-administrative, economic, political and, what was more important for our study, religious and cultural centres. Both Indian and European cities were places of most revered and magnificent temples, shrines, monasteries and hospices; pilgrims flocked there, religious education, theological studies and discussions flourished; festivals were celebrated in luxury and pomp unheard-of in the countryside. Though true devotion to God required ascetic renunciation in a calm and peaceful atmosphere of a hermitage or monastery, many priests and theologians preferred noisy cities and even court life. Donations to temples and shrines, patronage and protection of all clerics were immediate duties of a ruler both in India and in the West. The unsophisticated souls of the villagers were considered by some medieval authors to be more pure and closer to God. Still urban people were looked upon as "civilised" (in many North Indian languages the word *nāgara* means both "urban" and "refined"; compare, for instance, with the English *urbane* from the Latin *urbanus*). Urban style of religious life was supposed to be more rightful and regular than the superstitious practices of the rural folk. Both medieval Indian and European authors mocked the ignorance and churlish manners of the village people, while in the Western medieval romances like *Le Charroi de Nimes* or *Yvain* a European peasant was described as an ugly monster and worshipper of Muhammad.[1]

As far as differences are concerned, two points are to be specifically stressed. Firstly, no religion in India has had such a strict and regular system of organisation as it was established by the Roman Catholic and

Russian Orthodox Churches. The very notion of church is irrelevant to Hinduism,[2] Jainism and even to the more structured Islam. Of course, every temple or mosque in India, with the exception of those which enjoyed a region-wide or a country-wide popularity, has usually had a more or less fixed number of worshippers residing in a neighbourhood; some shrines or temples belonged to certain castes or communities; the institution of family or community priests has been widespread, but there has been nothing equal to the system of parishes which has played an extremely important role in Europe. Influencing to a considerable extent all spheres of political and social life, neither Hinduism, nor Islam, nor any other religion in India created structures of power.

Secondly, medieval Indian cities, especially since the beginning of the so-called "Islamic period" of history, differed from their European counter-parts as concerned an extremely important aspect of life. While the pre-Reformation cities of the West were by and large homogeneous as concerned confessional composition of population with relatively small clusters of non-Catholics (mostly Jews), in India the majority of pre-modern cities exhibited a rainbow of religious communities. Muslims remained a minority throughout the whole period under review, as well as later, but their share in urban population was considerable, in some places coming upto 50 per cent or even more. Apart from Hindus and Muslims among the townspeople there were followers of Jainism, Zoroastrianism, Christianity, later on Sikhism. If we take into consideration that for many parts of India a city with population of 1,00,000 was considered a medium-size one, while some metropolitan cities like Delhi, Ahmadabad or Lahore had by the seventeenth century between half a million and a million of population each,[3] we see a picture quite different from that of pre-modern European cities.

In medieval European cities the non-Catholic residents usually lived in separate blocks; the sinister word *ghetto* originates from *geto* (foundry), a place where a special Jewish quarter was established in Venice in 1516.[4] It was easy to isolate the non-Catholics and to reduce their contacts with the majority of population to business traffic only, as it did happen in many European cities. In India the situation was different. There existed Hindu and Muslim *moḥalla*s (along with mixed ones)[5] but no ghetto-type clusters of religious minorities, for in the context of big cities in India a "minority cluster" might have had a population of tens or hundreds of thousands.

The Muslim rulers of India, no doubt, considered their faith to be the only true and styled all non-Muslims as infidels. Though some fanatical *'ulemā* urged the Muslim kings to offer their Hindu subjects the only choice of "death or Islam",[6] political reality and common sense pressed upon even the most bigoted Muslim kings to be tolerant to the Hindus who constituted an overwhelming majority of tax-payers. In the Hindu principalities Muslims were looked upon as a tolerated minority occupying its particular place in the caste hierarchy. The history of medieval India abounds in examples of the Muslim kings donating lands and money to the Hindu shrines and Hindu Raja patronising mosques and *madrasahs*.[7] But apart from these manifestations of the rulers' political wisdom and spiritual pursuits (in the case of Akbar both rolled in one), there was everyday life of the crowded cities where Hindus and Muslims were destined to live, work, suffer and rejoice together, rubbing shoulders in the narrow streets and noisy bazaars.

Many descriptions of medieval Indian cities stressed the above-mentioned peculiarity of urban life. For example, Vidyapati Thakur, the great poet from Mithila (second half of the fourteenth century-beginning of the fifteenth) left a colourful picture of the populous city of Jaunpur: 'Here Muslims pronounce "bismillah" and slaughter cattle, there Hindus offer sacrifices to the Gods; here they perform namāz, there they perform pūjā; here dwell the Ojhas, there reside the Khwajas'.[8]

No doubt, peaceful coexistence of Hinduism and Islam in urban environment was hardly possible without tension or sometimes clashes-in Vidyapati's words, "what is being looked upon as dharma by one kind of people is but a mockery according to another."[9] The bigoted policies of some rulers also added fuel to fire. But on the whole medieval cities of India were rather places of tolerance, making it possible for the followers of different religions to not only perform their rituals freely, but to cooperate and even have some common values, attitudes and sacred objects.

This phenomenon is to be explained by a number of socio-religious factors, but here noteworthy are those connected with the specific features of urban life. The very fact of concentration of the huge masses of population belonging to the two different faiths (Zoroastrians and Christians were small communities residing in a number of places only; Jains and later on Sikhs were generally looked upon as Hindu sects) appealed to the common sense and reason of the people who just wanted to live in peace and allowed others to do the same. Both religions and. philosophical traditions allied to them have had premises for the ideas of coexistence as well as for the ideas of the opposite character. But a social aspect peculiar to urban life is worth discussing.

The Muslim community in India has always been and is now heterogeneous, a rainbow of ethnic, cultural and social groups. They have entered the intricate system of the Hindu caste society and established their own hierarchy of castes, clans, sects. As a result many professions and social grades in the urban society were represented by a parallel structure of Hindu and Muslim castes. This may be described as a negative development leading to communal clashes and social discord,[10] but there was another side also.

This parallel structure of Hindu and Muslim caste divisions pertaining to a majority of urban professions and social groups, from nobles to craftsmen, made it possible for the followers of different religions to feel the community of their lifestyles, joys and sorrows. No doubt, every one considered his own faith to be the best, but in the city bazaar a Hindu weaver (*korī* or *tantī*) and his Muslim counterpart (*julāhā*) had their shops side by side; both equally suffered from poverty and oppression. From the available sources we know that religious differences were no obstacle for business and intellectual contacts, as well as friendship and other kinds of human relationship; all attempts by the orthodox teachers of every religion to limit the contacts were in vain.[11] This parallel structure was a peculiarity of the Indian cities; in the villages where population was relatively small and a different type of social hierarchy existed, nothing of this kind was possible, although a certain experience of communal harmony was developed by the villagers as well. Of especial significance here was the fact that many Muslims were converted Hindus who continued to be loyal to many traditions and practices of their pre-Islamic past. As a result a unique feeling of community emerged which made a Hindu and a Muslim, bound together by the same profession, social status, regional identity and language, feel closer to each other than to their respective co-believers who belonged to higher or lower social strata or other regions. This factor explains to a certain extent why quite a number of Muslims supported the anti-Mughal movements and in some cases fought for the Sikh *Khālsā* or Maratha *Swarājya*,[12] as well as why some Hindu princes struggled on the Mughal side against their co-believers. In this sense Mughal India differed much, for example, from the Christian domains of the Ottoman Empire where Muslim minority was a ruling elite opposed to the "infidels", also from European countries where non-Catholic communities were segregated and confined to a limited number of professions.

It was but natural that cities as centres of religious life, as places where huge masses of population were concentrated became the stage for the activities of so many heretical sects and movements. Throughout the whole of medieval period, from Britain to Japan, one could have observed the spreading of urban heterodoxies. It would hardly be an over-estimation to presume that this was an objective law of historical and social development of medieval societies, different as they were. Given all diversities of forms, ideological background and historical destinies of these sects, all of them had much in common and perhaps had been brought to life by the same historical process.

The essence of this process was the growing discrepancy between the socio-economic, political and cultural development of a given society and the postulates of the "official" religion, its philosophical and ethical norms as well as the whole social order sanctified by it. In different countries this disparity was realised in peculiar forms. In the West they just compared the principles of the early Christian communities with the real situation to arrive at the conclusion that "virgin Church became a harlot".[13] In India many factors of socio-economic, technological and ethno-cultural development made the real role of various castes and social groups totally different from what had been prescribed by the holy books of Hinduism.

Perhaps the ideal caste society of the "laws of Manu" had never existed at all, but the growing fragmentation of castes, especially due to the development of new technologies and labour division in urban industries, changes in the caste hierarchy, social uplift of traders and craftsmen along with the degradation of so many brahmans, the domination of the Muslim *mlecchas* – all these and other such developments had brought the Hindu society too far from the traditional social norms. Urban life was especially responsible for the emergence of new professional occupations as well as changes in social structure and laws of caste purity: in Vidyapati's words, so thick was the city crowd that "one's caste mark was stamped on another's forehead and a Brahman's sacred thread was found hanging around an untouchable's neck".[14] A Muslim also had to see violations of his holy law everywhere and was forced by the very course of life to break it all the while. In any case both in India and in Europe this discrepancy was looked upon as an ungodly anomaly, a deviation from the true road of God's behests; so changes were in demand, especially in the sphere of religion and social life.

Medieval reformist sects and movements have been well studied in the European environment. Medieval India also produced a wide and variegated picture of urban heterodoxies and mystical sects. These are known under two general terms: those based upon Islam as *Taṣawwūf* or Sufism, those based upon Hinduism as *Bhakti*. In the latter case it has to be noted, however, that there was nothing heretical in *Bhakti* itself – as a path of communion with God it has been an integral part of the Hindu religion since the earliest times of its history. But it were medieval sects that proclaimed *Bhakti* to be the main and most effective pathway to God, superior to all other ways and, contrary to what the orthodox brahmans taught, open to men and women from every caste and social group. Hence our discussion of *Bhakti* will concern this spiritual phenomenon only as the religious and ideological foundation of medieval heretical movements within the fold of Hinduism. One of the *Bhakti* sects later on emerged into a separate religion, Sikhism. Each of these trends of heretical thought was indeed a rainbow of sects sometimes holding polar views on the most important matters of religious and social life. None of the medieval sectarian movements in India was exclusively urban in origin or composition: they harboured people from all walks of life, but, much like the West, in India leading role was played by urban traders and artisans, at least when the movement had reached its maturity.[15]

Notwithstanding the civilisational and confessional differences the preachers of medieval heresies in Europe and India had a number of similar conceptions, attitudes and socio-ethical norms. For all of them the inner sincerity of devotion had a doubtless priority over the formal, outwordly sides of religious cult. They stood as if united in their opposition to idol worship, ceremonies, fasts, pilgrimages, asceticism. Kabir the weaver from Varanasi, one of the greatest *Bhakti* preachers, argued:

> Holy tirthas are but water, there is nothing in it, see.
> The image of God is dead, brother, and mute, see.
> The Puranas and the Quran are mere words, unveil thy soul.
> Kabir judges by experience: all these are but trumpery, see![16]

Similar views were held by the Lollards who insisted that "holy watir halwed be a prest is of no mor effect than the watir of the river or of a welle", that "no worship ne reverence oweth be do to any ymages of the Crucifix, of Our Lady, ne noon other Seyntes for all such ymages be but ydols and. maade be working of mannys hands".[17] The God worshipped by medieval reformers both in India and in the West dwelt neither in the churches nor in the temples but in a true devotee's sincere heart, as well as in all Nature around. Thus, according to the Lollards, "material churches be but of litel availe, for every mannys prayer said in the field is as good as the prayer said in the churche".[18] Kabir's God addressed his devotees as follows:

> Where dost thou search for me, oh slave? I'm just nearby.
> Neither in the temple am I, nor in the mosque, nor in Ka'aba,
> nor in Kailasa.
>
> Nor in any funeral rites, nor in asceticism, nor in yoga.
> Whoever looks for me, will find me in no time . . .
> Hari's abode is in the East, Allah's abode is in the West,
> But in thy heart do thou search, there is Karim, there is Rama.[19]

Same was the position of many Sufis who preferred "going around the Ka'aba of heart" to the formal rituals of Islam.[20] While for the followers of a number of European heretical sects human body itself was a church and God's abode,[21] Basava, the twelfth century South Indian *Bhakti* saint, said:

The rich raise temples, but, poor as I am,
This shall I do: my legs for pillars,
My body for sanctum, my head the golden kalaśa complete.[22]

Mysticism was supposed to be the most genuine and trustworthy link between devotee's heart and God in a situation when the "official religion" had emerged as a religion of mere observances and, in the words of S. E. Ozment, was featured by "an absence of the institutionally valid lay piety."[23] Mysticism was an inseparable part of medieval heterodoxies both in India and in Europe; these mystical approaches were in many cases the same as it was, for instance, demonstrated by S. Eveland's comparative study of the mystical poetry by Mechthild von Magdeburg and Mirabai.[24] Comparative studies of this kind bring out interesting results. The Sufis preached that, in the words of the famous nineteenth century mystic Sharafuddin Maneri, God was "the beloved of souls and the desired of hearts",[25] and the ocean of Sufi poetry, Indian, Persian, Arabic, Turkish, etc., was a priceless evidence of the creativity of this attitude. Perhaps in India medieval mysticism produced a greater variety of forms and emotional experiences. The followers of *Bhakti*, especially in its *Saguṇa* type, offered the God-seekers a variety of pathways correlated with a rich variety of human emotions and psychological states[26] like parental tenderness, loyalty of a friend, slavish reverence and erotic passion. It required a lot of dramatic changes in the very core of religious consciousness so that Krishna the mighty and frightening god, the one who had scared even the fearless hero Arjuna, gave way to Krishna the merry butter-thief, the darling of the Vrindavan milkmaids.[27] Medieval European mystics also looked for alternative to the morbid "official religion" and this quest brought them to the same way of love and devotion. Thus Quillaume Farel, the contemporary of Mirabai, wrote that the essence of religion was "an affection, an experience and a true knowledge that God our father is good, perfect, powerful and wise",[28] while for Sebastian Franck "the very science of piety" was just "pressed into the tablets of our heart . . . by the finger of the living God".[29] It is noteworthy that the absence of erotic pigment in the palette of the Christian religious emotionalism (correlated with the general view of sexual love as a sin) was felt and filled to a certain extent by the Christian mystics, in whose writings erotic allusions were present,[30] but in not as colourful and poetic way as in *Saguṇa Bhakti.*

Perhaps the stages and emotional-psychological experience of Indian and European mystics were different but what really united them was the negation of all intermediaries between God and devotee, who, in Maneri's words, "received the truth and divine knowledge directly from God without intermediaries".[31] Both Indian and European mystics and heretical teachers held a very negative attitude towards professional priesthood and monkhood. In their satirical exposition of the hypocritical and greedy brahmans and mullahs, ascetics and yogis the *Bhakti* and Sufi poets were worthy counterparts of Ulrich von Hutten, Erasmus and other celebrities of the Reformation in their biting anti-clericalism.[32] The idea of priesthood of all believers, equally promoted by the Lollards, Hussites, Anabaptists, other protestant sects as well as Sufis and *Bhaktas*, including Sikhs, quite logically came out of the negation of formal religion and all mediators between God and man. "Every Christen man is a prest",[33] – said the Lollards, and the quest for the "institutionally valid lay piety" led practically all medieval reformers to the conclusion that real piety was not in formal ceremonies or theological scholarship (the latter was treated in an equally negative way) but in sincere devotion, mercy and kindness.

Thus Diepold Peringer, a German protestant preacher and a participant of the famous sixteenth century peasant war, argued: "If you want to find Him, go over to your neighbour's house where small children lay sick and hungry and give them what you would otherwise uselessly squander or sacrifice to some idol."[34] Of the same opinion was Malukdas, a seventeenth century follower of Kabir:

> One who gives water to the thirsty is a true slave of the Prophet.
> One who gives food to the hungry will reach God at once.[35]

Representing in most cases the burger and plebeian masses, both Indian and West European heresy teachers looked with equal disdain upon all those "seeking God in books" along with all kinds of scholarly activities.[36] However medieval reformist movements were supported by the representatives of the educated elite, humanists, scholars and writers who tried to combine the ideas of religious reform with the quest for scientific discoveries and philosophical contemplations as well as working in the fields of literature and fine arts. Nevertheless for the majority of medieval dissenters God belonged primarily to the common people and spoke the unsophisticated language of their hearts. Hence there was no need for a canonical language, be it Latin, Sanskrit or Arabic. Indian and Western heresy teachers expounded their views and preached in vernacular languages, used folklore, proverbs, jokes, songs and fables to bring their message to the grassroots. In both cases it was a valuable contribution to the development of modern languages and literatures. But there was a noteworthy difference between Indian and Western realities.

All believers in Christ were equal in the eyes of God and had equal access to the churches and shrines as well as holy books though the latter were not recommended by the clerics for the "profane reading".

The Latin language and the hypocrisy of priests were considered to be the only obstacles barring the bürgers' access to the "genuine and unspoilt" word of God. Thus Luther's translation of the Bible was a logical and inevitable step. But in India low castes were not allowed to enter temples and read the holy texts, the main obstacle being not the language, but caste prejudices. Hence the Indian reformers who acted in the fold of Hinduism and in many cases themselves belonged to the lower castes, were engaged not in the translation of the Hindu holy texts into spoken languages, but in producing new versions which differed to a considerable extent from the Sanskrit original. Indeed, one can hardly define, for instance, the medieval *Rāmāyaṇas*, including Tulsidas' masterpiece, as mere translations of Valmiki's epic. In some cases like Sikhism, Kabir Panth or Dadu Panth they even created new holy scriptures based upon the utterances of the saints themselves.

These circumstances had a direct bearing upon the socio-ethical attitudes of medieval reformers. Both in India and in the West they were opposed to greed and ambition, excessive riches and pauperism. Their ideal was very much the same: a modest, hardworking craftsman, trader or peasant, his hands engaged in honest labour, his mind absorbed in God. The latter, according to medieval dissenters, needed no ascetic renunciation to serve him. A decent family life, a middle course between too much wealth and too much poverty along with charity, purity of heart and simplicity were supposed to be the most attractive and rightful paths of devotion. Even the apostles of the "protestant ethics" like Calvin or Zwingli were against usury and excessive profiteering; they urged their followers to work without any hope for enrichment or reward[37] – that would rather remind us of the passage from the *Bhagavad Gītā*,[38] not of "proto-capitalism".

According to Guru Nanak, only one who toiled for his bread and shared the fruit of his labour with those in need, knew the real path to God, contrary to those who styled themselves as teachers of truth and lived by begging.[39] The latter ideas was especially important for India where manual labour was traditionally looked upon as a defiling attribute of the low and untouchable castes and where there existed a distinction between "clean" and "unclean" kinds of work. Both Sufis and *Bhaktas* elevated labour and castigated the traditional attitudes to it. "Work is praiseworthy, all prophets did so", – argued Maneri, – but one has to work only to think about God".[40] All members of the Sufi brotherhoods were obliged to do some kind of manual labour; the Sikh gurus urged their followers to scorn no work. Even Ramdas, the famous Marathi saint, known to be more traditionalistic in his approaches refused to discriminate between "pure" and "impure" work and stressed the validity of labour.[41]

Bhakti devotion allowed the low caste members to overcome the inferiority complex, to obtain self-respect and spiritual protection as it happened, for instance, with the untouchable tanner Raidas (fifteenth century):

> Oh townspeople, all of you know,
> That I am a tanner and chamār by caste.
>
> But the noble brahmans bow to me since
> Raidas obtained shelter in (God's) name.[42]

The *Bhakti* preachers viewed all people as equal in God's eyes and the path of salvation offered by them was open to any one of whatever sex, caste, wealth or position. But they held different opinions as concerned social equality. Some saints like a number of early South Indian *Bhakti* poets, Tulsidas or Ramdas realised equality only in the spiritual context which had nothing to do with real life; some felt that preservation of caste hierarchy was a stronghold of social stability and well-being. They created their own Utopia like the kingdom of Rama, where all people strictly observed the laws of caste purity and at the same time were equally protected by Rama, the guardian of *dharma*. The radical *Bhaktas* as well as Sufis were bold enough to correlate the equality in God's eyes with the egalitarian ideas. Kabir, Raidas, Nanak, Akho Bhagat, Sarvajna, Purandara and other saints rejected the very foundation of caste system, i.e. the concept of purity. Kabir declared all thirty-six castes to be equal and pure; for him the untouchable Raidas was a holy man, while the purest brahman was "good-looking, but inside full of filth". Akho Bhagat, the seventeenth century Gujarati saint insisted that only fools boasted of their caste and even damned those observing *varṇāśrama* rules to be unhappy and childless.[43] Sarvajna from Karnataka argued:

> When light enters Pariah's house, is it also outcaste?
> Oh, talk not of high caste and. outcaste . . .
> We all tread the same Mother Earth.[44]

The social Utopia of the radical saints was not the caste idyll of the kingdom of Rama, but the Begampura (meaning at the same time the "Queen City" and "City of No Sorrows"). This city, created by the poetic imagination of Raidas, was an abode of prosperity and happiness, where "all were equal, no second or third class people", where "everyone could go wherever he wanted and entry to no place was prohibited".[45]

Medieval Hindu reformers are sometimes reproached by scholars for the limited and non-militant character of their egalitarian ideas which were aimed rather at "individual salvation or mystical union with God" and not so much at "a change in the living conditions of the masses".[46] Indeed, even the most persistent advocates of social equality in medieval India looked quite tame and inactive in comparison with the preachers of the radical Reformation in Europe. But here one has to bear in mind an important factor.

In medieval Europe the heretical sects and the Reformation preachers could avail themselves of the egalitarian principles of the early Christian communities, of the poverty of Jesus and his apostles, of the very doctrinal and social basics of Christianity where a noble knight and a base serf had equal access to the churches, shrines, festivals and all components of worship with no "pure" and "impure" in the realm of the faith itself. The memories of "good old days" of the primitive semi-tribal life of the rural communities were also helpful and enabled the reformers to ask: "When Adam delved and Eve span who was then a gentleman?" The Sufi saints also found support in the declared, albeit never fully realised, principle of equality of all Muslims.

The Hindu reformers had no such support. Neither in the holy books of Hinduism, nor in the contemplations of the sages nor in the popular tradition and dreams of the Golden Age was there a place for egalitarian principles. A low caste person or an untouchable were not just socially degraded, but they were looked upon as sources of pollution, as sinners partaking of the fruit of their evil deeds in previous birth; they were not only scorned and detested, but caused physical aversion.

Thus the task of medieval Hindu reformers was much more difficult than that of their Western counterparts: to change the society not in accordance with the foundations of the creed, but to change the very core of religion and the social order sanctified by it. The social criticism and reformism of the radical *Bhaktas*, moderate as it was in comparison with that of Muntser, Anabaptists or Hussites, required much more efforts and boldness. The Indian heretical teachers never tried to force all people to live according to the newly proclaimed rules. They just established a new social order in their sects and fraternities where admission was open to all. In many sects all caste differences were abolished, members were free to participate in communal feasts, cook and eat together. To become a Sikh or even to meet the Guru one had to share the food specially prepared in the *guru kā langar* (communal kitchen) with other members of the sect and even for the Mughal emperor Akbar no exception was made. Communal feasts were practised by the European reformist sects as well, but in India they were, no doubt, of special significance, since people belonging to different castes were traditionally prohibited to eat together and food was supposed to be polluted by a mere look by an untouchable.

Reformist sects and fraternities offered their members a new identity, allowing the humiliated and the oppressed to raise their heads. Thus the rules of the *Sādhs*, a Northern Indian sect which became popular in the late Middle Ages, stated: "When asked what you are, declare yourself a Sadh, speak not of caste". The same rules urged the members to "acknowledge but one God . . . to him is all the worship due, not to earth, stone, metal, wood (i.e. idols-E.V.)", to be modest, to respect other people's property rights, to avoid covetousness, to shun dances and music except holy hymns, also to avoid enjoying tales, theatre shows, etc. The *Sādhs* were obliged to wear plain white clothes, never to use perfumes and jewellery, betel, wine, tobacco. The rules also insisted: "bow not your head in the presence of idols or man, assume not mendicant's garb nor solicit alms".[47] These regulations perhaps might have been approved by Calvin and Puritans.

One should bear in mind, however, that all efforts to bring the egalitarian ideas into practical life of medieval society failed, both in India and in Europe. Many communities founded by the *Bhakti* saints as well as the Sikh *Khālsā* of Guru Gobind either got transformed into separate castes or became caste-ridden. This transformation was similar to that of the Hussite Tabor which had been established as a community of equals and gradually degraded into a typical medieval city with its guild-based industries and social oligarchy.[48] Nevertheless these experiences were in both cases useful as they helped to lay the foundation of further development of egalitarian and reformist thought. It was not by chance that the nineteenth and twentieth century reformers of social life and religion in India revered the Sufi and *Bhakti* preachers as predecessors.

There was, however, a sphere where the views of medieval Indian reformers and heresy teachers were absolutely different from the position of their Western counterparts. For a majority of *Bhaktas*, Sikhs and. for quite a number of Sufis all religions were equally true paths to the Universal God, the one and the same for the whole world albeit worshipped under different names. One could go to mosque, temple or church, address God as Allah, Vishnu or Jesus; but, as the Indian saints taught, it was only a pure heart and sincere devotion that really mattered while all outword forms of religious cult were looked upon as a "trumpery". The Indian saints spared no bitter words to condemn religious strife, fanaticism and discrimination between the "true" and "false" religion. In Kabir's mind, the priests of both Hinduism and Islam were equally vicious and hypocritical; none of them really knew "God's secret".[49] For Dadu Dayal, the sixteenth century saint from Ahmadabad, an infidel was not a follower of a "wrong" faith but one who spoke falsehood and did not keep his heart pure.[50] Garibdas, the successor and perhaps the son of Dadu, in his work *Anabhay Prabodha* (1608) listed all Hindu and Muslim epithets of God as equally rightful and summed it up with a line: "Innumerable are God's names, but Hindus and Muslims have the same creator".[51] In a passionate appeal for unity Malukdas wrote:

> Mecca, Medina, Dvaraka, Badrinath and Kedarnath-
> Without mercy all are false in Maluka's opinion . . .
>
> Elephant and ant, man and beast – God dwells in all of them.
> Should one kill a God's creature to be listed among heroes?
>
> Hindus and Muslims alike worship the same God,
> God's bliss is due to him only whose faith is solid.[52]

Gobind Singh, the Sikh Guru under whom this sect acquired a final touch of a distinct community, the valiant leader of the anti-Mughal war, stated: "One is a Hindu, another a Sunni, or Shia Muslim, but all of them belong to one caste, the caste of men". He also authored a hymn in which God was praised and worshipped equally by Hindus, Muslims and other peoples of the globe, including English and French.[53] For many Sufis kindness and tolerance towards the Hindus were but instruments in their proselytising activity; salvation was possible in their view only within the fold of Islam, the only true religion.[54] But there were Sufis who considered Islam and Hinduism as equally valid pathways to the Universal God. Thus Nur ud-din Rishi, a famous Kashmiri Sufi and a follower of the Shaivite woman saint Lalleshwari, said:

> Among the brothers of the same parents
> Why did you create a barrier?
> Muslims and Hindus are one.
> When God will be kind to his servants?[55]

The seventeenth century Sufi poet Barkatullah (note his *Bhakti*-style pen name Pemi) was bold enough to condemn Aurangzeb's bigotry and the destruction of the Hindu temples. He argued:

> Hindus and Muslims alike possess all the virtues.
> The same light illuminates both the temple and the mosque.[56]

A similar approach was adopted by the free-thinkers of later medieval India like Abu-l Fazl Allami, his brother Faizi, other "enlightened philosophers" of Akbar's court and further by Dara Shukoh, Prannath, etc. They combined the simple universalism of the Sufi and *Bhakti* saints with the rationalistic research and comparative analysis of different creeds like Hinduism, Islam, Christianity and Judaism to arrive at the conclusion that all religions had many similar values and none of them was free from obsolete dogmas and unreasonable practices; thus no faith was to claim superiority and no faith was to be condemned as false.[57]

One has to bear in mind that even the most liberal and daring minds of the Reformation and Humanism in Europe were not ready to acknowledge for the non-Christians the right to be just "other worshippers of God" (as Abu-l Fazl styled all non-Muslims). Tolerance and freedom of worship advocated by the Western humanists and reformers concerned Christians only; all others were to obtain salvation in the "true religion" or to be damned as pagans and enemies of Christ.[58] At worst the "unbelievers" were hated and persecuted, at best pitied and described as the poor souls ignorant of the only rightful faith; in both cases they had to be converted by coercion or by kindness; the only difference between the humanistic and the orthodox position here was in the former's emphasis upon more compassionate attitude towards the "ignorant pagans".

No doubt, India had enough fanatics to match Torquemada, Mary Tudor or Henri de Guise. But while in Europe the Reformation and the Counter-reformation held similar or nearly similar views concerning the non-Christians and their right to follow their creed, while the Protestants and their Catholic opponents were equally intolerant and oppressive towards each other, in India both Muslim and Hindu reformers, plebeian and elitist, were active opponents of fanaticism and advocates of communal amity. Their universalist approach, along with its development in the *ṣulḥe-kul* policies of Akbar (a contemporary, it would not be out of place to recall, of the bloody religious wars in Europe), was, in our mind, one of the most important contributions of medieval India to world culture and deserves to be studied more attentively.

Religious-reformist movements in India and in the West had a number of similar features like their predominantly urban origin, socio-ethical views and forms of activity. In both cases, as rightfully observed by K. Schomer, these movements were diverse and had a variety of mystical ways, philosophical and social doctrines.[59] The sects which for quite a long time preached humility and meekness, could, during social or national crises, grow militant and introduce significant changes into their ideology and practice. For instance, Sikhism had a number of features comparable with the Hussite movement. Indeed, each of them was a combination of liberation war against the "aliens"; religious reform and social protest, both began with a peaceful sectarianism and turned militant after the martyrdom of their spiritual leaders (Guru Arjun, Jan Hus and Jeronym Prazsky); both had radical elements in conflict with the moderates (the followers of Guru Gobind versus the *ṭāṭ* Sikhs; the Adamites and radical Taborites versus the Calixtines). Social composition, doctrinal approaches and ethic values of the two movements had much in common; both tried, and equally in vain, to implement their ideas in the "liberated zones" like Tabor or Anandpur.[60]

Now, the readers have every right to ask: does it really mean that medieval India has lived through "that very" Reformation similar to that of pre-modern Europe? Moreover, for any one who has studied history, especially in the Marxist perspective, Reformation means an overture to the advent of capitalism; the "potentialities" of the latter have been anatomised by Prof. Irfan Habib and the verdict was pronounced with no counter-appeal possible.[61]

It will bring our study too far from the chosen subject if we enter the "potentialities" discussion. As for the scholars' attitude to the concrete problem of medieval heterodoxies in India, K. Schomer, for example, has viewed *Bhakti* as "analogous in many ways to the Protestant Reformation of Christianity".[62] In her turn, Krishna Sharma has criticised the researchers in whose opinion *Bhakti* was an anti-feudal movement.[63] Reviewing the debates, E. Zelliot could not forbear scepticism: "The *Bhakti* movement has been seen as an Indian counterpart of the Protestant Reformation, with one or another of its poet-saints, usually Kabir, sometimes Chaitanya, filling the role of Luther". Further on she stated that "Kabir was certainly no Luther in terms of establishing an inclusive organized challenge to the established religion, but he was a Protestant".[64]

Indeed, Prof. Zelliot's scepticism is justified if one sees the only one "progressive" way of socio-cultural development and imagines the latter to be as straight as a modern urban avenue. But it was hardly so in reality and in many cases the components of what we understand now as "progress" were rather independent from each other. For example, one may take late medieval Germany, the land of Luther and Muntser, one of the major centres of Reformation. The "overture" to capitalism was impressive, no doubt, but the main show was much belated and even in the first half of the nineteenth century the major part of Germany remained a reservation of semi-feudal relations, lagging much behind other European countries.

It would be wrong, no doubt, to depict Kabir as a *dhotī*-clad Luther. Luther's role was to be performed by Luther only, not even by Wycliffe or Hus. But if we perceive the fundamental unity and boundless diversity of mankind, if we believe in equal validity of all socio-economic and cultural models of evolution, we may suppose that the medieval mysticism and heretical teachings in Europe, the analogous ideologies and practices in India, China, Iran, Russia, etc., and the Protestant Reformation were manifestations of the same above-mentioned law of historical development of medieval societies and religions. In every case the reform movements passed through different stages of development correlated with the most burning problems of a given epoch or civilisation. Sometimes it was a protest of the primitive communities against the feudal offensive and violation of "good old laws", sometimes it was an objective necessity to accelerate the socio-economic, cultural, ethnic or political evolution of a society and to remove all obstacles from its way; sometimes it was a deep structural crisis and the emergence of new socio-economic order.

Temporal characteristics and concrete implementation of this development varied in different countries and epochs. Thus Muqanna, Babek, Iranian *Sarbedārs* and early *Bhaktas* were more close to the early medieval mystics and reformist sects of Europe, like, for example, Albigenses or Waldenses. Kabir, Nanak, Malukdas had much in common with Wycliffe or Lollards while the Sikhs were comparable with the Hussites and other movements of the early Reformation. Different religions, dissimilar civilizations brought about movements and trends of religious, social and ethical thought which were to a considerable extent analogous in their approach to the problems of their respective societies. It is an example of the dialectical link between general laws and specific features of historical evolution, appealing to all of us, the researchers into the Oriental and Occidental civilisations, to keep constantly in mind that we study the parts of the integrate humanity and if we bring together and compare the results of our researches, we may come closer to the historical truth.

Notes and References

1. I have consulted the Russian translation of Chretien de Troyes' *Yvaine* by V. Mikushevich (Moscow, 1974, p. 37) and of *Le Charroi de Nimes* by Yu. Korneyev (Moscow, 1976, p. 240).
2. So much so, that some scholars like H. Von Stietencron even doubt the applicability of the term "Hinduism" arguing that what is having been usually meant by it is not a unified creed but a complex of different religions; vide: H. Von Stietencron, 'Hinduism: On the Proper Use of the Deceptive Term', G.D. Sontheimer and H. Kulke, eds., *Hinduism Reconsidered*, Delhi, 1991, pp. 11–27.
3. H. Kh. Naqvi, 'Shahjahanabad: An Introduction', R.E. Frykenberg ed., *Delhi Through the Ages. Essays in Urban History, Culture and Society*, Delhi, 1986, pp. 145–46; I. Habib, 'Non-Agricultural Production', I. Habib and T. Raychaudhury (eds.), *The Cambridge Economic History of India*, Vol. I, Cambridge, 1982, p. 171.
4. L. W. Spitz , *The Protestant Reformation 1517–1559.* New York, 1985, p. 356.
5. S. Nurul Hasan, 'The Morphology of a Medieval Indian City: A Case Study of Shahjahanabad', Indu Banga (ed.), *The City in Indian History*, Delhi, 1991, pp. 89–90.
6. Kh. A. Nizami, *Studies in Medieval Indian History and Culture*, Allahabad, 1966, p. 23; Muzaffar Alam, 'Indo-Islamic Interaction in Medieval North India', *Itinerario*, XIII 1989, I, pp. 51–54.
7. M. Athar Ali, 'Encounter and Efflorescence. Genesis of Medieval Civilization', *Presidential Address. 50th Session of the Indian History Congress. Proceedings,* Delhi, 1991 , p. 9.

8. Vidyāpati Ṭhākur, *Kīrtilatā.* Ed. by V. Agravāl. Jhānsī, 1962 , pp. 111–14.
9. Vidyāpati Ṭhākur, *Kīrtilatā*, p. 111.
10. For an example of such an interpretation vide A. L. Srivastava, *Akbar the Great*, Vol. III Agra, 1973, p. 56.
11. B. Ambastha, *Non-Persian Sources of Indian Medieval History*, Delhi, 1983, p. 22; A. J. Syed, 'State, Religion and Society: Medieval India. Problems of Interpretation', *Presidential Address. 47th Session of the Indian History Congress. Proceedings*, Delhi, 1986, pp. 212–13; M.P. Singh, *Town, Market, Mint and Port in the Mughal Empire 1556–1707*, Delhi, 1985, p. 274.
12. A. R. Kulkarni, 'Social Relations in the Maratha Country Medieval Period', *Presidential Address. 32nd Session of the Indian History Congress.* Reprinted in: A.R. Kulkarni, *Marathas and the Maratha Country*, Vol. I 'Medieval Maharashtra', pp. 118–20; Surinder Singh Kohli, *The Life and Ideas of Guru Gobind Singh*, Delhi, 1986, p. 8.
13. J. Hillerbrandt, *The Reformation: A Narrative History Related by Contemporary Observers and Participants*, New York, 1964, p. 223. The cited statement is by Thomas Muntser.
14. Vidyāpati Ṭhākur, *Kīrtilatā*, p. 86
15. The leading role of merchants and craftsmen was not a primordial feature of the *Bhakti* sects. It has to be noted that at the earlier stages of the development of the *Bhakti* ideology the majority of the preceptors and their followers belonged to the brahmanical and other high castes; for instance, note the descent of the leading alvar and nayanar saints of Tamilnadu [M. G. S. Narayanan and Kesavan Velluthat, 'Bhakti Movement in South India', S. C. Malik (ed.), *Indian Movements: Some Aspects of Dissent, Protest and Reform*, Simla, 1978, p. 48] or the later mystics like Dnyaneshwar, Basava or Caitanya. The leading role of merchants and craftsmen was more visible in the North Indian *Bhakti* traditions of the XVth-XVIIIth centuries, but there also *Bhakti* sects attracted people from nearly all social strata [cf. Satish Chandra, *Historical Background to the Rise of the Bhakti Movement in Northern India* – reprinted in: Satish Chandra, *Historigraphy, Religion and State in Medieval India Delhi*, 1996, pp. 126–31].
16. H. Dvivedī (ed.), *Kabīr*, Bombay, 1960, p. 262.
17. N. P. Tanner (ed.), *Heresy Trials in the Diocese of Norwich, 1428–1431*, London, 1977, pp. 57–58, 154.
18. N. P. Tanner (ed.), *Heresy Trials*, p. 58.
19. H. Dvivedī (ed.), *Kabīr*, pp. 230, 237.
20. M. Athar Ali, 'Sidelights into Ideological and Religious Attitudes in the Punjab During the XVIIth Century', *Medieval India: A Miscelanny*, Bombay, 1971, I, p. 188; Kh. A. Nizami, 'Impact of the Sufi Saints on Indian Society and Culture', S. S. Hameed (ed.), *Contemporary Relevance of Sufism*, Delhi, 1993, p. 141; J. R. Puri, T. R. Shangari (tr.), Bulleh Shah Amritsar, 1986, p. 458.
21. S. E. Ozment, *Mysticism and Dissent: Religious Ideology and Social Protest in the Sixteenth Century.* New Haven & London, 1973, p. 83.
22. S. T. D. K. Hakari (tr.), *Thus Spake Basava*, Bangalore, 1965, p. 36; also vide: K. V. Zvelebil, *The Lord of the Meeting Rivers: Devotional Poems of Basavanna.* Delhi, 1984, p. 28.
23. S. E. Ozment, *The Reformation in the Cities: The Appeal of Protestantism to the Sixteenth Century Germany and Switzerland*, New Haven & London, 1975, p. 22.
24. S. Eveland, 'An Enquiry into the Significance of Mysticism in the Poetry of Mira

Bai and Mechthild von Magdeburg', E. Polome (ed.), *Southwest Conference on Asian Studies: The Proceedings 1978*, pp. 1–7.

25. P. Jackson (tr.), *Letters from Maneri, Sufi Saint of Medieval India*, Delhi, 1990, p. 109.
26. On the psychological aspects of *Bhakti* mysticism vide T.R. Sharma, 'Psychological Analysis of Bhakti', Werner K. (ed.), *Love Divine: Studies in Bhakti and Devotional Mysticism*, London, 1993, pp. 85–93.
27. P. K. Varma, *Krishna: The Playful Divine*, Delhi, 1993, pp. 39–142.
28. S. E. Ozment, *The Reformation in the Cities*, p. 70.
29. S. E. Ozment, *Mysticism and Dissent*, p. 35.
30. Vide, for instance: D. Kinsley, *The Goddesses' Mirror: Visions of the Divine From East and West*, New York, 1989, pp. 229, 244–45.
31. P. Jackson, *Letters from Maneri*, p. 30.
32. Compare: H. Dvivedī, *Kabīr*, p. 271; W. M. Callewaert, P. G. Friedlander, *The Life and Works of Raidas*, Delhi, 1992, pp. 130, 141, 146, 210; *Sri Dasam Guru Grānth Sahībjī*. Hindi tr. by Jodh Singh. Lucknow, 1976, vol. 2, pp. 697–99; H. J. Hillerbrandt, *The Reformation*, p. 79.
33. N. P. Tanner (ed.), *Heresy Trials*, p. 86.
34. S. E. Ozment, *The Reformation in the Cities*, p. 67.
35. *Malukdāsjī ki Vāṇī*, Allahabad, 1946, p. 22.
36. H. J. Hillerbrandt, *The Reformation*, p. 223; P. Jackson, *Letters from Maneri*, p. 99; Swami Mahadevananda (tr.), *The Devotional Songs of Narsi Maheta*, Delhi, 1985, p. 132.
37. M. A. Mullett, *Radical Religious Movements in Early Modern Europe*, London, 1980, pp. 35–39; S.E. Ozment, *The Reformation in the Cities*, p. 65.
38. *The Bhagavad Gita*, Tr. by S. Radhakrishnan, London, 1948, p. 120.
39. *Selections from the Sacred Writings of the Sikhs*, London, 1960, p. 116.
40. P. Jackson, *Letters from Maneri*, p. 285.
41. T. D. Joshi, *Social and Political Thoughts of Ramdas*, Bombay, 1970, p. 43.
42. B. Śarmā (ed.), *Santguru Ravidās Vāṇī*, Delhi, 1978, pp. 90–91; W. Callewaert and P. G. Friedlander, *The Life and Works of Raidas*, p. 132
43. H. Dvivedī (ed.), *Kabīr*, pp. 231, 271; K. C. Singh (ed.), *Akśay Ras: Gujarat ke Mahan Santkavi Akhā kī Hindī Vāṇī*, Baroda, 1963, p. 206.
44. E. Rice, *Kanarese Literature*, Calcutta, 1921, p. 73; vide also: K. B. Prabhu Prasad, *Sarvajna*, Delhi, 1993, pp. 29, 36.
45. W. Callewaert, P. G. Friedlander, *The Life and Works of Raidas*, p. 198.
46. Savitri Cahndra, *Social Life and Concepts in Medieval Hindi Bhakti Poetry: A Socio-Cultural Study*, Delhi, 1983, p. 1; Satish Chandra, *Historical Background*, p. 110.
47. H. H.Wilson, *Essays and Lectures on the Religious Sects of the Hindus*, Reprint, Delhi, 1976, I, pp. 353–55.
48. H. Kaminsky, *A History of the Hussite Revolution*, Berkeley, 1967, p. 368.
49. H. Dvivedī (ed.), *Kabīr*, p. 326.
50. W. Callewaert (ed., tr.), *The Hindi Biography of Dadu Dayal*, Delhi, 1988, pp. 38, 93.
51. W. Callewaert, 'The Anabhay Prabodha of the Dadu Panthi Garibadas', *Orientalia Livaniensia Periodica*, 1974, V, p. 123.
52. *Malukdāsjī kī Vāṇī*, pp. 36–37.
53. *Hindī Kāvya Pravāh*, Allahabad, 1964, p. 689; M. A. Macauliffe, *The Sikh Religion, Its Gurus, Sacred Writings and Authors*, Oxford, 1909, V–VI, p. 275.

54. Muzaffar Alam, *Indo-Islamic Interaction*, pp. 37–51.
55. M. Ishaq Khan, 'The Societal Dimensions of the Mystical Philosophy of Nur ud-din Rishi Kashmiri', *Proceedings of the Indian History Congress, 46th Session*, Delhi, 1987, p. 259.
56. P. Chaturvedī (ed.), *Sūfī Kāvya Saṁgrāh*, Allahabad, 1967, p. 235.
57. By the present author: *Ideas and Society in India from the Sixteenth to the Eighteenth Centuries*, Delhi, 1996, pp. 59–85.
58. L. Spitz, *The Protestant Reformation*, p. 368; S. E. Ozment, *Mysticism and Dissent*, p. 50.
59. K. Schomer, 'The Sant Tradition in Perspective', K. Schomer and W.H. McLeod (eds.), *The Sants: Studies in a Devotional Tradition of India*, Delhi, 1987, p. 2.
60. By the present author, *Ideas and Society*, pp. 129–33.
61. Irfan Habib, *Potentialities of Capitalistic Development in the Economy of Mughal India*-reprinted in: Irfan Habib, *Essays in Indian History: Towards a Marxist Perception*, Delhi, 1995, pp. 180–232. The verdict is "no potentialities". For a different perception of the economy and society of pre-modern India vide: C. A. Bayly, *Indian Society and the Making of the British Empire: The New Cambridge History of India*, 1988, pp. 10–11,38, cf.; D. Washbrook, 'From Comparative Sociology to Global History: Britain and India in the Pre-History of Modernity', *JESHO*, XL, pt. 4 November, 1997, pp. 410–43.
62. K. Schomer, *The Sant Tradition*, p. 2.
63. Krishna Sharma, *Bhakti and Bhakti Movement: A New Perspective*. Delhi,1987, pp. 31–35.
64. E. Zelliot, 'The Medieval Bhakti Movement in History: An Essay on the Literature in English', B. I. Smith (ed.), *Hinduism: New Essays in the History of Religions*, Leiden, 1976, pp. 143, 158.

THIRTEEN ❖ Indo-Muslim Culture as a Synthetic Phenomenon

A. A. SUVOROVA

THE PROBLEM OF HINDU-Muslim cultural synthesis has been discussed for a rather long time and has got both defenders and opponents among the scholars. Some historians spoke of the predominant impact of Muslim thought on Hindu pre-modern mysticism in the form of *Bhakti* movement. Others, pointing out to the audacity of the poets like Kabir or *majẕūbs* like Shaikh Sarmad, believed that it was the Hindu *advaita* mysticism that gained a victory over Islamic monotheism. The third, who are in majority, spoke of correspondence between *Taṣawwūf* (Sufism) and *advaita vedānta* and made an attempt to bring an approximation between Muslim and Hindu thought – the idea that was viewed with great distrust by the orthodox elements from both sides.

The question that still awaits solution is whether this correspondence was of purely typological origin or whether it was a result of constant interaction and mutual influence. It would be hardly reasonable to discuss this very complicated and questionable matter in a superficial manner here. In this article our attention will be centred around only the aesthetic dimension of Hindu-Muslim synthesis as reflected in some pieces of Indo-Muslim literature.

The basis for the Hindu-Muslim synthesis in the field of literature was laid in the period of the Delhi Sultanate when certain local legends and love romances were selected and included in the body of Indo-Persian literature. The best example is the poetry of Amir Khusraw Dehlawi, in particular, his poem *Duvāl Rānī-o-Khiẕr Khān* (Duval Rani and Khizr Khan) based upon a historical incident. At that time the poetry that belonged to both Indian and Muslim traditions, was let through "the filter" of the latter one and partly transformed under its impact, and consequently came into mutual and constant contact within the limits of Muslim, mainly Persian, literature.

During the reign of the Great Mughals the process of synthesis of diversely originated elements gained intensity alongside the deepening Islamisation of some vernacular literary traditions like Sindhi, Punjabi, Dakhni, Kashmiri and Gujarati. A great diversity of forms emerged where a new literary self-consciousness could manifest itself. There are narratives like *maṣnawī, qiṣṣa, vāqe'ātī baitā,* as well as lyrics like *kāfi* in Punjabi, *vāi* – in Sindhi, *sūfiāna kalām* – in Kashmiri. The most perfect among them originated from the typological "sensitivity" of the pre-modern vernacular literatures, from their ability to combine the fragments of different traditions and to identify them on the basis of their mutual correspondence.

The forms that reflected the ideas of synthesis to the full extent were the local love romance which, as a rule, had got Sufi interpretation. It is generally known that while preaching the ascent of the soul to the Absolute the Sufis have used the wide-spread forms, popular legends and romantic plots where the characters' mundane love (*'ishq-i-majāzī*) served as an allegory of a divine love (*'ishq-i-haqīqī*).[1]

Along with the classical stories of Laila and Majnun, Shirin and Farhad, Yusuf and Zulaikha, Indian Sufi poets used local tales as well. These included ancient Indian legends of Nal and Damayanti, love stories of Madhumalati and Manohar, Padmavat and Ratansen; the Punjabi romance of Mirza and Sahiban, Hir and Ranjha, Sohni and Mahinval; the Sindhi legends of Sassi and Punhun, Lila and Chanesar, Marui and Umar; the Rajasthani stories of Dhola and Maru to mention but a few.

Though the structure of the Sufi love poems in the Indian vernaculars was mainly oriented towards their Persian prototype, their vivid originality stemming from their religious syncretism is indisputable. One of these original features attracted Annemarie Schimmel's attention.[2] What we have in mind is the personification of a soul longing for the transcendental love in the image of a female character and not a male, as it was usually the custom in the previous non-Indian Sufi tradition. Precisely, the presentation of a longing soul in the character of a woman occurred only once as the case of Yusuf and Zulaikha love story.

The striving of the soul of a mystic, personified in a female, for a union with her Divine Beloved, undoubtedly appeared in the regional Indian literatures under the impact of the *Bhakti* mysticism, its *Vaiṣṇava* version in particular. The classical example of this presentation is the Radha-Krishna mysticism. Sikh mysticism also adopted this imagery as well as the sacred songs-*gināns* of the Ismaili community.

As a peculiar feature of indigenous tradition, the bridal symbolism had rather early appeared in the Indo-Muslim literatures. For instance, a bridal soul longing for her Divine Spouse is encountered in the poems of the early Deccani mystics such as *Mi'rāj ul-'ashiqin* (The Ascension of the Lovers) by Muhammad Gesudaraz and *Khūsh nāmah* (Book of Contentment) by Miranji (fifteenth century) and in the poems of Muhammad Jiv Jan, who was one of the beginners of the Gujarati Sufi literature.

Especially vividly was this female type of the personification of the soul represented in the North-Western India, in the compositions of the Punjabi and Sindhi Sufi poets of the seventeenth and eighteenth centuries. Among them are Abdul Karim Bullri, Bullhe Shah, Shah Abdul Latif Bhitai, Waris Shah and others. In their works, both lyrical and narrative, the female characters of folk legends – Hir, Sohni and Sassi – acquired a strict allegorical connotation. "Hir is our soul", – says Bullhe Shah.[3] In the *Risālo* (collection of mystical poetry according to musical *rāgas*) by Shah Abdul Latif, Sohni is depicted drowning in the "ocean of souls".[4] Sassi punished for the "the sleep of heedlessness" is described as a repenting soul (*nafs-i-lawwāma*).[5]

It should be emphasised that in all other folk romances of this area, such as Lila and Chanesar, Marui and Umar, Nuri and Jam Tamachi, Momal and Rano, the woman is always the active part; it is she who seeks the beloved, who suffers and dies first. The descriptions of these female characters often contain beautiful imagery and are full of psychological insight.

Even prior to Sind and the Punjab, in the fourteen-sixteenth centuries, the genre of the love poem based upon the local folk romance, appeared in the area of the spread of the Hindi language dialects. Particularly famous are the poems written in the Awadhi dialect and titled after the names of their heroines: *Padmāvat* by Malik Muhammad Jayasi, *Candāyan* by Mullah Daud, *Mrigāvatī* by Qutban, *Madhumālatī* by Manjhan, *Citrāvalī* by Usman. They had a decisive influence upon the establishment of a literary narrative tradition in Northern India, which later on mixed with the Punjabi and Sindhi folklore through the Persian versions. In the seventeenth century a famous historian of Sind, Mir Ma'sum Nami for the first time presented the folk romance of Sassi Punhun in the form of a Persian *ma<u>s</u>nawī.* Another historian Idraqi Beglari versified the romance of Lila Chanesar in his *Canesar Nāmah.* Later on the Punjabi romance of Hir Ranjha was retold and elaborated in dozens of Persian *ma<u>s</u>nawīs.*

It is interesting to note that the Sufi poems in Awadhi Hindi were considered by Muslims as the examples of indigenous "Indian romance". This fact was particularly outlined by Manjhan in his preface to *Madhumālatī.*[6] However, from the view point of comparative literature, the plots of these poems show a dominating impact of the poetics of the Middle Eastern literatures, in particular, the Persian *ma<u>s</u>nawī,* the novelistic tradition of both Indian and non-Indian origin, and folk narratives of the *dāstān, qiṣṣa* and *hikāyat* types.

Of no less importance for the formation of Indo-Muslim romance were the narratives in Persian based upon the chronicles or presented as such. These poems were often focused on a tragic love between a Muslim man and a Hindu girl. That love was given an allegorical interpretation. The practice of composing such poems goes back to the *masnawī Duvāl Rānī-o-Khiẓr Khān* by Amir Khusraw Dehlawi and *'Ishq Nāmah* (Story of Love) by his contemporary Amir Hasan Sijzi.

Even still later poems, those written in Persian in the sixteen-seventeenth centuries may be also added to this list. These include: *Sōz-o-gudāz* (Burning and Melting) by Muhammad Nau'i and *Nāz-o-niyāz* (Amorous Playfulness) by Mukhsin Fani. They describe allegedly historic facts of the times of Akbar rule. Precisely this type of the poems, devoted to the loving couples separated by their faith, may be considered as a pattern for a big group of later vernacular poems.

A clear-out differentiation may be traced inside the genre of romance. Some of them closely follow the novelistic and narrative tradition. The Indian scholars sometimes call them "*dāstān*-like" (*dāstānī andāz*).[7] These traditions are mainly of the Near-and Middle East origin. Such poems are characterised by a comparatively long and developed narration. More often than not they have parallel plots and inserted stories, excessive fairytale fantasy and adventures, conventional place and time of action and an indispensable happy end. To this type belong, for example, the famous poems in Dakhni written in the seventeenth century. They include *Quṭb Mushtarī* (The Polar Star and Jupiter) by Mulla Wajahi, *Saif ul-Mulūk-o-Badī ul-Jamāl* (Saif ul-Muluk and Badi ul-Jamal) by Gavvasi, *Phūlban* (The Flower Garden) by Ibn-i Nishati, *Gulshan-i 'ishq* (The Rose-Garden of Love) by Nusrati.

Another type of love poem presents emphatically authentic stories with short and simple (at times even "meagre") plots deprived of any magic adventures. Such poems almost always end in the death of the loving couple. The moment of the lovers' death is marked by the motive of "miracle" which is absolutely different from the decorative fantasy of the "*dāstān*-type" poems. The plots of such poems (the earliest of them is probably *Ishq Nāmah*) had a vividly lyrical colouring, originated from local legends and traditions and more often than not contained some historical and geographical realities the aim of which was to create the atmosphere of pseudo-authenticity. Such poems show great similarity with the romantic ballads in different Indian vernaculars. We conventionally call them ballad-like in contrast to the *dāstān*-like type. To the ballad-like type also belong the early *masnawī Candārbadan-o-Mahiyār* (Chandarbadan and Mahiyar) by Muqimi in Dakhni-Urdu, *Sho'ala-i-'ishq* (Flame of Love) and *Dariyā-i 'ishq* (River of Love) by Mir Taqi Mir in Urdu-*Rekhtā*, some narrative parts from the chapters (*surs*) of *Shāh jo risālo* by Shah Abdul Latif in Sindhi, some *qiṣṣas* in Punjabi. By their veritable atmosphere the ballad-like romance also resembles the Sindhi *vāqe'ātī baitā* composed in the matter-of-fact style.

Precisely in the ballad-like poems the difference of faith (*dīn-o-imān*) serves as a tragic motivation of the plot. In the stories of Chandarbadan and Mahiyar, Sohni and Mahinval the heroines are Hindus, whereas the heroes are Muslims. Even if the lovers are of the same confession, they belong to different tribes (as Mirza and Sahiban in the Punjabi *qiṣṣa* by Hafiz Barhudar) and have to face the resistance of the society to their love. Usually this conflict is solved by the death of the hero and heroine either in water (as it is in the case of Sohni and Mahinwal) or in fire (as it is in the Momal and Rano case). The loving couple may be killed or commit suicide by poison or dagger. The love miracle is usually concomitant to their death. Their bodies merge together in an embrace after death and they cannot be broken apart.

There also exists one more interesting motif. The heroine remains indifferent to the hero, but his death gives rise to a reciprocal feeling and inspires her to embrace Islam. Inside the corpus of poems describing love between a Muslim and a Hindu girl there exists a certain genre stratification which proves that the main idea behind those works was a controversy between Hinduism and Islam in which the latter was the winner. In some way or other these poems were written with a proselytic aim in view.

No doubt, the first and foremost proselytic poem was *Candārbadan-o-Mahiyār* by Muqimi where a Hindu girl rejected a Muslim young man who was in love with her, but after his death she embraced Islam and died immediately after him. The miracle takes place after the death of the lovers. The hero and heroine who had died separately held each other in such a close embrace that they had to be buried in the same grave.

Close to this interpretation of the plot are such later poems as *Tālib-o-Mohinī* (Talib and Mohini) by Sayyid Muhammad Vala, *Bahlūl sādiq* (Faithful Bahlul) by Lutfi, *Shamā'-i 'ishq* (Candle of Love) by Anvar and *Sarāpā soz* (Totally Burning) by Akhtar in Urdu (all of them written at the end of eighteenth century). In all these poems the tortuous death of the Muslim hero provoked by unshared love proves to the Hindu heroine the superiority of his religion. By putting herself to death she, so to say, pays the penalty for her disregard of the true faith and the real *haqīqī* love.

It is easy to trace in this standing and widespread plot the scheme of a specific proselytic myth about the conversion to Islam by means of love which was advocated by the mystic brotherhoods of *Chishtiyya* and *Qādiriyya.* Moreover, the formation of such plots was also stimulated by the legends that cycled around the Muslim shrines and *mazārs* – the tombs of the Muslim saints.[8] The martyrdom or death resulting from unusual circumstances served as a rich soil for the origin of such legends which provided a stable plot paradigm by passing it over to the field of literature.

So, the Deccani chronicle of the eighteenth century, *Tuzuk-i Aṣāfiya* (Regulation of Asaf) by Shah Tajalli, described the Chandarbadan and Mahiyar tomb. The tomb, identified as a burial vault of Sassi and Punhun, was situated in the Las Bela area in Sind. Well-known were also the tomb of Hir in Jang and the *mazār* of Mirza and Sahiban. All of these were the objects of reverence and veneration, if not completely religious, then traditional, and possessed some wonder-working force (*baraka*).

There also existed another kind of poems about the love of a Muslim to a Hindu lady. In its basis was the possibility of free polemics between the two religions and the thesis about a conscientious and rational acceptance of Islam. A majority of this kind of poems were created in the seventeenth century Gujarat in Persian and Gujarati. They include the poems *Mughal-o-Nāgrānī* (Mughal and Nagrani) by an anonymous author, *Nāznīn-o-Pathan* (Nazneen and Pathan) by Hamid Surati, *Hīrā Lāl* by Parveen, *Natho Bāmanī* by Hajji Muhammad and so on. The plot scheme of all these poems contains the same motives: a discussion between the Muslim hero and the Hindu heroine trying to ascertain whose religion is better. Then comes the test to which the heroine subjects the hero by ordering him to jump down from the city wall, throw himself into fire or dive into water. The hero manages to stand the test with honour and as a result the heroine embraces Islam and becomes his wife.

In these poems as well the conversion to Islam with the help of love is the chief idea of action, but here it is deprived of the halo of martyrdom. This is the reason why the characters remain alive and get happily married. At the same time the poems of love miracle and the poems about the test of faith did not refute but supplemented one another. Both types represent the well known semantic opposition of "Turk-Hindu" peculiar to the Indian Islamic literatures.[9] Having been some time back addressed to the proselyte they later on formed a well-composed plot-genre concept of the ballad-like romance.

In the period of the late Mughals when the process of Islamisation in certain cultural spheres was almost over, the trends of synthesis weakened. But even at that stage some evidence of synthetic aesthetics can be traced in Urdu literature. The most colourful example of the identification of the elements belonging to both traditions is the early Hindustani drama and theatre.

The dramatic tradition in Hindustani (both Hindi and Urdu) emerged as a result of fusion of the Urdu *maṡnawī* and the Hindu religious performance – *rāslīla.* Therefore the development of the dramatic aesthetics was coupled with the formation of the synthesis in the field of performing arts, when the drama that was Muslim by its content, took up the scenic devices from Hindu traditional theatre.[10] The dramatic conflict originated from the basic Islamic concept of fate and destiny (*qażā-o-qadar*). There is no tragedy as a genre form in Hindustani drama, for the harmony between the Divine fate and human destiny is peculiar to providential Muslim theories.

But in spite of this purely Muslim content, the aesthetics of early Hindustani drama is usually described in terms of Indian *rasa* theory. The aesthetic transformation of life into art, the generalisation of emotions, and the identification of subject and object in the Muslim theatre are just the same as in the Sanskrit theory of *rasa.* Some of the prefaces to the plays are very important as they point out to the aesthetic values of the dramatic arts.

Thus the preface to Hafeez Abdulla's play *Savāneh-i Qais Maftūn* ("The adventures of fascinated Qais") states: "In his everyday life a man can't penetrate into hidden meaning of his personality (*shakhṣiyat*). Contemplating the transcendental truth (*ḥaqīqat*) and allegorical sense (*tamṣīl*) through art, he enlightens his hidden "self" and gets the bliss (*rāhat*)". Another playwright Mahmud Mian Raunaq in the preface to the play *Sāniḥa-i dilgīr* (The Terrifying Incident) developed the point by saying: "Those who are watching this story (*tamṣīl*), full of grief and sorrow, will reach the bliss (*rāhat*) and peace (*aman*)".[11]

The meaning of these remarks are quite similar to the concept of *rasa*: self-cognition (or "enlightenment of one's hidden self") is a result of certain aesthetic experience, and it can be nothing but bliss. The universalised emotions may be mournful or terrifying, but once transformed into *rasa* they can evoke bliss only. The consequence of that bliss will be the sentiment of peace – *aman,* or in classical terms, *śāntī rasa.*

The histories of Indian Islamic literatures (Urdu, Sindhi and to some extent, Punjabi and Gujarati) lack theoretical texts that might help to penetrate into literary self-consciousness of the local narrative tradition. The canons of borrowed genres as *ghazal, qaṣīda, qiṭ'a* and others were described by many poetics in Persian, but narratives, even Persian-like *maṡnawīs,* were never included in the poetological treatises. However, a great many of passages in *maṡnawī, dāstān, qiṣṣa* and local romances, let alone prefaces and postscripts thereto, present a sufficiently vast material for the reconstruction of this literary self-consciousness. Those prefaces and postscripts are most important for the reconstruction which disclose not only the literary and aesthetic principles of the genre but also its ideological foundations.

As a rule the following concept is presented in the prefaces: the

Divine Mercy (*raḥmat*) pours out into a poet's soul (*nafs*) capable of perceiving the spiritual light of inspiration (*nūr-i rūhānī*) and is transformed into a stream of individual ideas and images (*ma'na*) which possess a potential being. The right actualisation of these images in the verbal substance (*lafẓ*) brings to life a thing possessing an actual being – that is a literary work itself. In case of the correct perception by a sophisticated reader or connoisseur (*aḥl-i-ẕouq*) the literary piece produces a balancing effect on his soul suffering from excessive passions. The analysis of this theory and, in particular, of its technical terms bears witness to its Muslim origin. Still, in many of its aspects certain features may be seen that are traced back to the pre-Muslim period in the history of Indian literary thought.

One of the aspects in question is the teaching of the psychotherapeutic function of a literary work the Muslim origin of which is evident. This teaching has been expounded in medical, ethical and poetological manuals of Ibn Sina, al-Farabi and Nizami Aruzi Samarqandi. Its reflections may be found in the poems of Nizami, Amir Khusrau, Nava'i and in a great many of other works in Arabic, Persian, Turkish, Urdu languages belonging both to the high and popular forms of Muslim culture.

The psychotherapeutic effect is based upon the following process: the literary work, thanks to its beauty (*jamāl*), is perceived by the power of imagination inherent in the soul which subsequently makes the power of anger and the power of passion subordinate to imagination. Both powers arouse in the soul a certain affection under the influence of which the "cordial pneuma" expands (*inqibād*) or contracts (*inbisāṯ*). This action, provided the desired affection is reached, leads to the healing of a person. For example, Ibn Sina, speaking of the verbal healing of passionate love, recommended either to induce the opposite passion (anger) in the loving soul, or to effect a sublimation of a sort of the initial affection (love) by means of transference to another object and its subsequent extinguishing. The last method, often mentioned in Indo-Islamic romances, presents a particular interest.

However, the mention of Muslim roots of the psychotherapeutic theory does not solve the problem of its origin in India, since a psychotherapeutic effect of art is described in very similar terms in the forms which have not so much to do with Islam, such as, for instance, the *bārahmāsa* or early Hindustani drama the plot of which could be both Muslim and non-Muslim. The transformation of an actual heartache of a reader or spectator into aesthetic bliss became a general principle adopted by the local writers. And this principle of balancing passions may be very easily described in terms of aesthetic experience known as *rasa.*

The sources of *rasa* are inherent in human psyche i.e. stable psychic complexes – *sthāyibhāva* (love, fear, anger etc.) which have been formed as a result of the present and former rebirths, and preserved in the subconsciousness in the form of "impressions" (*vāsanā*). Through a description of their symptoms (*anubhava*), their stimulants (*vibhāva*), and their concomitant "transient emotions" (*vyabhicāribhāva*), the poet entices the connoisseur to "taste" or to "partake of" the *rasas* corresponding to the stable psychic complexes (erotic, comic etc.). Since a direct description of an emotion is unable to impart an aesthetic sentiment, the manifestation of a *rasa* is effected through *dhvani* ("sound", "echo"), a certain sense that is hidden, but capable of manifestation represented in description of symptoms, stimulants, and transient emotions.

The tasting of *rasa* is not only an emotional process. It is a kind of cognition, an immediate intuitive perception of an universalised object devoid of all individual specifications and representing the most generalised psychic qualities, by a universalised subject that renounced its "ego". This perception, effected through a complete identification of the subject and object (i.e. through dissolution of the subject-connoisseur in the object-hero), arouses the state of bliss in the soul of connoisseur. The experienced state of bliss (*camatkāra* – "admiration", "delight") is self-cognition of the subject free from limitations of the ego and distractions, the cognition identical with realisation of the absolute "self", or *Brahman*, with which *rasa* as such is identified in the individual "self". *Camatkāra* is the common principal underlying all *rasa*s which leads to the attainment of bliss regardless of the events described.

An echo of this theory we evidently perceive in the concept of healing "the pain of heartache and longing" both in narratives and dramatic forms of Muslim content. The perception of the universalised object and subject brings about the renunciation of the "ego" whose "agitation" is responsible for the "heartaches", and the attainment of blissfulness. According to A. Warder, "the operation of the aesthetic experience is as it were to sublimate emotions from the psychological to the aesthetic plane. In this process individual emotion is transformed into, or replaced by, an aesthetic experience – *rasa*. The individual forgets himself and attains a universality of outlook which also brings him the highest happiness".[12]

We may suppose that the *rasa* theory being a living heritage of the Indian literatures of different genres (*kāvya*, lyrics, drama) was also familiar to some Muslim poets of India who used for their speculations the plots of local romances and even Sanskrit classics (for example, *Nal-o-Daman* by Faizi and different Urdu and Persian versions of *Śakuntalā*). All authors of classical Urdu *ma<u>s</u>nawis* adopted the old schemes of Indian plot-making and emotional structure that may also be described in terms of *rasa*. In this case the literary self-consciousness of the vernacular authors turns out to be a "fact of twin motivation", motivated both by Indian and Muslim aesthetics.

The discovering of the correspondence between these two aesthetic systems and creation of a "typological glossary" of a sort, that made it possible to assimilate new ideological doctrines, constituted one of the most important qualities of Persian-Hindawi verses by Amir Khusrau, *Kitāb-i Nauras* (The Book of Nine Rasas) by Ibrahim Adil Shah of Bijapur, the *thūmrī* compositions by Wajeed Ali Shah, and many other samples of the so-called "mixed"[13] forms. It looks like it was the discovering of the correspondences and bilateral identification of elements of both traditions, and not just their mechanical mixture (although the latter has taken place too), that has determined the synthetic character of some Indian vernacular literatures.

We should not however think that this process was confined to a mere identification of elements of the old and the new, the Hindu and the Muslim. The closer to the core of the tradition, i.e. to the religious canon was the old concept to be "translated" into the new cultural "language" the more intensive this process became. One might point to quite a number of differences between the Indian and Muslim aesthetics. Notably, the Muslim concept of the soothing function of literary work had only psychotherapeutic and ethical character. It was related to the psychic plan or, to be more exact, to the plan of the animal soul as opposed to the intellect. It was believed that the beauty (*jamāl*) was able to deliver delight to the intellect only if represented in a poem as *tamṣīl*, that is as indirect expression of a certain meaning arousing intellectual activity. In any case, the bliss brought about by aesthetic object is understood by Muslim tradition as a result of balancing or purification of the psychic plan.

As concerns the Indian tradition, this state of blissfulness is conditioned by the transcending of this plan which opens the possibility of cognition of the Absolute. This difference accounts for the absence of the idea of a special aesthetic path in Islamic tradition in general.

There are a lot of Indian narratives that reflect the composite synthetic self-consciousness of a large group of Indians in the premodern period. What we have in mind is a story of a dead saint or a religious leader who left his spiritual message to both communities – Hindus and Muslims. The apocryphal biography of Kabir[14] is the best example of this message. Both communities considered Kabir to belong to their own respective faith, but Kabir himself was a *muwaḥḥid*, a unitarian, far removed from them all. When he was on his deathbed, the Muslim and Hindu disciples started to argue as to whether to bury or cremate his body. The saint told them that if his dead body was found they could do with it whatever they wished. Then he locked the doors and passed away. The end of story is well-known. When Kabir's cell was opened, nothing but flowers were found there, and the quarrel came to an end, for both Muslims and Hindus could share those flowers without any clash.

This beautiful legend is the allegory (*tamṣīl*) of the composite synthetic culture of India, the Indo-Muslim culture that was evoked by the early saints of the Delhi Sultanate, then flourished with the Great Mughals in poetry and narratives, the imposing architectural monuments, the *kathak* dance, the *khayāl* music, *qawwālī* singing and many other art forms.

Notes and References

1. Discussed in more details in: Anna Suvorova, *Masnavi: A Study of Urdu Romance*, Karachi, 2000.
2. Annemarie Schimmel, *Mystical Dimensions of Islam*, Chapel Hill, 1975, pp. 200–25.
3. Faqir M. (ed.), *Dīwān Bulleh Shāh*, Lahore, 1960, p. 58.
4. Elsa Kazi, *Risalo of Shah Abdul Latif: Selections*, Hyderabad, 1981, p. 87.
5. T. H. Sorley, *Shah Abdul Latif of Bhit: His Poetry, Life and Times*, Karachi, 1989, p. 175.
6. Quoted in: Rāmacandra Śukla, *Hindī sāhitya kā itihās*, Benāres, 1953, pp. 130–50.
7. Narang Gopicand, *Hindustānī kissŏ se makhūs urdū masnaviyā̃*, Delhi, 1962, p. 67.
8. A. A. Suvorova, *Musulmanskiye svyatiye yuzhnoi Azii XI-XV vv* (The Muslim Saints of South Asia, XIth to XVth Century), Moscow, 1999.
9. Annemarie Schimmel, 'Turk and Hindu: A Poetical Image and Its Application to Historical Fact', *Islam and Cultural Change in the Middle Ages*, Wiesbaden, 1975, pp. 107–26.
10. See: A. Suvorova, *U istokov novoindiyskoy drami* (At the Sources of New Indian Drama), Moscow, 1985, pp. 131–32.
11. Ibid., p.137.
12. A. K. Warder, *Indian Kavya Literature*, Delhi, 1970, p. 35.
13. The language itself identifies these vernacular literature forms as "impure", "mixed" like *rekhtā, milā julā, Gangā Jamnī* etc.
14. Dārā Shikūh, *Safīnat al-auliā*, Lahore, 1975, p. 74.

FOURTEEN ❖ # Dr Ambedkar's *Navayāna*: In Search for Democracy

E. S. YURLOVA

In 1990 Dr B. R. Ambedkar was posthumously awarded "Bharat Ratna", India's highest civilian award. But bitter polemic against those who seek recognition of Dr B.R. Ambedkar's contribution to social democracy and protection of human rights is still going on in India. Many are blamed for "worshipping false gods". There are others who try to look into the essence of this great man's endeavour. K. R. Narayanan, President of India, called him "a giant among the great men produced by the Indian nationalist movement", using "the term in its broadest sense". In this connection he writes, "If Mahatma Gandhi gave to the nationalist movement a mass dimension and a moral purpose and Jawaharlal Nehru an economic and socialist dimension, Dr B. R. Ambedkar gave it a profound social content and a challenging social-democratic goal".[1]

In his turn Justice V. K. Krishna Iyer reminds his readers that Ambedkar, being a staunch nationalist, condemned the British for their deportation of Tilak and transportation of Savarkar and the repressive Indian Press Act, 1910. Justice Iyer is quite convinced that "when the history of Indian Independence, in its many dimensions, comes to be written, Ambedkar's contribution will stand out as a fresh, fierce infusion of social democracy sans which political freedom stands on shifting sands". He insists that Ambedkar had been a historic necessity, a dialectical demand if social democracy was to be India's desideratum.[2]

In this article we intend to show Dr Ambedkar's search for democracy as a means to reform the socially stratified Indian society.

Ambedkar's heritage should be assessed in its totality. At the same time it has to be understood that it is difficult to sum up the main results of his creative work without taking into account the historical context of his life, the conditions in which he lived and developed. A historical approach to Ambedkar's teaching may help us understand the specificity of his path to Buddhism.

The social, economic and national upheavals during Ambedkar's lifetime could not but have an impact on the evolution of his outlook. These were the World War I, 1917 revolution in Russia, the Great depression of the 30s in the West, fascism and World War II, and the Cold War. And, of course, there were such historical events in his country as the freedom movement, attainment of independence, and India's search for its own path. In all of them Ambedkar participated very actively.

Ambedkar's world outlook represents a certain synthesis of different ideas borrowed from different sources. All of them in any case uplift furthered his main goal – to find a way to up lift the lower castes. Not incidentally he said: "I am prepared to pick and choose from everyone, Socialist, Communist or other. I do not claim infallibility and as Buddha says there is nothing infallible, there is nothing final and everything is liable to examination".[3]

His study of religions – Hinduism, Christianity, Islam, Buddhism, as well as the social and economic theories and their practical application – was only an instrument, a means to achieve his goal – the social liberation of the Untouchables. This became a focal point of all his endeavours and searches. And it was inseparable from his life – the life of a man who was born in a family of Untouchable *Mahars* and got his first and lasting experience there. This formed the background for his struggle and search for a better lot for the *Dalits*. One may say that Ambedkar got "enlightened" as a result of his long and sharp ideological and political struggle.

During the course of Ambedkar's lifetime, under the pressure of political events, significant changes took place in his views, which marked his adaptation to the new conditions. While studying the past he built bridges between that past and the present, which helped him uphold his new ideas. To make them more comprehensive not only in India, but also in the West, he used the method of comparative ideology and political science.

Ambedkar's *navayāna* became the final product of his spiritual and political development, of his critical evaluation of the experience accumulated by India and the mankind. Defining this term, Christopher Queen wrote, "By the mid-twentieth century CE a new form of Buddhism was evolving out of the dialogue between Asian and Western cultural values. Centering on social causes of human suffering – such as economic exploitation and racial and caste violence – and the collective action required to overcome them, this new Buddhism found an eloquent spokesman in Dr B. R. Ambedkar. Seeking a term for this socially engaged Buddhism, Ambedkar suggested *Navayāna* or New Vehicle".[4] In this sense his teaching could also be qualified as political Buddhism.

Ambedkar's refuge in the Buddha was a matter of principle for him. Having rejected Hinduism and everything connected with it in the religious, social and political life, as well as the possibility of converting to Christianity, Sikhism or Islam, Ambedkar was left with no other choice but to embrace Buddhism.

Ambedkar's *navayāna* was the result of his long search for the means of religious reformation of the existing social system with the aim to spiritually liberate the *Dalits* and create conditions for an egalitarian society.

Though he had been working on his *navayāna* for quite some time, his final decision to embrace Buddhism was made by him in the last hour of his life. The mass conversion of the *Mahars* into Buddhism arranged by him was a result of different circumstances and pressures – psychological, emotional, and political.

One of the most significant elements of Ambedkar's Buddhism was his philosophy of social justice. He was strongly wedded to the idea of equality from the early days of his involvement in public life till his last breath.

In the 30s Ambedkar believed that Western democracy (which he closely associated with capitalism) could not be totally applicable to Indian conditions because of the specificity of the social contradictions of the society based on caste. He came to such a conclusion after having studied the history of parliamentary democracy in Europe. That system of governance had, in his view, "all the marks of a popular Government, a government of the people, by the people, and for the people." But after a century of its universal acceptance there had been a revolt and discontent against it in many countries (Italy, Germany, Spain, Russia), which led to the failure of democracy. "Why did it happen?" – asked Ambedkar in 1943, when India was in the very midst of its freedom struggle, and ultimately had to choose its mode of government.

So, why did parliamentary democracy fail? Ambedkar writes with bitterness that it is the idea of freedom of contract that has ruined parliamentary democracy. This idea became sanctified and was upheld in the name of liberty. Parliamentary democracy took no notice of economic inequalities and did not care to examine the results of freedom of contract, whether they were unequal or not. Consequently, parliamentary democracy has continuously added to the economic wrongs of the poor, the downtrodden and the disinherited class. Parliamentary democracy has also failed to realise that political democracy could not succeed where there was no social and economic democracy.

In Ambedkar's opinion, democracy and equality are closely interlinked: "Democracy is another name of equality." At the same time he perceived that parliamentary democracy, as he witnessed it between the two world wars, did not strive to achieve equality in society, and shifted the emphasis to developing liberty instead. Thus the very principle of equality so dear to Ambedkar's heart had been transformed into a stepson of democracy. Parliamentary democracy "failed to realise the significance of equality and did not even endeavour to strike a balance between Liberty and Equality, with the result that liberty swallowed equality and has left a progeny of inequities."

Ambedkar also criticised parliamentary democracy for not being able to become the government by the people, as "the rulers are always drawn from the ruling class and the class of the ruled never becomes the ruling class". Thus parliamentary democracy "has not fulfilled the hope it held out to the common man of ensuring him liberty, property and pursuit of happiness".[5]

He opined that in a number of countries democracy was not able to solve the burning issues of life. In one of his public speeches in 1938, addressing the problem of the future government in India, he said, "Having regard to the present-day conditions in India, democracy is a most unsuitable system of government. At any rate, for some time India needs the strong hand of an enlightened autocrat".[6] One can see that Ambedkar was not a blind adherent of democracy the way it was practised in the West in the 1930–40s. At that time he did not treat democracy as an ideal to be pursued in all circumstances and in all claims.

After 1947 and specially with the adoption of the Constitution of India, whose primary architect Ambedkar was, and which proclaimed democracy as the main principle of governing the society, he had become a staunch defender of democracy. He could no longer limit himself only to criticism of the parliamentary democracy in spite of its weaknesses, hardships and failures. He moved further in developing the democratic principles, while addressing both the Indian and the Western practices and conditions.

In his book *The Buddha and His Dhamma* Dr Ambedkar presented Buddhism as a democratic system, and the Buddha as a great democrat. More so, he tried to install in the minds of his countrymen that India had produced its own wisdom, the Buddha's *Dhamma* or rather *navayāna*, which in fact had been Ambedkar's creation. According to Eleanor Zelliot, Ambedkar was interested in creating an image of the Buddha which represented his own vision. His search for a meaningful Buddhism focused on the person of the Buddha.[7]

According to Ambedkar, "rules applied by the Buddha to the meeting of the Bhikshu Sanghas, he must have borrowed from the rules of the political Assemblies functioning in the country in his time". Ambedkar argued that Buddhist *bhikśu sangha*s "were nothing but parliaments", they "knew and observed all the rules of parliamentary procedure known to modern times".[8] As democracy has been known to India since ancient times when its republics were acquainted with parliament and parliamentary procedure, India, Ambedkar said, had only to re-establish the long lost democracy, but on a different basis, which had to correspond to the modern demands, avoiding the mistakes and failures of the Western democracy.

His fundamental thesis that political democracy is not self-sufficient and it should correlate itself with social democracy, is very important for understanding his own socio-political outlook: "We must make our political democracy a social democracy as well. Political democracy cannot last unless there lies at the base of it social democracy".[9]

Democracy, in Ambedkar's understanding, was not attainable without social guarantees to safeguard the interests of the "small" man. He thought that the *sine qua non* of a successful functioning of democratic institutions in India would be a society in which there would be no class which had all the privileges and a class which had only duties. Otherwise the "microbes of bloody revolution" would remain in the society. He warned that clashes between classes should be avoided. Those clashes might happen not only on the initiative of the lower classes, but mainly because of the upper classes ignoring the interests of the former.

Therefore great importance was attached to the development of democracy in three spheres of human life – political, social and economic. According to Ambedkar, political democracy minus socio-economic democracy could create innumerable problems for human beings and society as a whole. Political rights are of no importance for an individual who does not enjoy economic freedom. Democracy would break down if it was not enlivened by social justice as its soul. He warned again that "these downtrodden classes are tired of being governed. They are impatient to govern themselves. This urge for self-realisation in the downtrodden classes must not be allowed to devolve into a class struggle or class war . . . the sooner room is made for the realisation of their aspiration, the better for . . . the country, . . . the better for the continuance of its democratic structure." How can this be achieved? Ambedkar's answer was: "By the establishment of equality and fraternity in all spheres of life".[10]

In Ambedkar's understanding, social democracy was a way of life which recognises liberty, equality and fraternity. At the same time these principles should not be treated separately, but in a trinity: "Without equality liberty would produce the supremacy of the few over the many. Equality without liberty would kill individual initiative. Without fraternity, liberty and equality could not become a natural course of things".

Why did Ambedkar consider fraternity as one of the inseparable parts of democracy? In his opinion, fraternity could be compared with the feeling of kinship for all Indians: "Fraternity means a sense of common brotherhood of all Indians, all Indians being one people. It is the principle which gives unity and solidarity to social life. It is a difficult thing to achieve." Thus fraternity was of a paramount importance for the leader of socially discriminated masses. He was of the opinion that because of the caste system the Indians could not consider themselves as a nation: "How can people divided into several thousands of castes be a nation? The sooner we realise that we are not yet a nation in the social and psychological sense of the word, the better for us." Castes are "antinational . . . because they bring about separation in social life. . . Without fraternity, equality and liberty will be no deeper than coats of paint".[11]

Therefore, to follow Ambedkar's logic, to achieve fraternity, the caste barriers are to be pulled down and the caste system eliminated. There is no other way to build up an Indian nation. In spite of the hardships confronting the society it has to overcome them before it could become a united, stable and democratic nation.

Before independence Ambedkar spoke of the "two enemies of the working class in the country and they were Brahmanism and Capitalism".[12] In very harsh terms he criticised the Congress and M. K. Gandhi in particular for not defending the interests of the poor and the downtrodden. Addressing a conference of the Depressed Classes at Masur in the Bombay province in September 1937 he told the audience that it was his confirmed opinion that Gandhi was not the man who would look to the interests of the working classes and the poor. Had the Congress been a revolutionary body, he would have joined it. But the Congress was not courageous enough to proclaim the ideal of social and economic equality. Later at the Sholapur district conference of the Depressed Classes in December, Ambedkar expressed a strong resentment at the treatment those classes got from the Congress which was ruled by the capitalists. It was necessary, he added, to form a united front against the capitalists, who were out to exploit them.[13]

That is why Ambedkar participated in joint actions with the communists and socialists to defend the economic rights of the workers. For instance, on the 6th and 7th November 1938 he took part in a mass demonstration against the attempt of the government of the Bombay province to pass the Bill on conflicts in industries, which he called The Workers' Civil Liberties Suspension Act. Ambedkar headed that successful public action along with the communists. But on the whole, before and after that demonstration, he had very difficult and complicated relations with them, saying more than once that for him there was no possibility of his joining the communists. He declared himself their confirmed enemy, because they "exploited the labourers for their political ends".[14] He even suggested that the communists change their name, because for many people it was associated with terror.

As far as the socialists were concerned he had closer relationship with them, though he announced publicly that he was not a socialist. Ambedkar complained that there was no clear understanding of socialism in India. "What is socialism, nobody is able to say. There is the socialism of the Prime-Minister, which he himself said he could not define. There is the socialism of the Praja Socialist Party; they don't know what it is. And even the Communists".[15]

In February, 1956 Ambedkar stated very decisively that the East had already become more important than the West, and he feared that if the Buddhist gospel was not adopted, the history of conflict in Europe would be repeated in Asia. This was how Ambedkar exercised pressure on the Hindu orthodox and conservative opinion in order to promote his social reforms. If the social structure of the Indian society is not changed, he warned, then any religion that could not provide an answer to communism would perish.[16] He said that the system was likely to collapse, and the alternative, if democracy did not work in India, was something of communism.[17]

Ambedkar insisted that his country had to choose between Buddhism and communism, or as he put it, "between the gospel of the Buddha and the gospel of Karl Marx".[18] This attitude of Ambedkar was also dictated by other, far deeper reason, – the very content of his social philosophy.

After having criticised Brahmanism and capitalism for their inability to solve the problem of inequality, Ambedkar was inevitably confronted with Marxism, as the ideology of the working class. He devoted much time and effort to studying the theory of Marxism and its practice in the Soviet Union. Ambedkar's interest in this matter is obvious when one reads his works. And he himself spoke about it on a number of occasions: "I have been a student of politics; I was a professor of economics, and I have spent a great deal of time in studying Karl Marx, Communism and all that . . .".[19] Addressing one of the mass meetings in Bombay, he claimed, a bit too emphatically, that the number of books he had read on communism exceeded the number of books read by all communist leaders put together.[20] His biographer Dhananjay Keer wrote, that on the 3rd December, 1956, a few days before he died, Ambedkar, as was his habit before going to bed, took among other books, "The Capital" in order to complete the last chapter of his essay *The Buddha or Karl Marx.*

In this essay Ambedkar expressed an opinion that though the major part of the Marxist creed had been disproved by history, its "residue" "was still very important". According to him, there were four items still alive in Marxism: "(*i*) The function of philosophy is to reconstruct the world. (*ii*) That there is a conflict of interest between class and class. (*iii*) That private ownership of property brings power to one class and sorrow to another through exploitation (*iv*) That it is necessary for the good of society that the sorrow be removed by the abolition of private property".[21]

For the leader of the *Dalits* the starting point in the Marxist theory was "exploitation in the world". "The poor are exploited by the rich because of the property that they hold, and they enslave the masses. And that enslavement results in suffering, sorrow and poverty." But the Buddha, according to Ambedkar, said "exactly the same thing": "There is *Dukkha* in the world". In Ambedkar's understanding, the Buddha did lay the foundation of his religion on what he called *Dukkha.* (The word *Dukkha* was interpreted by Ambedkar as "poverty".) And it had been done much earlier – some 24 centuries before Marx. Ambedkar saw "no difference at all" between Marx's "exploitation of the poor" and the Buddha's *Dukkha.*

Then Ambedkar compared the way Karl Marx suggested to get rid of exploitation with the Buddha's attitude toward property, and again found, as he said, "some close affinity" between them. According to Marx, in order to prevent exploitation, the State must own the instrument of production, that is property, so that no private owner might intervene and rob the worker of the profit of his labour. And according to the Buddha, no monk should have private property. However, the Buddha, Ambedkar argued, made the abandonment of private property a matter of "principle" and not of "rule" (except in the *bhikśu saṅgha*). For Ambedkar, the problem was to what extent this rule of denial of private property could be applied to the society as a whole. His answer to this question was: "That is a matter of expediency, time, circumstances, and development of human society". "But so far as theory is concerned, whether there is anything wrong in abolishing private property, Buddhism will not stand in the way of anybody who wants to do it, because it has already made this concession in the organisation of the Buddhist Sangha." Thus, Ambedkar saw no problem, at least theoretically, in abolishing private property to eradicate poverty and attain equality.

Comparing both the teachings, Ambedkar concludes that there is agreement between the Buddha and Karl Marx on these points, though "the language is different but the meaning is the same". So, he said, "the end is common to both", but "the differences are about the means", i.e. in the case of Marx – violence and dictatorship of proletariat.[22]

In his last speech on Buddhism, delivered at the International Buddhist conference held at Kathmandu in 1956, he juxtaposed Marx with the Buddha, saying that the Buddha aimed at achieving his aims by persuasion, moral teaching and love; he wanted to conquer the opponent by expounding to him the doctrine that love and not power could conquer anything. So the Buddha would not allow violence, said Ambedkar, but the communists do. Then he posed a question: "They can get quick results by using force. But will it last long?"

According to Ambedkar, the Buddha's way was a long, but the surest one, it was "the safest and the soundest". That is why, Ambedkar argued, "it is unnecessary for the Buddhist people to go to Karl Marx to get the foundation. The foundation is already there, well laid". Repudiating violence and dictatorship as a means of achieving aims, he considered Buddhism as an antidote to Marxism, and claimed that its moral and humanitarian aspects appealed to Indian people and suited them best of all, because the system of Buddhism is democratic.

One can say that while appreciating some of the aspects of Marxism, Ambedkar did not accept it, did not agree with its basics. At the end of his life Ambedkar declared that he had found "a way of life which was better than what was supplied by the Communist way of life". In a very pathetic way he passed his verdict in favour of Buddhism: "Buddhism could be a substitute for Communism".[23]

Ambedkar's personal relations with the Indian communists – from cooperation to open hostility – had to no small degree predetermined his approach to Marxism. His very negative attitude towards the Soviet Union, China and other socialist countries which he blamed for lack of freedom and democracy, was reflected in his writings and speeches in the 50s.

Ambedkar tied up very closely the social aspects of *navayāna* with democracy. In order to appreciate it, one must take into account his main ideas related to the development of man and society. In the first place, it is his assumption that there is no justice in the world. Secondly, it is his urge to find a way to eliminate this injustice.

Quite often Ambedkar puts his own arguments in the mind of the Buddha. So he says, "The Buddha realised that there were two problems. The first problem was that there was suffering in the world and the second problem was how to remove this suffering and make mankind happy" . . . "That suffering and unhappiness in the world the Buddha thought was an incontrovertible fact. . . . It is, therefore, on this problem – how to remove suffering and unhappiness – that He concentrated his mind".[24] Next comes the demand to reconstruct the unjust society based on self-love, avarice and private property. According to Ambedkar, "knowing that there was so much unhappiness in the world the Buddha realised that it was wrong for Him to sit as a sanyasi with folded arms and allow things to remain as they were. He realised that . . . what is necessary is not escape from the world. What is necessary is to change the world and to make it better".[25] By such pronouncements Ambedkar demonstrated his personal activism.

Another important point in Ambedkar's Buddhism relates to the necessity of obtaining freedom for man and the society. Without freedom man cannot realise himself in his life. "What is the use of man's existence if he is not free?" – Ambedkar asks this crucial question. "What is the use of man's intelligence if he continues to believe in supernatural causes?"[26]

The relations between man and man, and not between man and God, were most important for Ambedkar. This he considered as the real meaning and significance of a true religion, which he called *Dhamma.* Ambedkar says that according to the Buddha "the centre of religion lay not in the relation of man to God. It lay in the relation between man and man. The purpose of religion is to teach man how he should behave towards other men so that all may be happy".[27]

Proceeding further Ambedkar argues that "what the Buddha calls *Dhamma* differs fundamentally from what is called Religion". Contrary to religion which is personal and which one must keep to oneself, "Dhamma is social. One man if he is alone does not need Dhamma. But when there are two men living in relation to each other they must find a place for Dhamma whether they like it or not. Neither can escape it".[28] The purpose of religion, continues Ambedkar, is to explain the origin of the world. The purpose of *Dhamma,* as a social teaching, is to reconstruct the world.[29]

Ambedkar's book *The Buddha and His Dhamma* had a very clear social message. It was meant to solve the problem of social conflict between the Untouchables and caste Hindus by liberation of the downtrodden from social oppression. Salvation was to be found in this life and the lowliest and the lost had to know how to get rid of the social pollution syndrome. One way to do so was to denounce "the law of *Karma* as formulated by the Brahmins", as it "was calculated to sap the spirit of revolt" against injustice (see Chapter l, verse 40). In this book Ambedkar pays attention to the conversion of the "low and the lowly", the "fallen and the criminals," and women.

Inequality and social injustice of brahmanical Hinduism felt most of all by the lowest castes during long centuries were confronted with attempts of those groups to shed off the stigma of untouchability. Their efforts were crowned by Ambedkar's activities which were intended to help the *Dalits* attain their dignity, and instill in them faith in their ability to struggle for social equality and ultimately acquire it.

In his speech in the Constituent Assembly on 25th November, 1949, Ambedkar raised the question he had been concerned about for many years: "How long shall we continue to deny equality in our social and economic life?" and warned: "If we continue to deny it for long, we will do so only by putting our political democracy in peril." Thus Ambedkar pressed for the solution of the problems of the low-born masses without delay. In fact it was a demand for equality both in social and economic life. In the Indian society, based on the principle of graded inequality, he pointed out, "it means elevation for some and degradation for others. As a result some have immense wealth as against many who live in abject poverty". And if this contradiction, that is inequality in the social and economic life, is not removed, political democracy will be threatened. It might happen that "those who suffer from inequality will blow up the structure of political democracy which this assembly has so laboriously built up".[30]

As a statesman, political thinker and ideologue, Ambedkar always found strength in one fundamental principle – equality for all human beings. This was the core of his creed and the basis of his lifelong activities. Equality and social liberation for his submerged fellowmen was his primary obsession and aspiration, his burning passion.

Discussing the problem of morality as a spiritual and social category, which is synonymous to *Dhamma*, Ambedkar considered it as an instrument of management of society, which regulates relations between its members. Devoid of morality, society is prone to anarchy and extinction.[31] Morality had to become the law of life. The ability to independently take decisions based on morality should exclude the use of double standards in political and social life – one set of standards for the have-nots and another for the haves.

Ambedkar battled for the holistic humanism of one man, one value. His ideology was fortified by a political will, a deep devotion to his cause and a perception of himself as a Messiah, who must liberate his low-born brethren and level up the lot of the menial masses. But he also fought for the philosophy of social equality and against any kind of discrimination characteristic not only for the Indian caste system but for all the stratified systems of inequality in the world. And in this sense he was not a mere *Dalit* leader but a defender of human rights of those people whom F. Dostoevsky called "the humiliated and insulted".

Notes and References

1. K. R. Narayanan, "Babasaheb Ambedkar", *Mainstream*, 8 August, 1992, p. 23.
2. Justice Krishna Iyer, *Dr Ambedkar and the Dalit Future*, Delhi, 1990, pp. 34, 38, 42.
3. B. Das (ed.), *Thus Spoke Ambedkar*, Vol. III. Bangalore, 1979, p. 187.
4. Christopher Queen, "Ambedkar and the Rise of the Fourth Yana", *International Conference "Reconstructing the World: Dr Babasaheb Ambedkar's Understanding of Buddhism"*, University of Pune, 7–9 October, 1998.

5. B. R. Ambedkar, 'Speech on Labour and Parliamentary Democracy', *Dr Babasaheb Ambedkar Writings and Speeches*, compiled by Vasant Moon, Bombay, 1991, pp. 107–9.
6. D. Keer, *Dr Ambedkar: Life and Mission*, Bombay, 1981, p. 298.
7. Eleanor Zelliot, 'Dr Ambedkar and the Search for a Meaningful Buddhism', *International Conference "Reconstructing the World: Dr Babasaheb Ambedkar's Understanding of Buddhism"*, University of Pune, 7–9 October, 1998.
8. B. Das (ed.), *Thus Spoke Ambedkar: Selected Speeches*, Vol. II, Jullundur, 1969, p. 184.
9. Ibid., 186.
10. Ibid., p. 189.
11. Ibid., p. 187–88.
12. D. Keer, *Dr Ambedkar: Life and Mission*, p. 303.
13. Ibid., pp. 297–98.
14. Ibid., p. 296.
15. B. Das (ed.), *Thus Spoke Ambedkar*, Vol. III, p. 176.
16. B. Das (ed.), *Thus Spoke Ambedkar*, Vol. II, p. 139.
17. D. Keer, *Dr Ambedkar: Life and Mission*, p. 447.
18. Ibid., p. 447.
19. B. Das (ed.), *Thus Spoke Ambedkar*, Vol. II, pp. 134–35.
20. D. Keer, *Dr Ambedkar: Life and Mission*, p. 301.
21. B. R. Ambedkar, "Buddha or Karl Marx", *Dr Babasaheb Ambedkar Writings and Speeches*, compiled by Vasant Moon, Bombay, 1987, p. 444.
22. Ibid., pp. 444–45.
23. B. Das (ed.), *Thus Spoke Ambedkar*, Vol. II, pp. 127–34.
24. B. R. Ambedkar, *The Buddha and His Dhamma*, Bombay, 1974, p. 55.
25. Ibid., p. 78.
26. Ibid., pp. 174–75.
27. Ibid., p. 178.
28. Ibid., p. 226.
29. Ibid., p. 231.
30. B. Das (ed.), *Thus Spoke Ambedkar*, Vol. II, pp. 186–87.
31. B. R. Ambedkar, *The Buddha and His Dhamma*, p. 232.

❖ Contributors*

ALAYEV, L. B. (b. 1932), D.Litt, Professor, research scholar in the Institute of Oriental Studies, Russian Academy of Sciences. Author of a number of articles and books on village community in India including *Sotsialnaya struktura indiiskoi derevni (territoriya Uttar-pradesha, XIX vek* (The Social Structure of the Indian Village the Uttar Pradesh Territory, the XIXth century, Moscow, 1976); Selskaya obschina v Severnoi Indii. Osnovniye etapi evolutsii (The Village Community in Northern India. Main Stages of Evolution, Moscow, 1981). He has also contributed chapters 'The Systems of Agricultural Production: South India' and 'Non-Agricultural Production: South India' to: Irfan Habib and Tapan Raychaudhuri (eds.). *The Cambridge Economic History of India,* Vol. I, (Cambridge University Press, Cambridge, 1982).

KALANDAROVA, M. (b. 1953), Ph.D. (History), research scholar at the Centre for Indian Studies, Institute of Oriental Studies, Russian Academy of Sciences. Author of a number of articles on India-Central Asia relations in the XIXth century, including 'The Bokhara Burnes', *Contemporary Central Asia,* Vol. 3, no. 3 (December, 1999).

KASHIN, V. P. (b. 1954), Ph.D. (History), research scholar and Member Secretary of the Centre for Indian Studies, Institute of Oriental Studies, Russian Academy of Sciences. Author of a number of articles on Russo-Indian relations, freedom movement and partition of India, including 'Sardar Patel', *Aziya i Afrika segodnya (Asia and Africa Today),* No. 12, 1999; 'Nezavisimaya Indiya i Sovetskii Soyuz (po materialam rassekrechennogo arkhiva (Independent India and the USSR;

*Only some of the contributors' works have been cited here with special reference to those published in English.

Materials from the Declassified Archive)' *Vostok* (Orient), No. 1, 2001; 'Rossisko-indiiskoye regionalnoye sotrudnichestvo (Russo-Indian Regional Cooperation)', *Indiya segodnya* (India Today), No. 1, 2001;' "Misssiya kabineta" i pozitsiya veduschikh indiiskikh partii (The Cabinet Mission and the Position of the Leading Indian Parties)', *Pamyati I. M. Reisnera* (*I. M. Reisner Memorial Volume*, Moscow, 2000).

KOMAROV, E. N. (b. 1927), Ph.D. (History), research scholar in the Institute of Oriental Studies, Russian Academy of Sciences. Author of a number of articles and books on national liberation movement, agrarian history of India, recent socio-political developments, such as 'Bengalskaya derevnya i krestyanskoe khozyaistvo vo vtoroi polovine XVIII veka. (The Village and Peasant Farming in Bengal in the Late XVIIIth and Early XIXth Centuries)', *Ucheniye zapiski Instituta vostokovedeniya* (Memoirs of the Institute of Oriental Studies), Vol. XVIII, (Moscow,1957); 'Development of Socio-Political Thought and Egalitarian Concepts in India of the 19th-20th Centuries', *Soviet Oriental Studies. South and South-East Asia,* (Calcutta, 1970); *Indo-Soviet Cooperation: Historical Background and Present Day Developments* (Allied Publishers Pvt. Ltd., Delhi, 1976); 'Indian Liberation Movement: Impact of Revolutionary Russia-the USSR', *The Calcutta Journal of Political Studies,* Vol. 3, Winter, 1982; 'The Party Structure of India: Evolution and Socio-Economic Correlates: 1962– 1982', *Changing South Asia: Politics and Government,* (Asian Research Service, Hong Kong, 1984); *Lenin and the National Liberation Movement in India: Historical Essays,* (Panchasheel Publ., Delhi, 1986); 'Elitist Modernization in Colonial India: Some Specificities of Generation and Concentration of Power Resources', *Democracy in the Modern World: Essays for Tatu Vanhanen,* Tampere, 1989.

KOTOVSKY, G. G. (1923–2001), Ph.D. (History), research scholar at the Centre for Indian Studies, Institute of Oriental Studies, Russian Academy of Sciences, Deputy Co-chairman of the Indo-Russian Joint Commission on Cooperation in Social Sciences. Author of a number of books and articles on agrarian history and modern socio-economic situation in India, including: *Agrarian Reforms in India* (People's Publishing House, Delhi, 1964); 'Agrarian Relations in Maharashtra in the late 19th and early 20th Centuries', *Tilak and the Struggle for Indian Freedom,* (People's Publishing House, Delhi, 1966); 'Agricultural Development and Planning in the Underdeveloped Countries outside the Socialist Sphere: Comment', *Policies, Planning and Management for Agricultural Development. Papers and Reports. 14th International Conference of*

Agricultural Economists (Oxford, 1971); *The History of India*, Vol. I and II. (Progress Publishers, Moscow, 1978) (co-authored by G. M. Bongard-Levin and K. A. Antonova); 'Economic Organisation and Social Structure of Rural Society in Contemporary India (A Conceptual Approach)', *General Problems of Anthropology and Ethnology in the South Asia* (Moscow, 1978); 'Certain Trends in India's Socioeconomic and Sociopolitical Development', *Asian Survey*, No. 12, 1984); 'India and Russia Versus Challenges of the New Century', *Mainstream*, Annual 1998; 'Socio-Class Struggle of Indian Countryside', *Social Scientist*, No. 154 (1999); 'Objective and Subjective in Inter-Ethnic and Inter-Communal Conflicts', *Mainstream*, Vol. XXXVIII, No. 25, (10 June, 2000).

MITROKHIN, L. V. (b. 1934), Ph.D. (History), research scholar at the Centre for Indian Studies, Institute of Oriental Studies, Russian Academy of Sciences. Jawaharlal Nehru Prise winner (1985). Author of a number of articles and books on the history of freedom movement in India and Soviet-Indian relations, including *Friends of the Soviet Union: India's Solidarity with the USSR during the Second World War in 1941–1945* (Allied Publishers Pvt. Ltd., Delhi, 1977); *Lenin in India* (Allied Publishers Pvt. Ltd., Delhi, 1981); *Lenin and Indian Freedom Fighters* (Panchsheel Publ., Delhi, 1988).

SAMOZVANTSEV, A. M. (b. 1949), D.Litt, research scholar at the Institute of Oriental Studies, Russian Academy of Sciences. Author of a number of books and articles on ancient history of India, including *The Legal Text of the Dharmasastras*, (Moscow, 1991); *Kniga mudretsa Yajnavalkyi* (The Book of the Sage Yajnavalkya – an annotated translation of the law chapters from the Yajnavalkya Smriti, Moscow, 1995); *Kniga mudretsa Narady* (The Book of the Sage Narada, an annotated translation of the law chapters from the *Narada Smriti*, co-authored with A. A. Vigasin, Moscow, 1998); *Society, State and Law in Ancient India* (Sterling, Delhi, 1985; co-authored by A. A. Vigasin).

SHAUMIAN, T. L. (b. 1938), Ph.D. (History), research scholar at the Centre for Indian Studies, Institute of Oriental Studies, Russian Academy of Sciences. Author of a number of articles and books on India's foreign policy, Asian security, etc. including the recently published 'Who is Fighting in Kashmir and Why' (Moscow, 2000) and *Tibet: The Great Game and Tsarist Russia* (Oxford University Press, Delhi, 2000).

SUVOROVA, A. A. (b. 1949), D.Litt, Head of the Department of Literatures of the Institute of Oriental Studies, Russian Academy of Sciences. Translator into Russian of the Urdu *masnavis* by Khwaja Alibeg

Surur and Nihalchand Lahori as well as *Dilruba* by Qurratul Ain Haidar. Author of a number of books and articles on Urdu literature and theatre, Sufism, history and culture of the Indian Islam and Hindu-Muslim cultural syncretism, including: *Nostalgia po Lakhnau* (The Lucknow Nostalgia, Moscow, 1995); *Musulmanskiye svyatiye yuzhnoi Azii XI-XV vv* (The Muslim Saints of the South Asia, XIth to XVth Century, Moscow, 1999); *Masnawi: A Study of Urdu Romance* (Oxford University Press, Karachi, 2000).

TYULINA, E. V. (b. 1957) Ph.D. (History), research scholar at the Centre for Indian Studies, Institute of Oriental Studies, Russian Academy of Sciences. The translator of the Savitri episode from the *Mahabharata* into Russian. Has recently completed and prepared for publication the Russian translation of the Book II of the *Garuda-purana* with comments and cultural-cum-historical analysis. Author of a number of articles on the cultural and historical analysis of the *puranas*, including 'Traditsionniye predstavleniya o cheloveke v Garuda-purane (The Traditional Notions of Man in the Garuda-purana)', A. D. Litman, L. R. Polonskaya (eds.), *Obschestvennaaya mysli Indii: problemy cheloveka i obschestva* (The Indian Thought: Problems of Man and Society, Moscow, 1992); 'Cosmological Notions in Memorial Ritual (according to Garuda-purana)', *Journal of the oriental Institute*, Baroda, Vol. 39, No. 3–4 (March-June, 1990); 'Skazaniye o Shrimati (The Russian Translation of the Srimati Episode. From the Linga-purana)' *Vostok* (*Orient*), No. 12, 2000.

VANINA, E. YU. (b. 1957) Ph.D. (History), research scholar at the Centre for Indian Studies, Institute of Oriental Studies, Russian Academy of Sciences. Author of a number of books and articles on medieval India, including: *Ideas and Society in India From the Sixteenth to the Eighteenth Centuries* (Oxford University Press, Delhi, 1996); 'Urban Industries of Medieval India: Some Aspects of Development', *Studies in History*, (Delhi, July-December, 1989) NS, V: 1–2.; 'Madhavanala-Kamkandala by Alam: A Hindi Poem of Akbar's Epoch', *The Indian Historical Review*, Vol. XX, No. 1–2, 1993–1994, published in 1996); 'Of Russian Spies and Itinerants: Different Perceptions on Eighteenth Century India', *Indian International Centre Quarterly*, Spring, 1997; 'Baji Rao and Mastani, A Family Tragedy in the XVIIIth Century Maharashtra', I. Glushkova and R. Vora (eds.), *Home, Family and Kinship in Maharashtra*, (Oxford University Press, Delhi, 1999); 'Communal Relations in Pre-Modern India', S. Settar and P.K.V. Kaimal (eds.), *We Lived Together*, (Pragati Publications and ICHR, Delhi, 1999)

VIGASIN, A. A. (b. 1946), recently appointed Head of the Department of India and South Asia, Institute of Asian and African Countries, Moscow State University. Author of a number of books and articles on the history of ancient India and the history of Indian studies in Russia, including: *The Image of India: The Study of Ancient Indian Civilisation in the USSR* (Progress Publishers, Moscow,1984; also available in Hindi); *Society, State and Law in Ancient India* (Sterling, Delhi, 1985; co-authored by A. M. Samozvantsev);' Asoka's Third Rock Edict Reinterpreted', The *Indian Historical Review,* Vol. XX, No. 1–2, 1993–1994; 'Some Aspects of Asokan Edicts', *Indologica Taurinensia,* Vols. 23–24, 1997–1998.

YURLOVA, E. S. (b. 1932), Ph.D. (History), research scholar at the Centre for Indian Studies, Institute of Oriental Studies, Russian Academy of Sciences. Author of a number of books and articles on the social position of Indian women, the *Dalits* and B. R. Ambedkar, including: 'Social Aspects of Female Employment', *India: Problems of Development* (Moscow, 1982); 'Communal Relations in Colonial India and the Harijans', *Communal Relations in South Asia: Past and Present,* (Institute of Oriental Studies, Moscow, 1988); *Scheduled Castes in India,* (Patriot Publishers, Delhi, 1990); B.R.Ambedkar's Birth Centenary in Moscow'. *Patriot,* 26 January, 1991. 'Political Emergence of the Scheduled Castes Ethnocommunity'. *Mainstream,* 12 October, 1991; 'Emergence of Scheduled Castes as a Political Power', K. S. Singh (ed.). *Ethnicity, Caste and People: Proceedings of the Indo-Soviet Seminars held in Calcutta and Leningrad, 1990.* Anthropological Survey of India, New Delhi, Institute of Ethnography, Moscow (Manohar Publishers, Delhi, 1992); 'Untouchables and the Nationalist Movement in Maharashtra', I. Glushkova and R. Vora (eds.), *Home, Family and Kinship in Maharashtra,* (Oxford University Press, 1999).

ZAGORODNIKOVA, T. N. (b. 1952) Ph.D. (History), research scholar at the Centre for Indian Studies, Institute of Oriental Studies, Russian Academy of Sciences. A compiler of the collections of archival documents *Russko-indiiskiye otnosheniya v XIX v* (Russo-Indian Relations in the XIXth Century, Moscow, 1997) and *Russko-indiiskiye otnosheniya v 1900–1917* (Russo-Indian Relations in 1900–1917, Moscow, 1999).

❖ Index of Names, Places, Terms and Titles